Quality Money Management

Process Engineering and Best Practices for
Systematic Trading and Investment

The Financial Market Technology Series

Series Editor

Benjamin Van Vliet

The Financial Market Technology Series is a partnership between Elsevier, Inc. and the Institute for Market Technology (i4mt) to publish cutting-edge books covering topics concerning the integration of technology with financial markets, including:

- automated trading,
- building trading and investment systems,
- operational issues in back office processing,
- clearing and settlement, and
- compliance and governance issues as they relate to technology.

The goal of the series is to promote increased understanding and competency with technology in the finance industry through publishing high-quality books on the latest areas of research and practice for professionals working in the financial markets.

Series Editor: Ben Van Vliet is a Lecturer at the Illinois Institute of Technology (IIT), where he also serves as the Associate Director of the M.S. Financial Markets program. At IIT he teaches courses in quantitative finance, C++ and .NET programming, and automated trading system design and development. He is vice chairman of the Institute for Market Technology, where he chairs the advisory board for the Certified Trading System Developer (CTSD) program. He also serves as series editor of the Financial Markets Technology series for Elsevier/Academic Press and consults extensively in the financial markets industry.

Mr. Van Vliet is also the author of "Modeling Financial Markets" with Robert Hendry (2003, McGraw Hill) and "Building Automated Trading Systems" (2007, Academic Press). Additionally, he has published several articles in the areas of finance and technology, and presented his research at several academic and professional conferences.

We welcome proposals for books for the series. Please go to www.books.elsevier.com/finance where you will find a link to send us your proposal.

Quality Money Management

Process Engineering and Best Practices for Systematic Trading and Investment

Andrew Kumiega
Benjamin Van Vliet

ELSEVIER

AMSTERDAM • BOSTON • HEIDELBERG • LONDON • NEW YORK • OXFORD
PARIS • SAN DIEGO • SAN FRANCISCO • SINGAPORE • SYDNEY • TOKYO
Academic Press is an imprint of Elsevier

ACADEMIC
PRESS

Academic Press is an imprint of Elsevier
30 Corporate Drive, Suite 400, Burlington, MA 01803, USA
525 B Street, Suite 1900, San Diego, California 92101-4495, USA
84 Theobald's Road, London WC1X 8RR, UK

Design Direction: Joanne Blank
Cover Design: Joe Tenerelli
Cover Images © Corbis Corporation

This book is printed on acid-free paper. ∞

Library of Congress Cataloging-in-Publication Data
Kumiega, Andrew.
  Quality money management : best practices and process engineering for systematic
trading and investment / Andrew Kumiega, Benjamin Van Vliet.
      p. cm.
  Includes index.
  ISBN-10: 0-12-372549-6 (hardback : acid-free paper)
  ISBN-10: (invalid) 0-12-372549-3 (hardback : acid-free paper)
  ISBN-13: 978-0-12-372549-3 (hardback : acid-free paper)
  1. Electronic trading of securities. 2. Finance—Mathematical models.
3. Investments—Mathematical models. 4. Financial engineering. I. Vliet, Benjamin
Van. II. Title.
  HG4515.95.K86 2008
  332.6—dc22

                                                                    2007052636

British Library Cataloguing-in-Publication Data
A catalogue record for this book is available from the British Library.

ISBN: 978-0-12-372549-3

For information on all Academic Press publications
visit our Web site at www.books.elsevier.com

www.charontec.com

Working together to grow
libraries in developing countries

www.elsevier.com | www.bookaid.org | www.sabre.org

ELSEVIER   BOOK AID   Sabre Foundation
              International

Contents

Preface

This book began several years ago as an attempt to provide a detailed road map for students to follow from the theoretical quantitative finance taught in graduate school to building a trading/investment system to manage real money in the real world. From our years of consulting and experience in building funds and through academic research, discussions with working students, and feedback from many colleagues, our perspective grew from writing a classical money management book with detailed equations for calculating trading signals and risk calculations to process engineering, statistical process control, Six Sigma, and software design. The original shift back to industrial engineering was slow in the beginning, but we kept going back to manufacturing examples to explain how to build trading/investment systems. Every class, job, and consulting assignment led us away from the financial literature toward process engineering. Eventually, we both realized that the true missing theory in finance was not another equation, but a concise methodology to implement theoretical concepts.

At colleges and universities around the world and in most industry publications, the mathematics of markets and trading is most often taught from a theoretical perspective using clean sample data, in spite of the practical nature of the discipline as well as the fact that most students are pursuing the knowledge for purely professional reasons. While most academics prefer to teach students highly mathematical theory, working students want to learn how to implement those theories in the real world and turn them into profitable ideas and careers. While academics prefer to find and explain degrees of market efficiency, working students hope one day to find and exploit inefficiencies. Students who lack experience in the real-world financial markets study mathematics diligently only to fail in interviews that ask for real-world knowledge. A gap exists between students of the markets and the educational service providers.

Furthermore, students learn by doing. An ancient Chinese proverb states, "I hear and I forget, I see and I remember, I do and I understand." No class or homework assignment is sufficient for one to become a good trading/investment system architect. Due to time constraints, students will not build their own components but rather buy off-the-shelf ones. The value is in learning how to test components and glue the pieces together to build a complete system. Does the school attempt to organize its curriculum around a process for solving real-world problems, similar to engineering disciplines, or does it more or less offer a smattering of courses in mathematics related to finance? Just as with product teams, for students to implement financial theory in the real world, they need a step-by-step process to follow. Other engineering disciplines have confronted this same problem and chosen to design courses around building products using real-world machines and real companies.

In this book, we present an overview of the body of knowledge of finance, linking topics to create a linear progression of steps toward solutions to a business problem—how to build trading and investment systems. We have not written in-depth chapters on areas that are covered in detail in dozens of other books and hundreds of papers.

We had a difficult time drawing the line between adding in-depth quantitative finance information and focusing solely on higher-level processes. Like graduate students doing research, we often wandered off the path to smell the surroundings, only to force ourselves back on the road to present a process map. For the interested reader who intends to sniff the mathematical and technological flowers close up, we recommend the readings in the end notes or searching the Internet for papers and books on topics of interest.

As one can imagine, additional credit for completion of this project must be given to many friends, family, and colleagues, in particular to the many individuals who read drafts of the chapters and provided invaluable feedback, including Bruce Rawlings, Debbie Cernauskas, Fabian Valencia, Mulianto The, Dr. Zia Hassan, Assad Fehmy, Jason Malkin, Batavia, Larissa J. Miller, Dr. Joe Wojkowski, Matt Lech, and Josip Roleta; and all of our colleagues at the Illinois Institute of Technology's Stuart School of Business: Russell Wojcik, Dr. Michael Gorham, Keith Black, Dr. Michael Ong, Dr. John Bilson, Dr. Michael Kelly, and Jodi Houlihan. Also we would like to thank the many students at IIT who have also provided valuable feedback. Certainly without their help and the help of many others this book would never have been completed.

Andy Kumiega also thanks Megan, Kayla, Carrie, and Therese Kumiega for their long-term support. He also thanks Dr. Miller, Dr. Rice, and Dr. Cesarone for their guidance and support in graduate school. Ben Van Vliet thanks his wife Julia for putting up with late nights and long weekends of research and writing.

We hope you learn from our research the topic of process engineering for trading and investment systems and are inspired to delve deeper into the topic. Please provide us with any feedback you may have.

CHAPTER • 1

Introduction

In the financial markets, the competition gets tougher every day. Today, the difference between 25th and 75th percentile performance of money managers in some sectors of the industry is measured in basis points. The only trading and money management firms that survive now are the ones that continually discover cutting-edge position selection strategies and technologies to build better quality trading and investment systems. Where once traders and money managers based decisions on greed and hope, now rational self-interest controls discovery processes that promote fact-based decisions and implement proven research.

Entrepreneurs refer to the discovery process as knowledge-based innovation. In finance it has begotten a new discipline: systematic trading and investment, the reasoned study of financial markets using the scientific method to explain and replicate market phenomena and the use of computer automation to make profitable trading/investment decisions. Today, entrepreneurial activity in financial markets revolves around the practice of systematic innovation[1] to build new (and shut down old) trading and investment systems.

A top-rated hedge fund company stopped accepting new money in 2004 and started liquidating positions. In 2005 management shut down the fund completely. Their diligent and continuous research made it clear that their models were no longer working. There was a fundamental shift in their ability to arbitrage convertible bonds and they told their investors to take their money back. Every investor is waiting anxiously for them to open their next fund. (Compare that to Long Term Capital Management.) Ideally, the hedge fund manager should have been building new strategies ahead of time so that they could have kept the customers' money by switching funds.

The key determinant of sustainable competitive advantage is the ability to continually discover, build, and operate better trading/investment systems. Which is to say, in financial markets the new business model is quality: higher returns, lower risk, and lower cost, all at a faster time-to-market. This model is complicated, though, by the tendency of many skillful fund managers, traders, and financial engineers to fall short when it comes to process engineering.[2] Other industries have faced this same problem.

In manufacturing plants, small margins demand reductions in waste and costs of reworking defective parts. High quality is necessary to gain and maintain market share.

1

Most engineers already know how to design machines that make parts; that research went on in the 1930s and 1940s. Over the last 30 or 40 years, manufacturing research has focused on production engineering. At Toyota and Honda, for example, research focuses on designing processes that generate less random variation. This type of research led to the well-known quality discipline Six Sigma and calculation of defects per million parts. The additional cost of Six Sigma processes is acceptable.

Quality and its effects are all around us. Manufacturers, software developers, aerospace, and many other industries use quality techniques everyday. This is especially true for mission critical projects. Here are two examples:

- When was the last time you heard about a plane crashing because of a software glitch?
- How often do computer problems cause nuclear power plants to melt down?

The answer to these questions is virtually never, because stringent quality management techniques have reduced the probability of failure to essentially zero through well-tested and redundant systems. For service firms, quality has a different slant. Controlling delivery at a service firm involves designing foolproof processes, communicating with and training employees thoroughly, and making certain that all personnel understand procedures and expectations.[3]

Should trading and money management firms be any less concerned about the quality of their trading or investment systems, especially when time-to-market is a key competitive advantage? Of course not. Since the late 1980s and early 1990s, the thrust of financial research has been on stochastic calculus for derivatives pricing, a place not dissimilar to manufacturing in the 1930s and 1940s. With most of the new mathematics now understood, research is focusing on the design of the production systems around the calculations.

1.1.   A Brief History of the Quality Revolution

Many years ago, manufacturing industries faced many of the same production engineering issues that trading and money management firms are facing today. Manufacturers turned to quality for solutions. The quality revolution started as far back as the 1920s with the idea of managing production with statistical process control. The concept was essentially this: use the central limit theorem to measure process outputs and control stochastic processes.

According to the central limit theorem, sample means from a population will be normally distributed, even if the underlying distribution is not. Thus, when the mean of samples from a process, such as a manufacturing process, shifts (say plus or minus three standard deviations), engineers consider the process to be out of control. It may seem like a simple idea, but back then it was revolutionary.

Dr. W. Edwards Deming, often called the "Father of Quality," built an entire philosophy of management around this simple idea, teaching quality management concepts across Japan after World War II. The Japanese readily accepted his ideas, implementing them at such world-class companies as Sony and Toyota, which went on to become high quality/low cost producers. The quality revolution nearly crushed the U.S. automotive industry. American manufacturers converted to quality just to survive and now compete successfully with foreign firms. (Many industrial firms find that they are now even legally required to be quality certified according to ISO 9000 standards, though the emphasis for service firms is still largely on fiscal and regulatory issues, not on the processes and procedures that determine the quality of the service.)

Deming laid the foundation for transforming a company into a quality firm in his book *Out of the Crisis*.[4] In his second book, *The New Economics*, Deming laid out his System of Profound Knowledge (SoPK), which consists of four parts:

- **Appreciation for a System.** All the parts of a business are interdependent. Successful management aims to optimize the performance of the system. Optimizing only one part will cause other parts to suffer.
- **Knowledge about Variation.** A system may be in statistical control or it may not be. "The variation to expect in the future is predictable."
- **Theory of Knowledge.** "Management is prediction. Rational prediction requires theory and we build knowledge through systematic revision."
- **Psychology.** People are different and management must optimize everyone's abilities.[5]

The goal of Deming's management methodologies is to create an organizational culture of continuous improvement in order to reduce waste, enhance productivity, lower costs, and generate higher profits and consistent long-term growth. Initial applications of quality principles to new product development started with attempts to force quality into products and services through inspections. But, companies quickly learned to stop reacting to inspection events, and started using process patterns, such as Design for Six Sigma, to design quality into the product from the start, building according to specification.[6] Many of Deming's ideas can be applied to trading and money management firms involved in systematic innovation.

1.2. A Brief History of Finance and Engineering

Over the last hundred years or so, the sciences of finance and engineering have become linked through the efforts of famous theoreticians like Louis Bachelier, Harry Markowitz, Fisher Black, and Myron Scholes. Black and Scholes' parabolic differential equation for the pricing of options is, mathematically, of the same type as the heat, or diffusion, equation from engineering.[7] Their equation became a foundation of the options trading industry and won a Nobel Prize. The success of engineers and mathematicians at explaining complex financial instruments and markets has encouraged thousands of Ph.D.s in these disciplines to join trading and investment firms to build new and better pricing, forecasting, and risk management models for all manner of listed and over-the-counter securities and derivatives and portfolios.

These quantitatively oriented professionals brought with them to Wall Street many of the tools of their prior trades: operating systems like Unix, programming languages like C++, and engineering software tools like MATLAB and Mathematica. However, it often seems that some engineering tools were left behind, namely the tools of quality.

Here is the question: if quantitative analysts in the financial markets hail from predominantly the same engineering-related backgrounds as the people that put planes in the air and nuclear power plants online, why is it they end up building so many trading/investment systems that are riddled with the kinds of mathematical and technological errors that have been responsible for some spectacular financial disasters? To solve these problems, the financial industry is now focusing on quality. In the new world of competing trading systems where competitive edges are razor thin, even small errors and waste are becoming too costly.

1.3.   Quality and Trading/Money Management

The most successful financial firms operationalize quality through trading/investment system design and development processes. Leading a proprietary trading firm, hedge fund, or mutual fund organization successfully requires managing in a systematic manner—understanding the product team's work and learning to better allocate their efforts. Success results from continually improving systematic knowledge-based innovation and the effectiveness of value-stream processes.

Firms that clarify the fuzzy front end of new trading/investment strategy development and rapidly investigate hundreds of opportunities, either discarding them (and failure should be celebrated) or exploiting them, now succeed at the expense of slower firms. Firms that minimize new trading/investment system development time and expenses, ongoing management costs, and operational risk provide better returns relative to firms that are less efficient.

As with all services, however, simply monitoring outputs of a trading/investment system will render a firm almost completely helpless to affect the outcome. Traders cannot inspect returns and prevent delivery of imperfect performance. Once a hedge fund loses all of its investment capital, it's too late. Does this mean that quality methods, such as Six Sigma, design of experiments (DoE), and Lean, cannot be applied to trading and money management services? Certainly not, but it can only be done by controlling the ex ante processes that deliver the trading/investment performance, where performance and risk data feed back into the system's trade selection and execution algorithms. So, two processes, or systems, exist and can be controlled in trading and money management:

1. The process of designing and developing a trading/investment strategy and its required technologies controlled with product realization (or value stream) processes.
2. A working trading/investment system generating measurable performance metrics controlled with statistical process control (SPC) since the underlying processes are non-stable, stochastic, and uncontrollable.

Now a common misconception is that quality takes too long. Since individual trading/investment ideas may be profitable for only a short time, speed to market is paramount. Anything that appears to slow development is skirted if at all possible. (This is human nature and generally only addressed after catastrophic failure.) If, in the end, a particular idea has potential for long-term profitability, only then is adding quality control even considered. More mature industries, like manufacturing, have overcome this shortsighted view and adopted quality management techniques. Quality it turns out actually speeds, not hinders, development.

1.4.   Managing the Process of Trading/Investment System Development

Management at trading and money management firms face many obstacles to successfully managing the development and operation of trading/investment systems. These obstacles are not unique to finance. They are the same problems facing just about every firm that is engaged in new product development and launch.

1.4.1. Assembling Product Teams

The complexities of trading and investment today are too much for one person; no one person can know all the math, all the technology, and all the strategies. So, managers hire talented financial engineers, traders, and programmers, often those in the top percentiles academically. Smart people do not necessarily work well together, though. Poor communication, egotism, politics, and out-of-control design processes can (and often do) still lead to failed development projects. Often, too, managers push "fast-track" projects, setting unrealistic time lines, despite the weight of research that schedule pressure can lead to up to four times the normal number of defects. The blame-game usually starts at the first sign of trouble—traders blame the financial engineers, the financial engineers blame the programmers, and the programmers blame the financial engineers and the traders, who in return blame the programmers.

Somehow, no one ever seems to blame themselves. Certainly, management never blames itself for not having clearly defined and documented plans for development. The real problem is a lack of proper team building and project management. Better managers help traders, financial engineers, and IT professionals improve the process of their work through coaching and mentoring. In the end managers, who only manage the numbers, never gain the confidence of their employees. Poor management results in high turnover when employees feel no loyalty to the firm; they behave like free agents, always seeking out the highest bidder.

Successful technology and engineering firms have found that product teams, composed of individuals from each of the three functional areas along with, potentially, a marketing or salesperson, work better. In a team setting, individuals are better motivated to contribute long-term innovations, and accomplish vital improvements in product, service, and quality, but only when they can work without fear: fear of taking a risk, having their ideas stolen, or of being fired for missing short-term goals. (If an employee is fearful of telling others what's wrong, or of suggesting a better way, how will things ever improve?)

A firm hired a Ph.D. financial engineer who found an incorrect formula in a valuation equation and pointed it out to the president of the firm. A book even explained the correct formula with code. The engineer was fired soon after for proving the president wrong. This type of closed-mindedness is continually being driven out at world-class firms before it leads to catastrophic failure.

This management style can be compared to 3 M, a recognized leader at discovering and launching new products.

3 M sought to encourage innovation through a variety of means including awards for innovation as well as in-house grants for innovative projects. The company also allowed staff to spend 15% of their time to explore new ideas outside of assigned responsibilities.[8]

New trading/investment firms often gain traction by stealing employees and intellectual property from existing firms. Overstressed people, tired of short-term deadlines and patches instead of fixes, prefer to work for new firms, where they hope they can do things right. New firms with even slightly better processes can win talent and clients because older firms are not investing in long-term quality and process improvement.

At SAS, a world leader in business analytics software, their business model is simple: "satisfied employees create satisfied customers." SAS reaps the rewards of having loyal employees and attracts the brightest minds in the business. Oprah featured SAS in a segment called "The Best Place to Work."[9]

If systematic innovation and quality techniques are to succeed, management must create a culture:

- Where all employees feel free to voice their ideas or to suggest that a certain process is a problem and in need of improvement.
- That supports the continuous improvement concept.
- With open, omnidirectional channels of communication.
- Where management is actively involved and honestly promotes quality in all aspects of the organization and its financial products.
- Where employees feel loyalty to the other team members (and hopefully their managers).

In the broader business world, firms have found great success employing process management techniques, providing product teams with systematic processes for moving new products through the various steps from idea to launch. Firms like 3 M and SAS have invested in this concept for decades and benefited by continual growth.

1.4.2. Managing Documentation

Managing processes means documentation, but money management organizations are (and should be) concerned about getting hung up on documentation instead of the pursuit of a working trading/investment system. Documents can be cumbersome in a highly dynamic, research-oriented area like trading/investment system development. Nevertheless, the best firms recognize the importance of verbal and written communication. (After all, engineers often spend 50 to 70% of their time communicating.) "The rewards are high for those who can communicate effectively."[10] But, effective communication does not come by chance.

As Joseph Cascio says, "word of mouth information rarely is communicated consistently. Only written information—clearly written—is constant,"[11] while documents, on the other hand, can't and don't contain all of the information the reader needs to know. There is a simple rule to follow, Martin's first law of documentation: "produce no document unless its need is immediate and significant."[12] Or, we might add, as required by law.

Increasingly, investors as well as regulators are requiring more transparency, more disclosure, and more documentation regarding trading and investment strategies, and back and middle office processes. Good or bad, this trend is likely to continue and proper documentation, process-driven generation of disclosures, and regulatory filings will continue to increase.

1.4.3. Overseeing and Prioritizing the Portfolio of Trading/ Investment Systems

Management must also answer the question, how should we most effectively invest our research and development resources? Which new trading/investment system development projects, from the many ideas the firm has, will it fund? And, which ones will be given priority. This is exactly what "portfolio management" in this context means—allocation of scarce resources and prioritization of competing projects, viewed as a portfolio of real options. Portfolio management is the balancing between financial risk versus return, maintenance of existing systems versus growth of new product lines, and new (and uncorrelated) trading/investment systems. Diversifying a portfolio of trading/investment systems, either by market, timeframe, or trading strategy employed, reduces risk, even when using the same basic trading rules.[13] Much in the same way that equity fund managers optimize their portfolios, top management can optimize their research and development investments—defining the right new trading/investment system strategy for the firm, selecting the winning new trading/investment system projects, and achieving the right balance of projects.

1.5. Operational Risk

Understanding trading/investment system development processes and managing those processes reduces operational risk, the probability that technology-related problems, either internal or external, will interrupt a firm's business.[14] (External disruption is a stoppage of business processes due to systems failures outside the firm, including, for example, failure of an exchange, administrator, credit provider, counterparties, or other third-party provider. Systems maintenance is also a stoppage of business processes due to the firm's technological failures, including, for example, software problems, systems that are outdated and unable to handle the firm's needs, computer viruses, system integration risks, and system developments being delayed or over budget.)

In *The Six Sigma Way*, the authors define Six Sigma as "a comprehensive and flexible system for achieving, sustaining, and maximizing business success. Six Sigma is uniquely driven by a close understanding of customer needs, disciplined use of facts, data, and statistical analysis, and diligent attention to managing, improving, and reinventing business processes." Several top firms in the financial markets apply best practices to reduce back office and operational risk, including performance measures, analytics, and improved capital and financial management techniques. Operational risk is an important area of quality management research, but we prefer to think of operational opportunity. That is, the opportunity for gain resulting from better internal processes, people, and systems. Six Sigma processes, applied in the front office, reduce operational risk and enable firms to beat their competition.

1.6. Project Risk

A subset of operational risk is project risk, the probability of loss due to events that adversely affect the success of a project. Such adverse effects could be "in the form of diminished quality of the end product, increased costs, delayed completion, or outright project failure."[15] Don Shafer's project risk management plan defines 12 categories of potential risk which can easily be adapted to trading/investment system development:

1. **Mission and Goals.** All trading/investment system development projects must fit within the organization's mission and goals.
2. **Organization Management.** All selected trading/investment system projects must be buildable within the current or planned organization. A primary risk in trading/investment system development is a subset of this risk we call internal team politics risk, where infighting between cross-functional product team members may cause project failure.

3. **Customer.** All projects must have a strong seed capital provider support.

4. **Budget/Cost.** Experience and good historical data from similar projects reduce this type of project risk.

5. **Schedule.** Trading/investment system development teams must be part of developing and modifying the project schedules; management must not impose them externally.

6. **Project Content.** Existence of documentation of trading system specification and design will ensure that knowledge will not be lost.

7. **Performance.** Complete performance testing of all modules and interfaces is crucial. Inadequate testing contributes to project risk.

8. **Project Management.** Managers need experience and understanding of trading/investment system project management processes.

9. **Development Process.** New trading/investment system development processes should be focused on quality assurance and analyses of alternative processes.

10. **Development Environment.** The lack of adequate physical environment and development tools contributes to project risk.

11. **Staff.** Clearly, having an experienced and proven product team reduces project risk.

12. **Maintenance.** This category of project risk includes maintenance and vendor issues, and software bugs after the trading/investment system has been implemented.[15]

As David Hulett points out, "project managers who assess the risk that the project will overrun its cost estimate or schedule, or will fail to meet performance objectives or specifications often improve their likelihood of a successful project."[16]

1.7.   Buy versus Build

If you work in the front office, you may say, "we buy all of our indicators and tools from third-party vendors; they take care of all that development process and testing stuff for us." But even if this is the case, ask yourself a simple question, "If a third-party piece of software contained an error—say, it calculates the price of options incorrectly—how much would knowing that be worth?" You should benchmark off-the-shelf components in order to isolate the performance of individual pieces of a trading/investment system. Benchmarking will expose their strengths and weaknesses, maybe even errors and problems in the underlying assumptions used to create them.

Here is an analogy. Suppose you want to race stock cars. The layman with little or no understanding of engineering might test drive several muscle cars at the local dealer and purchase one with good performance. Now, no one would be under the impression that such a car and a driver could compete with professional racing teams. Stock cars are in fact highly customized. Professional racing teams have engineers who understand the workings of race cars inside and out. They know what components to buy and what to machine themselves and how to put the pieces together to maximize performance. Part A may be used on hot days, while part B may be used on cold ones. Automotive engineers even use computer simulations that test different gears and shift points on the track for faster speeds. Without this depth of understanding, though, you cannot even begin to discuss which parts to buy and which to build for better performance, let alone compete on the NASCAR circuit.

To the lay investor, building a trading/investment system might be as simple as the NASCAR example—buy a few off-the-shelf parts and away you go. But, unless you truly understand the workings of a trading/investment system inside and out, you cannot even begin to discuss how to fine tune performance in the real markets, against real competition. Real professionals understand that a fully functioning trading/investment system blends together off-the-shelf and proprietary components and algorithms. Benchmarks additionally enable the running of real-world and what-if scenarios.

1.8. A Quality Approach to Development

Over the course of this book we apply quality techniques to systematic trading and investment. A systematic, methodical approach can control development, evaluation, and ongoing management of financial trading/investment systems. Furthermore, a process approach will provide a consistent framework for stepped allocation of seed capital for development and knowledge and team management. Applying a quality development methodology will satisfy the most important quality principle—customer satisfaction—as well as the interests of seed capital providers, employees, and regulators.

Our four-stage DTIM (Design, Test, Implement, Manage), 16-step trading system development methodology forms the structure of this book. The four DTIM stages spiral in a Plan-Benchmark-Do-Check (PBDC) framework, revolving around quantitative methods, data, technology, and portfolio monitoring, respectively. (Our methodology is in sync with the investment process proposed by Grinold and Kahn— "researching ideas (quantitative or not), forecasting exceptional returns, constructing and implementing portfolios, and observing and refining their performance" as set forth in their seminal book *Active Portfolio Management*. We have implemented some of Grinold and Kahn's methods at investment firms, and for the underlying financial concepts we have chosen not to address, we strongly recommend their text. This is also true of the books published by Jacobs and Levy. This text focuses on the engineering aspects of implementing the concepts presented in these and the many other books on quantitative finance.)

In each stage and at each step of a trading/investment system development project exist both risk and opportunity. For example, research into quantitative methods gives rise to model risk. Prototyping in Excel/Resolver gives rise to spreadsheet risk. Backtesting gives rise to data cleaning risks and optimization risk. Deming also presented seven deadly diseases to articulate certain risks. We have developed our own list of seven deadly diseases for trading/investment system design and development. They are a lack of:

1. A skilled, balanced, multifunctional product team.
2. Understanding of investment cycles and lack of a marketing plan that incorporate investment cycles.
3. Complete description of the trading or investment strategy.
4. Adequate backtesting and execution system testing for shadow trading.
5. Data and misunderstanding of data.

6. Project time line with firm deliverables and gates.

7. Clearly defined gate documents and review for initial and continuing capital funding.

The methodology presented in this book should cure these diseases. At each step of our methodology, we will provide best practice medicines to mitigate relevant operational and project risks. Quality, built in from the start, can control all manner of risk.[17]

> For automated, high-frequency trading systems, annual maintenance costs can exceed $5 million a year in addition to start-up costs of as much as $10 million according to the *Wall Street Journal*. Already, "we're seeing banks that only [a few] years ago made a decision to build their own trading systems now cutting back, because they weren't able to turn around large projects fast enough" or bear the projects' expense, according to a vice president of one software firm.[18] Further, as hedge fund attorney Paul Roth notes "most hedge funds fail for operational reasons rather than for poor investment decisions."[19] Development of and adherence to a systematic process of trading/investment system evaluation and implementation drives competitive advantage. Management costs and operational risk control clearly differentiate superior from inferior performers.[20]

1.8.1. Goals of Our Methodology

The goal of our methodology is Quality Money Management. More specifically, we define the goals of Quality Money Management to be as follows:

- Build trading/investment systems that deliver better performance to investors.
- Shorten the trading/investment system design and development cycle, the time it takes to turn a trading idea into a finished, working system.
- Formalize the process and increase the speed with which new trading ideas are evaluated and either discarded or promoted, called strategy cycling.
- Formalize the process and increase the speed of recognizing and shutting down trading/investment systems that no longer have a competitive advantage.
- Reduce the total cost of trading/investment system design and development.
- Provide seed capital investors with a real options model for capital burn rates and stepped commitment of capital.
- Formalize a process of developing, building, and packaging working trading/investment systems for sale to larger institutions.
- Enable seed capital providers to better allocate scarce resources and prioritize individual trading/investment systems within a portfolio of competing systems.
- Lengthen the maturity stage of working trading systems through continuous improvement.
- Satisfy the demand by investors and regulators for greater transparency through greater and standardized documentation.
- Create a taxonomy of risk for trading/investment system development and management and employ best practices to reduce risks.
- Provide a mechanism for effective self-evaluation, the preferred form of oversight in the financial industry.

In general, applying the techniques of quality to money management (Quality Money Management) will provide better trading/investment systems for seed capital providers, investors, and employees.[21] (While this book is written from a new product development perspective, because we believe in continuous process improvement this book can also be read from K|V 1.1 as the steps a product team would engage in to implement a fix or an enhancement to an existing system.)

1.9. Who Is This Book For?

This book is primarily for financial professionals involved in trading/investment system design and development, risk managers, seed capital providers, and even auditors performing due diligence or SAS 70 audits. If you fall into this category, you are already well aware of the drive toward automated trading, money management, and execution tools and systems, and this book should provide valuable techniques for implementing quality. As you will see, our methodology (the Kumiega|Van Vliet methodology, which for shorthand we call "K|V") applies to development and evaluation of disparate trading/investment systems, regardless of strategy, holding period, benchmark, or market, including:

- Fully automated, or algorithmic, trading/investment systems including both market making and market taking style systems.
- Partially automated trading/investment systems.
- Trade execution systems.
- Trading/investment systems that use third-party indicators, execution, and position selection software as opposed to building proprietary ones.

Our methodology is strategy independent and will work equally well for:

- Hedge fund style trading strategies.
- High frequency trading systems.
- Mutual fund style money management systems.
- Managed portfolios. (Especially for those implementing an asset allocation process where the portfolio and the investment strategy are rebalanced systematically.)
- Algorithmic trade execution systems.

If you are an investment capital provider, that is, you allocate investment capital to money managers, we believe you will also benefit from reading this book. As an investor you are undoubtedly aware of the bewildering array of investment strategies and vehicles available, not to mention the cost of money management, even maybe too the cost of hiring consultants to sift through the hoards of investment strategies and managers. If you sit on a pension or endowment fund board, we suggest you ask prospective money managers to discuss quality and how they apply quality management techniques to their investment strategy design and development process. Our guess is you will not get much of a response, or at best a very vague response. We recommend you consider investing only with money managers who take quality seriously, who employ transparent, Quality Money Management techniques with the investor-first goal of providing better performance at lower cost.

1.10.   THE KEY: Design Your Own Process

Trading and investment firms and strategies come in all shapes and sizes, and there are certainly various methodologies in use in different sectors of the financial industry. To simplify, we will apply our concepts to a trading/investment firm consisting of top management and financial engineering, trading or portfolio management, information technology, and risk management departments. Within this structure, we will assume that top management provides seed capital for trading/investment system development and provides investment capital either on its own or through a distribution mechanism. Additionally, we will assume that management oversees selection of trading/investment systems as well as management of the portfolios of new and working trading/investment systems. We will provide steps and best practices for a full-scale, fully automated trading system, which you may apply at your firm to manage large-scale development projects that take months to complete. Whatever your firm's actual structure and your project's scope, we believe all trading/investment organizations will need to account for, or at least consider, the functions laid out in the ensuing chapters. We do not expect, nor do we advocate, that anyone or any firm follow our methodology exactly.

We expect that different companies and trading groups will modify and adjust our standardized approach to suit their own cultures. Some will prefer a more agile approach (though one thing is immutable: the first step is to decide what trading/investment system to build, the second is to backtest it, the third is to build it, and the fourth is to manage the working system). We fully expect you or your firm to draw from the concepts we present in this book to design processes that work in your unique business culture, or for your unique trading/investment systems. Even if you are not developing trading/investment systems at all, you can easily adapt our methodology to work well for risk management systems and back office systems.

You may think to yourself "Quality theories don't apply to us, our situation is different." Be sure, your situation *is* different, but the principles that will help improve quality and performance of your trading/investment and back office systems are universal.

1.11.   Summary

Trading is an entrepreneurial activity and systematic, knowledge-based innovation is the key to beating the competition with better, faster, and cheaper-and-faster-to-build-and-run trading/investment systems. Too often, however, trading innovations fail due to a lack of effective management, reasons unrelated to the individual talents of traders, financial engineers, and IT professionals or to the validity of the trading/investment strategy.

Over the course of this book we apply quality principles and best practices to the process of trading/investment system development. Through systematic application, quality can drive competitive advantage, solve management problems, speed time-to-market, and reduce operational risk. So, make no mistake, processes are important and necessary. But we advocate processes and documentation that are lean, where work is guided by direction, not burdened by paperwork. Being lean means no wasted steps and no waiting. By implementing quality, trading and money management organizations:

Can...	AND...
Deliver better performing trading systems	Lower the cost of development and management.
Create more strategies	Develop and evaluate them more quickly.
Build more robust systems	Shorten the design and development time.
Reduce operational risk	Make entrepreneurial reward.
Satisfy fiduciary responsibility	Prove effective self-evaluation.

John Bogle in his book *The Battle for the Soul of Capitalism* states that "the fund industry operates under an institutionalized system of managers' capitalism" at the expense of the investing public.[22] As the use of derivatives and complex strategies become ever more pervasive and as hedge funds become available to a wider audience, doing things right, using quality standards, with the "national public interest and the interest of investors" first, will be the rule in money management. Value is created by the producer, but defined by the ultimate customer.[23] According to ISO, "organizations depend on their customers and therefore should understand current and future customer needs, should meet customer requirements and strive to exceed customer expectations."[24]

John Bogle goes on to point out that money management has mutated "from the industry's traditional focus on the stewardship of shareholder investments to salesmanship."[25] Good stewardship, through quality, is the best sales tool of all.

> Quality encompasses every aspect of our firm and is actually an emotional experience for the customer. Customers want to feel good about their purchases, to feel that they have gotten the best value. They want to know their money has been well spent, and they take pride in their association with a company of a high quality image.[26]

In summary, the largest problem facing trading and money management firms in the twenty-first century is not the lack of mathematical or technological understanding but rather an inability to manage the entrepreneurial processes of systematic innovation, development, and continuous improvement. Trading, hedge fund, and money management firms that learn the quality management lesson will thrive at the expense of firms that do not, but learning and implementing quality is not easy, nor is it done through a one-day seminar or reading this book for that matter. It takes a lot of work, but now is the time to start.

By evaluating our methodology and applying the principles that are relevant to your particular business model, you can strengthen your firm's practices. This book offers a framework and guidelines, not rigid formulas. We recommend you tailor our standard process to suit your projects and your organization's culture. In the end we expect that many of you will succeed in changing your approach to building trading systems. Others of you, however, will read this book and yet continue to put projects on the fast track with daily deliverables and blame the financial engineers and the traders and the programmers for failure. Only in retrospect, then, will you learn the true value of quality.

CHAPTER ◆ 2

Key Concepts and Definitions of Terms

The disciplines of trading, quality, technology, and new product development each have their own concepts and vocabularies. In this chapter, we describe key concepts and define key terms that we will refer to in later chapters. We have placed this chapter up front because an understanding of the concepts and definitions presented in this chapter is absolutely essential before proceeding with the rest of the book.

2.1. Benchmarking

A benchmark is a standard against which to compare performance. Over the course of this book, we will use the term benchmark to mean two different but related things:

1. An **index, sector, or peer group benchmark** is a reference point against which trading/investment system's performance measurements can be made. In this respect, we compare a system's performance to an index like the S&P 500, or industry sector, or direct competitors. All trading/investment systems must have a benchmark. An execution benchmark is also a reference point (usually VWAP or an implementation shortfall, or pretrade) against which trade execution performance measurements can be made.[1]

   Sailboat racing is a good analogy. In sailing, speed is proportional to length; sailboats do not plane for long periods of time. Weight is a second major factor; light boats plane before heavy boats. As a result, sailboats are handicapped according to a formula, which determines the overall speed of a boat given optimal sailing in a given weather condition.

   To make races "fair," organizers group sailboats with similar handicaps into sections. To win the race, sailors must first win their section. Nonetheless, weather is a key factor. If the weather favors smaller boats, the winner of the section grouping small boats tends to win overall.

   The same can be said about trading/investment systems. Market conditions at any given time may tend to favor one classification or section of trading/investment systems, for example, small cap funds or large cap funds. The media holds up the winner of the section as the winner overall for, say, the past year. This process is repeated year after year with a new winner in each.

In sailboat racing, the sailors that win their section are considered to be excellent sailors; the sailors that win overall are just lucky. (Incidentally, this is why the Olympics has very stringent rules on the boats, crew weight, and sail material, and runs multiple races before declaring a winner.) The same thinking should hold for fund managers. Applying quality by way of our methodology will not necessarily make your trading/investment system the winner overall, but over time it will make you one of the rare traders or money managers that consistently beats your sector benchmark.

2. **Process benchmarking** is, according to the American Society for Quality, "the search for best practices, the ones that will lead to superior performance."[2] This definition requires organizations to investigate industry practices and to accurately assess their own performance and that of their trading/investment systems. Process benchmarking demands that firms understand the best practices of its competitors to the extent possible and to research new ideas and methods, in order to gain and maintain competitive superiority.

So, process benchmarking is not just copying what some other firm does, it is rather a continuous self-improvement process in which firms measure performance against that of best-of-breed competition, determine how those competitors have achieved their performance levels, and use the information to improve the firm's own strategies, operations, and business processes. In trading/investment system design and development, we will benchmark four processes:

- Quantitative methods, including trade selection and execution algorithms.
- Data cleaning and backtesting processes.
- Technological architecture.
- Portfolio and risk management techniques.

Benchmarking is not just a buzzword. Management must actively structure benchmarking methods to ensure thorough and accurate investigations.[3] In any case, benchmarking will usually require several iterations to arrive at a best practice.

Process benchmarking requires a significant expenditure of resources: time, people, and money. It is possible to expend large amounts of time in a process benchmarking study and receive little in return for the effort. We know of trading firms that spend years researching and millions of dollars on salaries, hardware, and software, only to end up with nothing. The selected process benchmarking project must have the potential to result in a return on the investment.[4]

Process benchmarking focuses effort on how to improve a trading/investment system by exploiting best practices, not best performances. A best practice may not be the same for every system because each has its own data, technology, and underlying stochastic processes. As trading/investment systems most often integrate off-the-shelf components, we define component benchmarking as the method of comparing the performance of third-party hardware or software against known best practices.

In the dynamic, fast-paced financial markets, finding and adapting best practices is no longer an option; it is a necessity for firms that intend to survive.[5] A sought-after trading algorithm may be unique; the true best practice is unknown, maybe even unknowable. Nevertheless, we will use the term to mean the continuous search for better practices that will yield a competitive advantage.

2.2. Best Practices

Best practices are techniques or processes that are more effective at delivering a particular outcome than alternative ones. It is important to recognize that as financial markets change and technology evolves, best practices also change. So, the term "best practices" is better defined as a learning process for continual improvement.[6]

Best practices in trading, according to Philip Weisberg, CEO of FXAll in their publication *Best Practice in Foreign Exchange Markets*, "all stem from a few core goals—control, transparency, efficiency and responsibility to clients, whether this means best execution or advising them on the most appropriate financial product." Weisberg also notes that "to add value to our clients we have to create efficiencies right across the life cycle." Furthermore, "there is growing pressure on hedge funds to save money and cut operating costs." And, "it is clear that technological and administrative capabilities, such as automated trading and post-trade operational efficiency, are becoming increasingly important to hedge funds."

"The rapid advance of technology in markets is driving the movement towards best practices. Systems and processes that might have been unattainable are now within the bounds of possibility—and hence of best practices."[7]

In the end, Paul Wilmott too predicts that "importance of good business practices will return, replacing blind reliance on mathematical models."[8]

2.3. Capital

With respect to trading/investment system start-ups, we distinguish between types of capital, provided by two separate groups of investors:

1. Seed capital, which enables the management company to progress through the design and development process.
2. Investment capital, which the management company invests according to the trading/investment strategy on behalf of clients, to whom the firm has a fiduciary responsibility.

2.4. Conformance

If the performance metrics, that is, process outputs, that a trading/investment system is generating are consistent with those generated during backtesting or with the benchmark, we say that the system is in conformance, or conforming to specifications, and only common cause variation exists. The presence of defects, or special cause variation, events that are inconsistent with the backtesting or benchmark, implies nonconformance with specifications.

2.5. Continuous Improvement, or *Kaizen*

ISO defines continuous improvement as "recurring activity to increase the ability to fulfill requirements." In trading, continuous improvement describes the ongoing firmwide effort to better:

- existing trading/investment systems through more effective trade selection algorithms, position management techniques, risk management techniques, and faster and more robust technology, as well as,
- the process of trading/investment system development and refinement.

The Japanese word *kaizen*, meaning "to change for the better" or "improvement," is often used in quality-related research to refer to continuous improvement.

2.6.   Customer, Client, and Investor

Since only the customer can define quality, both top management and product teams should fully understand who their customers are and what their needs are. (The definitions of the terms "client" and "customer" are not identical though we will use the terms interchangeably. A client is a person that uses professional services, whereas a customer is one who purchases goods or services. Quality requires a customer focus, while professional services require client focus.) With respect to trading/investment system start-ups, we distinguish between two investor groups we consider to be clients, or customers:

1. **Seed capital providers** in the management company. For clarity, we will identify seed capital providers as such, or as seed investors. The customer in this sense may be a proprietary trading house for whom the product team works, a traditional money management or mutual fund firm, a hedge fund, a group of venture capitalists, or an individual or group of individuals. Seed investors provide capital for development and operation of a trading/investment system. They also earn the management fees.

2. **Investment capital providers**, to whom the product team owes fiduciary responsibility. Anyone who provides capital for the investable sum of a trading/investment system will fall under the term investment capital provider, or simply investor or client. An investor may also be the proprietary trading house for whom you work, a traditional money management or mutual fund firm, a hedge fund, a group of venture capitalists, or an individual or group of individuals.

As with all quality, in our methodology customer focus is the top priority. In this sense, the term customer applies to both seed capital providers and investment capital providers. While this book covers processes for design and development, understand that the product team's attempt to satisfy demands of both of these groups drives all processes. For the purposes of our discussion of quality and trading/investing, we will assume that customers, that is, investors of all kinds, demand better returns and lower risk relative to an associated benchmark and at lower cost.

2.7.   Corrective Action

According to ISO, corrective action is any "action taken to eliminate a detected nonconformity." Accordingly, corrective action is a fix and not a patch or containment of nonconformity. Corrective action may be taken in response to nonconformity of a trading/investment system, as well as to the process of trading/investment system development.

2.8.   Delphi Techniques

The well-known Delphi method is a forecasting mechanism based on a systematic, iterative gathering of independent, open-ended inputs from a panel of selected experts. It solves problems by establishing consensus among panel members through repeated problem definition, discussion, and feedback. Usually, in later iterations, panel members rate the relative importance of individual items. The Modified Delphi approach begins with a pre-defined set of items, which typically better controls the process.

The Wideband Delphi method, made popular by Barry Boehm in *Software Engineering Economics*, uses interaction and consensus to forecast effort, therefore lending itself well to trading/investment system development projects. Boehm's steps are

- Panel coordinator distributes a form outlining a specification and a section for estimation.
- Panel coordinator convenes a meeting where panel members discuss issues related to forecasting and estimation.
- Panel members then fill out their forms anonymously.
- Panel coordinator prepares and distributes a summary of the individual written estimates.
- Panel coordinator convenes another group meeting to focus discussion on points where summary estimates vary significantly.
- Panel members fill out forms again and the process is run again until consensus is reached.[9]

The Wideband Delphi method is useful because it raises and builds consensus on several issues important to the trading/investment system development process, including work breakdown structures, scheduling, project assumptions, as well as risks to the development process. Wideband Delphi can sit on top of other estimation methods, for example, a scoring model, improving them by incorporating additional participants, and iterative feedback and refinement.

2.9. Design and Development

Design and development is the set of processes that transforms requirements, generally defined in a Money Document, into a working trading/investment system. This includes ongoing position and risk management. Design and development is sometimes referred to as product realization.

2.10. Document

The *American Heritage Dictionary* defines a document as "a written or printed paper that bears the original, official, or legal form of something and can be used to furnish decisive evidence or information."[10] Our methodology uses documents to verify that product teams follow proper processes and procedures over the stage and, furthermore, that the outputs of that stage meet the input requirements of the following stage.

2.11. Financial Engineering

According to the International Association of Financial Engineers website, the primary definition of financial engineering is as follows:

Financial engineering refers to the application of various mathematical, statistical and computational techniques to solve practical problems in finance. Such problems include the valuation of derivatives instruments such as options, futures and swaps, the trading of securities, risk management and regulation of financial markets.

No single set of mathematical tools, computational techniques or financial theory describes financial engineering. Rather, it is the synthesis of a variety of these elements. Financial engineering is a practical field and a practitioners' field by its nature. It is driven in large part by practical problems that arise in the course of daily business; the nature of the problems demand that practitioners draw from as broad a palate of tools as possible to find the best solutions to their problems.[11]

Financial engineers on the trading side come in two flavors: multifactor quants and arbitrage quants. Multifactor quants use multifactor models to develop funds that can quickly switch between sectors and investment styles to take advantage of changing market trends. Arbitrage quants use derivatives, short-selling, and leverage to take advantage of small, short-term inefficiencies in markets. Multifactor quants develop multifactor and filter systems, whereas arbitrage quants develop filter and trigger systems.

2.12.   Gate

Our methodology borrows gates from Dr. Robert G. Cooper's Stage-Gate® method.[12] Gates are meetings where go/kill decisions are made, where weak projects are weeded out, and scarce resources are reallocated toward more promising projects. Gates act as checkpoints along the new product development process. Where traditional gates allow only for two outcomes—either a go or kill decision—K|V allows for five potential outcomes: go, kill, hold, return, trade.

2.13.   Innovation

Innovations are essentially new ideas, in the form of new products, methods, or even simply new improvements to old ideas. More concrete are our definitions of bottom-up and top-down innovation.

- **Bottom-up innovation** is research-driven innovation, where product teams invent new strategies with breakthrough research. Systems built in this way may then be offered to customers. This is essentially a quality engineered solution in search of a market need.
- **Top-down innovation** is driven by explicit customer needs, where investor research uncovers demand for certain types of risk. A product team then focuses on developing a trading/investment system to satisfy that demand. This is the more traditional customer need in search of a quality solution.

Management should cultivate several forms of both of these types of innovation. Whatever the driver of innovation, in either case, both customer quality, that is, investor satisfaction, and engineered quality must be achieved.

2.14. Life Cycle

Trading/investment systems have life cycles in the way that any new product does. Shorter-term, higher frequency systems tend to have shorter life cycles, whereas longer-term, more fundamentals-driven systems tend to have longer life cycles.

- **Design stage.** Trading strategy design, idea inception through Stage 1, where the product team benchmarks requirements according to the vision and scope set forth in the Money Document.
- **Testing stage.** During design and development (i.e., during the product realization process), shadow trading in Stage 2 of our methodology and probationary trading in Stage 3 will generate measurable performance indicators that may or may not be indicative of those encountered during maturity.
- **Growth stage.** During the growth stage, investable assets are gradually being allocated as qualified opportunities arise, though the full sum has not yet been invested.
- **Maturity stage.** During the maturity stage, the available funds are fully invested and performance should conform to test results and/or the benchmark. Maintaining maturity requires continuous improvement to prevent decline.
- **Decline stage.** During the decline stage, trading/investment system performance fails to conform to test results and/or the benchmark. Continuous improvement measures may not be effective and the trading/investment system may be shut down.

Continuous improvement (kaizen) processes should extend the maturity stage of any trading/investment system that would otherwise use static algorithms and technologies.

2.15. Modeling Software

As we define it, the term modeling software will refer to whatever software is being used to model or prototype quantitative and risk management methods. By use of the term, we mean to include Excel, Resolver, MATLAB, Mathematica, SAS, Zack's, or any other similar software package.

2.16. Preventive Action

The ISO definition of preventive action is "action taken to eliminate the cause of a potential nonconformity" or special cause variation. Our definition applies this to trading/investment system nonconformity. The key word is eliminate, as opposed to reduce or contain a nonconformity. Many firms use a patch to quickly contain problems. A patch does not eliminate the problem.

2.17. Process or System

The *American Heritage Dictionary* defines a process as "a series of actions, changes, or functions bringing about a result" or "a series of operations performed in the making or treatment of a product."[13] According to Deming, "a system is a network of interdependent components that work together to try to accomplish the aim of the system. A system must have an aim. A system must be managed."[14]

Furthermore, processes or systems can be either singular or continuously recurring. From an engineering perspective, a process consists of actions that take time, expertise, and other resources, to create changes in the properties of one or more objects under its influence. Our methodology looks at two continuously recurring processes or systems:

1. The process of interdependent human components cooperating to design and develop trading/investment strategies and enabling technologies, called product realization in ISO 9000. (Essentially, this system creates the second process or system.)
2. A working trading/investment system generating measurable performance metrics.

While the two terms are used interchangeably in literature relating to quality, we will for clarity attempt to refer to the first definition above with the term "process" and the second with the term "system."

All work is accomplished through processes, and trading/investment system development is no different. The methodology presented in this book is essentially a set of interrelated processes that transform inputs into outputs, which in the end transform raw financial and market data into a working trading/investment system.

2.18.   Process Approach to Management

A process approach requires a trading or money management firm to view its operations as a series of interrelated and interacting processes. Such an organization must identify and understand its processes for trading/investment system design and development and consciously manage them. Furthermore, such an organization should measure, monitor, and analyze trading/investment system performance to ensure conformity and implement preventive and corrective actions necessary for achievement of results and continuous improvement.

2.19.   Product

A product is the outcome of a product realization process. As we use the term, a product is a working trading/investment system that conforms to backtesting results. Several resources are required to design and develop a product—people, machines, facilities, and money.

2.20.   Product Realization

Product realization is the process that brings a product into reality. Product realization processes are those that conceive of the product in response to customer requirements; define, implement, and operate the means of production; and at the same time verify or validate the design and the production processes. As we use the term, product realization consists of the design and development, testing, implementation, and ongoing management of a new trading/investment system.

2.21. Product Team

A cross-functional business team includes all the people who will be associated with the trading/investment system design and development project: financial engineers, traders or portfolio managers, programmers, and marketing personnel. The product team may require one or several people from each of these groups to work together daily until the project is completed.

2.22. Quality

ISO 9000 clause 3.1.1 defines quality as the "degree to which a set of inherent characteristics fulfills requirements." That definition is a bit abstract because in the end quality can only be defined by the customer. Nevertheless, we can talk about aspects of quality, such as fitness for use, and meeting or exceeding customer requirements and expectations. We can also discuss quality characteristics such as waiting time, safety, reliability, security, responsiveness, competence, dependability, accuracy, and effectiveness of communications. Whatever quality characteristics are important to customers should be measured, monitored, and analyzed to identify areas for improvement.

ISO also defines a quality management system as a "management system to direct and control an organization with regard to quality." Quality management principles include:

- Customer focus.
- Leadership.
- Involvement of employees.
- Process approach.
- System approach to management.
- Continuous improvement.
- Factual approach to decision making.
- Mutually beneficial vendor relationships.

Over the course of this book, when using the term quality we mean to include quality itself as well as the quality-related disciplines Six Sigma and Lean.

2.23. Quality Money Management

Quality Money Management (QMM) is composed of all the procedures for development, research, testing, implementation, and management of trading/investment systems, including delineation of responsibility, all deliberately aimed at achieving performance levels consistent with or above the objectives of seed capital providers and investors. This is not a onetime effort. QMM requires ongoing commitment to improve continuously the systems of trade selection, execution, risk management, and all other trading/investment system processes and the performance of statistical process control on risk attributes. When these procedures are taken together, they define how management of the trading/investment organization operates.

2.24. Quality Planning

Part of quality management focuses on setting quality objectives and specifying necessary operational processes and related resources to fulfill Quality Money Management objectives. A quality plan is a document specifying which procedures and associated resources will be applied by whom and when to a specific project.

2.25. Software Quality Attributes

A software quality attribute is an observable characteristic of a system. A quality attribute requirement is the threshold value a system must meet with respect to a quality attribute.

- **Functionality.** These usually represent the main product features that are defined within the business domain of the solution being developed.
  - **Capacity.** For example, can the software listen to 50,000 options at the same time?
  - **Extensibility.** For example, can I add new markets to the system sometime in the future? Can the software be augmented?
  - **Interoperability.** For example, will the system work with our legacy execution system?
  - **Availability.** For example, will the system be up over night?
  - **Scalability.** For example, can I add 10,000 more options?
  - **Security.**
  - **Recoverability.** For example, what if I have positions over night? What if the network fails?
- **Usability.**
- **Performance.** For example, how many milliseconds will it take for my order to reach the exchange?
- **Reliability.** For example, does it ever make a mistake?
- **Supportability.**

Quality assurance testing in K|V 3.4 will make sure all requirements are met.

2.26. Stable or Stationary System

A stationary process or system, also called an in-control process, is a stochastic process whose probability distribution is constant, that is, the mean and variance do not change over time. We can also describe a stable or stationary system as one that contains no special cause variation, only common cause variation. A stable system can also be a process where all the causes of variation are known and accounted for, leaving the system to be governed only by common causes of variation, so that process outputs are then fairly predictable. Several conditions will indicate that a process is "out of control." Such conditions are often viewed in control chart tests. Stability involves achieving consistent and, ultimately, higher process yields through the application of an improvement methodology.

2.27. Standard

A standard sets out specifications and procedures designed to ensure that trading/investment system design and development processes, trade selection, position management, or risk management algorithms meet their respective purposes and consistently perform to intended use. Standards solve issues ranging from efficient development to addressing investor suitability concerns. Standards also simplify trading/investment system design and development and reduce non-value-adding costs.

2.28. Statistical Process Control

Statistical process control (SPC) is a method for recognizing and controlling special causes of variation in a process, often with control charts. By using the central limit theorem, SPC controls processes with stochastic outputs. When the mean of samples from a process shifts (say plus or minus three standard deviations), we consider the underlying process to be out of control.

2.29. Timeboxing

Timeboxing fixes the completion date for an iteration, or loop. (An entire project may also be timeboxed.) If the planned requirements for a loop in the spiral cannot be met within the timebox, the scope should be reduced to meet the completion date. In this way, each intermediate prototype or implementation of a trading/investment system will always be stable and tested, and delivered on time. Of course, over our four-stage methodology, all timeboxes need not be of the same length. Nevertheless, shorter, simpler iterations are better than long, complex ones. In the end, timeboxing will increase focus and productivity.

2.30. Top Management

Product teams operate trading/investment system value streams. Top management has the authority and responsibility to oversee and direct the activities of product teams. Within its function, top management provides seed capital for trading/investment system development and either provides investment capital with its own funds or gathers investment capital through a distribution network. Additionally, management oversees the peer review function for selection of trading/investment systems as well as management of the portfolio of new and working trading/investment systems. At many firms, the management function is performed by a cross-functional peer group acting as a product approval committee.

2.31. Trading/Investing

We define three stages of a trading or investing system:

1. **Shadow trading**, sometimes called paper trading, is simulated trading, where a system generates real-time signals, but executes only dummy orders.

2. **Probationary trading** is live trading, where a system generates signals, but executes trades in small quantities.

3. **Full trading** is live trading, where a fully functioning trading/investment system generates signals and executes orders in their total quantities.

2.32. Trading/Investment System

This book presents solutions to several risks that commonly arise during the development of trading and money management systems, which we will group together under the term trading/investment systems.

A trading/investment system consists of the interacting position selection and execution algorithms, that is, the rules and business logic necessary to enter into and exit from positions in the financial markets, as well as the technology required to partially or fully automate the trading, benchmarking, portfolio, and risk management processes. Such rule-based trading/investment systems apply the science of financial engineering to the management of portfolios of securities and derivative instruments. Trading/investment systems can take on the form of traditional long-only mutual funds, hedge funds, and proprietary, high frequency trading systems.

While the ideas and methods presented in this book focus on trading/investment systems, they will work equally well when applied to creation of other quantitatively focused financial systems, including execution, risk management, accounting, and other middle and back office systems.

2.33. Trading/Investment System Maturity Model

We use the structure, but modify the wording, of the Software Engineering Institute's Capability Maturity Model (CMM)[15] to apply to trading/investment system development. Each level of this model is a well-defined step toward achieving a mature trading/investment system design and development process.

Level 1: **Initial.** The trading/investment system development and management processes are ad hoc. Few processes are defined and success depends on individual effort. At this level, schedule and cost targets are regularly overrun and firms often implement trading/investment systems using inappropriate tools.

Level 2: **Repeatable.** Basic design and development processes are established to track costs, schedules, and trading/investment system specifications. Successful processes on one project are repeated on subsequent projects that are similar.

Level 3: **Defined.** Design and development as well as ongoing management processes are documented, standardized, and integrated into the culture of the firm. All projects use an approved, tailored version of the standard process for design and developing of trading/investment systems.

Level 4: **Managed.** Detailed measures of the development process and trading/investment system quality are collected. Both the development process and working systems are quantitatively understood and controlled.

Level 5: **Optimized.** Continuous process improvement is facilitated by quantitative feedback from the design and development process as well as from working systems, fostering new ideas and technologies.[16]

2.34. Value Stream and Value-Stream Mapping

For our purposes, a value stream consists of the activities required to design and develop a working trading/investment system from concept to launch to ongoing management. Identifying the entire value stream for each financial product is a step which trading and money management firms rarely attempt but which almost always exposes enormous amounts of waste.[17]

Our methodology is essentially a trading/investment system value stream map in that it identifies the activities along the value stream and their flow.

2.35. Variation

Performance of a system can be measured. Measurements will reveal two types of variation:

- **Common cause variation** is fluctuation caused by unknown factors resulting in a stationary, but random, distribution of process output around a mean. Furthermore, common cause variation is a measure of the potential of a process or system, that is, how well the system will perform after all special causes of variation have been removed. Common cause variation is also called random, nonassignable, or noncontrollable variation or noise.

- **Special, or assignable cause, variation** is that fluctuation caused by known factors, or root causes, and resulting in nonrandom outputs. Special cause variations shift process output and are caused by specific process inputs. Once accounted for, corrective action can potentially remove special cause variations.

2.36. Vendor

A vendor is a company that sells processes or technology for trading/investment system implementation. By vendor, we mean to include companies that sell software, such as order management systems or FIX engines; hardware, such as servers and leased lines; data and databases; and analytics, such as risk management processes or market indicators.

2.37. Summary

The field of quality has a vocabulary unto itself. Because over the course of this book we will intersperse the languages of financial markets and quality (and by use of the term quality we mean to include Quality, Six Sigma, and Lean), clarity is important. Additionally, we have defined several terms from finance that are not necessarily clear with respect to trading/investment system development.

CHAPTER ◆ 3

Overview of the Trading/Investment System Development Methodology

Any business process can be managed and trading/investment system design and development is no different. It can and should be managed. Too often, though, poor quality of execution dooms projects. What financial firms need is a more systematic approach to conceive, design, develop, and manage new trading/investment systems. Prior to implementation, though, the process of development of such a system should follow a well-defined, well-documented flow of steps according to a development methodology. The organization should establish controls over the sequence and interactions—of how the output of one process acts as the input for a subsequent process, in total, forming the product realization process.

While at times new trading/investment systems may be designed, developed, built, and tested using a ready-made process, more often a new process will be needed for each new system. Learning from experience, the organization can determine what new or additional verification, validation, monitoring, inspection, and testing processes will be needed for a new trading/investment system. Top management must also determine acceptance criteria for the product, the basis or test results upon which the product will be accepted or rejected, and define what documented evidence they will expect.

The problem is, as trading/investment system development progresses, traders and financial engineers like to make changes. No matter how hard they try to freeze the design, product teams may not be able to do so. The ability of any methodology to respond to change often determines the success or failure of a trading/investment system design and development project. Plans and methodologies must be flexible and ready to adapt to changes in the market and technology. If something changes during design and development, our methodology allows product teams to revert to a previous stage and rapidly progress again.

We have designed our incremental development methodology so as to ensure a rapid development cycle with quick deliverables and consistent quality standards. Before development can begin, however, the product team must raise money to fund the development. To raise money a product team needs a Money Document.

3.1.   The Money Document

Trading and money management is a business and in order to succeed, product teams need to raise research and development capital as well as trading capital, from either inside the firm or outside it. Either way, the product team will need to describe in a persuasive manner why a system can potentially be better than competing systems and worthy of seed capital. As with most business proposals, a focused, professional business plan is essential, especially in a start-up stage.

As a template, we present the Money Document, the primary deliverable before fully laying out a trading/investment system's business plan. A well-done Money Document serves as a Vision and Scope Document by outlining the business goals of a proposed trading/investment system in a clear and concise fashion in order to persuade management or outside investors (that is, collectively, seed capital investors) to provide the initial capital needed for research and subsequently for development of a trading/investment system according to our four-stage methodology. The Money Document answers the fundamental question, "Is this a business worth investing seed capital in?"

While the Money Document comes before entry into our methodology, its own development should follow an iterative process, forcing the product team to focus on building a business. The resources allocated to a project, subsequent to the delivery of a Money Document and management approval, will permit entry into our development methodology.

Our methodology owes its structure to a combination of the traditional waterfall of Royce[1] and spiral methodology of Boehm[2] from software, the Stage-Gate® methodology of Cooper[3] from new product development, and Lean, Six Sigma and Agile development, combining aspects of these well-known methodologies, seeking to gain from their respective strengths and overcome their respective weaknesses.

3.2.   Waterfall Methodology

Royce's traditional waterfall methodology for software development consists of four stages—analysis, design, implementation, and testing—that vaguely map to the four stages of our methodology, as you will see.

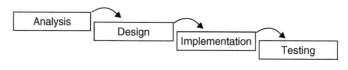

FIGURE 3-1

In sum, the waterfall methodology forces a development team to plan before building and requires a disciplined approach to development. Using the waterfall methodology, teams avoid the pitfalls of creating systems before project plans are precisely defined and approved. But, the waterfall methodology has at least two drawbacks.

The first drawback is that the waterfall methodology tends to put too much emphasis on planning; all details must be defined up front before design and implementation can begin. As a result, it leaves no room for error and no process for handling feedback on problems that inevitably occur during design and development. In the fast moving financial markets, where trading opportunities come and go, the waterfall methodology on its own is not flexible enough to react to new information and knowledge. (Project managers and IT professionals sometimes misunderstand that trading system specifications are rarely, if ever, fixed up front.) To overcome this shortcoming of the waterfall methodology, the spiral methodology was developed.

The second drawback is that prior to progression to each new stage, the waterfall methodology does not include a gate process—a management decision as to whether to or how to continue development based upon the system's potential. For this reason, our methodology includes gates after each stage.

3.3. Spiral Methodology

In the spiral methodology, a smaller amount of time is initially devoted to the four stages—research, planning, implementation, and testing—followed by several iterations or loops over each. As the loops progress, and the spiral gets larger, development teams add more detail and refinement to the project plan. At some final level of detail, each stage will be complete.

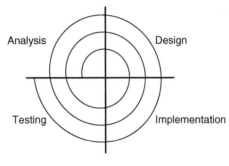

FIGURE 3-2

In this way, the spiral method allows for feedback as problems arise or as new discoveries are made. Problems can then be dealt with and corrected, unless they are fatal. So in a spiral project view, intermittent or prototype implementations provide important feedback about the viability and profitability of a trading/investment system.

As with the waterfall method, though, the spiral method is not without drawbacks. In the spiral methodology, the loops can grow without end and there are no constraints or deadlines to terminate iteration. This can lead to scope creep, a loss of project focus, messy logic, and unnecessary digressions, where the project plans may never contain a clear and concise design. (This can lead to a fuzzy front end of never-ending spirals, where researchers pursue new and better knowledge instead of working systems.) For example, spiraling has no criteria for transition from one tool set to another, say from Excel to C++. So, the looping process demands clear conditions for termination. K|V borrows from the waterfall and Stage-Gate® methodologies to overcome this weakness.

3.4. Stage-Gate® Methodology

Our methodology applies concepts from the science of new product development, including idea generation and screening, business analysis, development and testing, technological implementation, to trading/investment system development. Unlike new products, though, there are no external customers of the trading/investment system or enabling software itself. Rather, investors buy the results, or track record, of the system and its interaction with the trading team. Nevertheless, we can all benefit from an understanding of new product development methodologies, in particular Dr. Robert G. Cooper's Stage-Gate® method, from which we borrow the concept of gates. Gates are management meetings with product team members where go/kill decisions are made and where weak projects are weeded out and scarce resources are reallocated toward more promising projects.

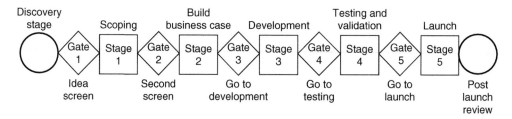

FIGURE 3-3

Gates act as checkpoints or screens along the new product development process. In our methodology, gates are an opportunity to check whether or not the business reason for developing the trading/investment system is still valid and whether additional seed capital is warranted. New in our methodology, however, is the set of gate outcomes. Where traditional gates allow only for two outcomes—either a go or kill decision—K|V allows for five potential outcomes:

1. **Go.** Go on to the next stage of the waterfall.
2. **Kill.** Kill the project entirely.
3. **Hold.** Hold development at the current stage for reconsideration at a future date.
4. **Return.** Return to a previous stage for additional research or testing.
5. **Trade.** Trade the existing prototype. (Should only be allowed for short-lived strategies, e.g., event trading algorithms.)

Well-organized gate meetings will each have a unique set of metrics or criteria for passage to the next stage. If the project is allowed to continue or is sent back to a previous stage, the gate meeting should also outline the plan for moving through the next stage and define the deliverables expected and the criteria for evaluation at the next gate meeting. The criteria for each gate should include a check on the deliverables, minimum standards, potential for profitability, competitive advantage, technical feasibility, scalability, and risk. Gate decisions give rise to risk of error:

- **Type I gate error.** Allowing to "go" a system that either cannot be built or will not succeed in its competitive advantage.
- **Type II gate error.** Killing a system that can be built and can achieve a competitive advantage.

We consider gates to be real option expirations. When management chooses to invest seed capital in a new trading/investment system development project, it is essentially buying a call option on that project, an option that expires at the next gate meeting. At the gate meeting, management can choose to exercise the option and fund the next stage, or allow the option to expire worthless, killing the project. This decision should be based on estimates of future cash flows and probability of those cash flows. So, gates predefine incremental releases of capital. An optional release structure limits seed capital providers' loss potential by tying capital to deliverables, predefined real option valuation techniques, and gate-passage criteria. Essentially, at each successive gate, management must make a progressively stronger commitment to the trading/investment system development project. In the end, well-organized and well-run gate meetings will allow losing projects to expire worthless, and allow worthwhile projects to proceed to the next stage.

3.5. Six Sigma, Lean, and Agile Development

Our methodology also benefits by including concepts from Six Sigma, Lean, and Agile development as well. As with Design for Six Sigma, the goal of our methodology is to drive investor needs into the product design, increasing performance and decreasing process variation. The by-products of Six Sigma are a reduction of defects and an improvement in profits and employee morale and the quality of trading/investment systems. Also, as with Lean principles, our methodology focuses on reducing waste in order to reduce production time. Like Lean Six Sigma, our methodology combines both Lean and Six Sigma to focus on both speed and quality. The goal is to build a better trading/investment system at a better cost in a shorter amount of time.

Lastly, as with Agile software development methodologies, our methodology attempts to compromise between too much process and no process, welcoming change by allowing for reversions to previous stages and minimizing risk through iterative prototyping. Furthermore, our methodology emphasizes real-time face-to-face communication through team-based development.

3.6. Trading/Investment System Development Methodology

As we have said, in order to overcome the respective shortcomings of each methodology, we combine them into a single paradigm for trading/investment system design, development, and management. Our four stages progress in a waterfall design-test-implement-manage (DTIM) framework, but within each stage four steps are connected in a spiral structure. The activities of each timeboxed spiral are organized into a four step plan-benchmark-do-check framework focusing on in order: quantitative methods, data, technology, and risk management, respectively.

Note that our plan-benchmark-do-check framework differs from the traditional plan-do-check-act methodology from quality due to the heavy research component in trading system development. Benchmarking consists of critical comparisons of available quantitative methods, data cleaning algorithms, technological implementation, and risk management methods that will yield a competitive advantage. Unlike standard software or manufacturing models, where there are clearly defined methods and goals up front, in trading system development the methods and goals are fuzzy, or poorly defined, and solutions will be highly complex. Most of these solutions need to be researched and replicated prior to moving forward. Furthermore, without benchmarking, firms cannot know if methods either derived in-house or those provided by vendors are correct.

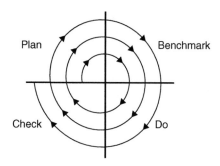

FIGURE 3-4

- **Plan.** Determine the problem to be solved, gather information, and then plan and document a course of action to solve it (i.e., what do we need to do?).
- **Benchmark.** Research and compare alternative solutions to arrive at the best practice (i.e., what is the best way to do it?). Over the four stages of our methodology, we will benchmark quantitative methods, data cleaning and optimization algorithms, technology, and portfolio and risk management processes.
- **Do.** Carry out the best practice course of action (i.e., we do it).
- **Check.** Check to see if the desired results were achieved along with what, if anything, went wrong, and document what was learned (i.e., how did we do?). If results are not satisfactory, repeat the cycle using knowledge gained.

The four-stage spirals consist of, for the purposes of this book, three loops. (In practice, they may consist of more or fewer as needed.) Each loop consists of one pass over each of the steps in the stage spiral.

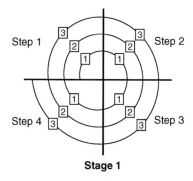

Stage 1

FIGURE 3-5

(We will refer to the activities of each stage, each step, and each loop in the following way:

K|V *Stage Number.Step Number.Loop Number*

For example, the shorthand K|V 1.3.2 would refer to Stage 1, Step 3, Loop 2.)

Again, at the completion of each stage is a gate that will allow top management to kill the project, return to a previous stage, hold until some future time, continue to the next stage of development, or trade the existing prototype. After completing the fourth and final stage, the methodology requires that we repeat the entire four-stage waterfall for continuous improvement.

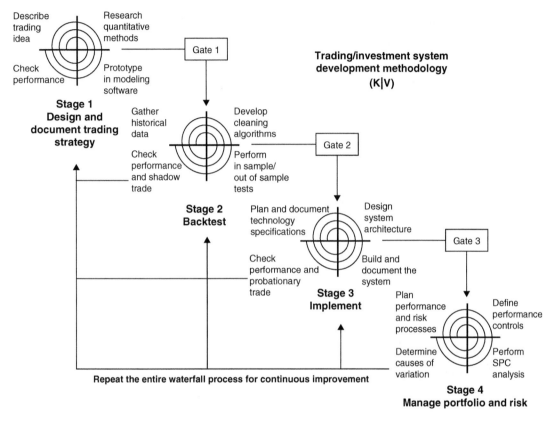

FIGURE 3-6

Here are the four stages of our methodology and their respective components:

Stage 1. Design and document trading/investment strategy

1. Describe trading/investment idea (K|V 1.1)
2. Research quantitative methods (K|V 1.2)
3. Prototype in modeling software (K|V 1.3)
4. Check performance (K|V 1.4)

Gate 1
Stage 2. Backtest

1. Gather historical data (K|V 2.1)
2. Develop cleaning algorithms (K|V 2.2)

3. Perform in-sample/out-of-sample tests (K|V 2.3)

4. Check performance and shadow trade (K|V 2.4)

Gate 2
Stage 3. Implement

1. Plan and document technology specifications (K|V 3.1)

2. Design system architecture (K|V 3.2)

3. Build and document the system (K|V 3.3)

4. Check performance and probationary trade (K|V 3.4)

Gate 3
Stage 4. Manage portfolio and risk

1. Plan performance and risk processes (K|V 4.1)

2. Define performance controls (K|V 4.2)

3. Perform SPC analysis (K|V 4.3)

4. Determine causes of variation (K|V 4.4)

Repeat the entire waterfall process for continuous improvement

The rest of this book is dedicated to developing trading/investment systems according to these 16 steps, but first we will provide a brief overview of each.

3.7.   Design and Document Trading/Investment Strategy (Chapter 7)

It is more fun to do than to plan. This very human trait is only driven out by years of schooling and experience. The problem with planning in the financial markets is two-fold; one, most traders prefer to trade rather than plan; and two, most planners never get the opportunity to trade since the management in financial firms generally rises from the trading ranks. Consequently, proprietary trading and money management firms tend to optimize for the short term, and wind up building trading/investment systems that are not unique, making it difficult to persuade investors to invest in the new strategy and not existing ones with long track records instead.

These types of systems, however, do not generally result in maintainable excess returns and are very often not scalable. This could explain why the vast majority of money managers underperform their benchmark index and why so many hedge funds close each year for underperformance. Complex systems that will generate long-term returns are built one step at a time and evolve along the way as new knowledge is gained.

3.7.1.   Describe Trading/Investment Idea (Chapter 8)

This first step is often the hardest one. The more complex the trading idea, the more difficult it becomes to plan and communicate it clearly. Before any development on a system begins, we must first be able to fully articulate the business logic and quantitative methods of the system. We have, though, already started the description process—the description created for the Money Document will serve as a starting point. Over the iterative research process, planning each loop will require team members to define goals and set boundaries for that research.

3.7.2. Research Quantitative Methods (Chapter 9)

Very rarely do we dream up completely new trading/investment ideas. Rather, we build on ideas of the past and add new twists. Many times new trading strategies are essentially copies of old ones that proved to be successful.

The next step is to research and benchmark the relevant mathematical and logical models, which may include deriving proprietary algorithms and/or applying publicly available research from journals, books, the Internet, or white papers. The research process may also include gaining an understanding of the trade selection and execution methodologies of other successful systems. The goal of research is to speed and refine our path to the best algorithms, which will form the basis of a Business Rules Catalog for the system. Building and maintaining a proprietary library of unique quantitative methods is key to the long-term success of a firm.

3.7.3. Prototype in Modeling Software (Chapter 10)

As we have said, despite its shortcomings, Excel as well as other modeling software (such as Resolver, MATLAB, Mathematica, or Zack's) are rapid development environments for testing trade selection and execution algorithms. The goals of prototyping are to quickly build several generations in order to evaluate whether a particular idea warrants further investigation and to promote risk-based iterative development, where the hardest pieces of the project are investigated first.

Currently, many trading/investment ideas are immediately built as working systems if confidence is high that the trader and/or the system will make money. This type of development often proceeds without proper definition prior to implementation despite understood software risks. Prototyping algorithms enables us to clearly define algorithms, GUI and data requirements, and develop a baseline application for regression testing. These prototypes will form a foundation of the Technology Requirements Specification document in later stages. Baseline regression with prototypes enhances defect detection and removal more than any other strategy.

3.7.4. Check Performance (Chapter 11)

We will use prototypes as a starting point in the discussion of how we are going to measure the performance of the system. Without a clear plan on how to measure performance and define success and the variability of the trading system, we cannot proceed to the next stage.

We define three types of trading/investment systems and each type will require a unique mechanism for performance testing. The three foundation types are:

1. **Trigger systems.** A good example of trigger trading/investment systems are ones built on technical or valuation indicators.

2. **Filter systems.** This is the traditional system for mutual funds.
3. **Signal strength systems.** These systems are typically highly quantitative in nature and use blending or regression algorithms.

(In reality, few trading/investment systems fit neatly into a single, simple category; more complex systems combine aspects of two or even all three. Nevertheless, our methodology applies to all types, simple and complex.)

If at this first checkpoint performance measurement shows system failure, the methodology necessitates a looping back to previous stages. The goal is to quickly stop development on trading/investment systems with a low probability of success.

3.8.   Gate 1 (Chapter 12)

In order to pass through a gate, several questions need to be answered and as we will see Gate 1 has several such questions. If the questions are answered to the satisfaction of the customer (usually top management), development will be allowed to proceed to Stage 2.

This gate will prevent development of the trading/investment system from moving to the backtesting stage until the required activities and deliverables have been completed in a quality manner. Furthermore, at the gate meeting we will chart the path ahead by ensuring that plans and budgets have been made for the backtesting stage.

For the remainder of the book we will use the term "well defined" to mean that a trading/investment system has passed through this first gate. The implicit assumption is that the methodology has been rigorously followed in a quality fashion.

3.9.   Backtest (Chapter 13)

Complete system analysis necessitates research into and optimization over past market movements as a way to analyze and validate the system—a process called backtesting. A backtest is a simulation and statistical analysis of a trading/investment system's inputs and outputs against historical data and would be a unique process for each system. A backtest will prove the capability of the trading/investment system to meet investor requirements and is based on statistical measures. Such proof will demonstrate that the system exceeds the traditional buy and hold sample path.

3.9.1.   Gather Historical Data (Chapter 14)

Once the initial prototype has shown a system to be worthy of further investment of time and resources, the real task of backtesting begins. Prior to building and implementing the system, we must test it over a relatively large set of historical data and preferably for a large sample of instruments. As a result, firms build a customized database of historical data and purchase or build a software tool that allows for proper backtesting of the system.

While it may seem elementary, planning and investigating the availability of data is very important. Required data may either not exist at all or is prohibitively expensive based upon the prospective returns of the trading/investment system.

3.9.2. Develop Cleaning Algorithms (Chapter 15)

One of the major obstacles to building a profitable trading/investment system is dirty data. Virtually all data contains errors, outliers, which may or may not be errors, and point in time problems. Even data purchased from reliable vendors has errors. As a result, the identification and removal or correction of errors and known issues in the calculation data prior to optimizing the trade selection and position management algorithms is very important. Development of a Data Transformation Management System (DTMS) that will scan data for errors and irregularities is essential.

A DTMS should implement data cleaning algorithms that can operate on live-time as well as historical data. Algorithms that cannot be run in real time prior to trade selection should not be used on historical data or the cleaned, historical data will skew the results. The benchmarked cleaning algorithms will be added to the Business Rules Catalog begun in Stage 1.

3.9.3. Perform In-Sample/Out-of-Sample Tests (Chapter 16)

Performing a proper in-sample/out-of-sample test is perhaps the most critical step in the process. Financial engineers are keenly aware of the extent to which in-sample results may differ from out-of-sample results and trading/investment algorithms must be examined against both before progressing to the implementation stage. A well-developed, optimized system will perform similarly out of sample as it does in sample, so it is of utmost importance to hold back some historical data for out-of-sample testing. Such a test will result in one of three outcomes for a trading/investment system:

1. Profitable both in sample and out of sample.
2. Profitable in sample, but not out of sample.
3. Unprofitable both in sample and out of sample.

If the system is profitable both in sample and out of sample, it will very likely receive capital to begin implementation and trading as soon as possible. If a system is profitable only in sample, it will likely be allocated additional resources for continued research. If, however, the system proves to be unprofitable both in sample as well as out of sample, it will likely be scrapped altogether.

3.9.4. Check Performance and Probationary Trade (Chapter 17)

At this point, we acknowledge that traders may very well demand to trade the prototype. However, it should be understood that the only purpose this should serve is to fully understand the performance monitoring tools that will be required by management in the later stages. Be aware that the performance of shadow trading may not be indicative of the performance of the completed system, largely due to the lack of SPC controls placed around the prototype system. The lack of controls at this stage can lead to, for example, overweighted sector bets.

Shadow trading may also occur in order to more fully understand the behavior of the system and as mentioned to understand what reporting tools management will need. As before, checking the performance of the system will prevent additional time and resources from being spent on unprofitable projects. We may need to loop back to the initial research stage and reassess the quantitative methods and algorithms.

3.10.   Gate 2 (Chapter 18)

As with Gate 1, Gate 2 has several questions we must answer before proceeding to Stage 3. If the passage criteria are met, to the satisfaction of seed investors, they will release capital and development will proceed to Stage 3.

This gate will prevent development of the trading/investment system from moving to the implementation stage until the required backtesting activities and deliverables have been completed in a quality manner. Furthermore, at the gate meeting we will chart the path ahead by ensuring that plans and budgets have been made for the implementation stage.

3.11.   Implement (Chapter 19)

Building a fully or even partially automated trading/investment system is in many respects a software development project. As a result, implementation will require:

1. Connectivity between and interoperability with disparate software and hardware systems for trade execution.
2. Object-oriented software design to encapsulate trading logic.
3. Other processes such as optimization and data storage.

This will require creation of plans and blueprints before programming in a language like C# or C++ begins.

3.11.1.   Plan and Document Technology Specifications (Chapter 20)

The purpose of technology specifications, such as the IEEE Software Requirements Specification (SRS), is to fully define the functionalities and performance requirements of the trading/investment system. The specification documents allow the team of hardware engineers and programmers to quickly build the system with the correct functionalities and to the proper specifications. As with all high-level planning documents in engineering, we expect these to be revised in an orderly process as we spiral through the development. (This is no different from the revision process of quality management using ISO 9000.)

Prior to constructing a trading/investment system we will have essentially completed a project Vision and Scope Document in the form of a Money Document. The specifications include all of the required features and functionalities and all of the items that hardware and software engineers will need to design, build, and modify the production system. Further, the specifications should clearly define the steps for the project along with documenting all of the detailed information about the network and hardware requirements, trading algorithms, including data dictionary, data flow maps, GUI requirements, error handling maps, and report generation maps. Fortunately, much of this work will already be done and the specification documents will largely be based upon the proto-types and descriptions created in earlier stages of development.

3.11.2. Design System Architecture (Chapter 21)

Architecture documents are blueprints of the hardware and software that will form the architecture of the trading/investment system, including the financial calculations, real-time data and user interfaces, order routing connections, reporting functionalities, and any other necessary processes.

As with architecture, the bigger and more complex the building or trading system, the more important blueprints are to the success of the project. The more complex a trading/investment system becomes, the more important it is to create detailed architectural plans, using an agreed-upon set of notations, as with the Unified Modeling Language (UML), which enables project designers and programmers to communicate the details of system design. Through the use of a common notation, problems can be solved in an object-oriented way before programming begins. As much of the technological implementation depends on interoperability and connectivity, glue code, computer programming code that is written to connect reused commercial off-the-shelf applications, should be well documented in the architecture documents.

3.11.3. Build and Document the System (Chapter 22)

Once the hardware is built and network connections are completed, the process of construction will be a step-by-step march through the architecture documents. Since the architecture documents themselves will be evolving as the team spirals through implementation, the ideal solution is to continue to add and refine it as the system is built.

The data maps will continue to grow along with adding new dictionaries to clearly show both the calculation of each field and where it came from and where it is used. A GUI section also will grow to include a screen shot of each form. The error handling section will continue to grow to list all known open issues.

The product team should produce a user manual that will allow a junior trader to operate the system and a junior programmer to maintain it. (Actually, the product team should be writing this manual over the course of the entire development process. By this stage and step, the production of a user manual should be a process of assembling already-written documents.) While junior-level people are not overseeing the system, the documentation should be placed at that level. It is assumed that since the systems we are building are proprietary in nature we will not need commercial-level user documentation. Documentation should be treated as a trade secret so staff external to the product team cannot steal its intellectual property.

3.11.4. Check Performance and Probationary Trade (Chapter 23)

Once the completed system has been built, probationary trading can progress to find any design flaws in the trading algorithm or the technology prior to trading the full investment sum, officially beginning the track record period, or managing customer funds. The second purpose of probationary trading is to allow the trader or money manager time to use the trading tools and determine what additional reporting tools need to be built to properly manage the embedded risks. Management tools should contain, for instance, displays of underlying data for calculations and trade reports. At this point, the performance of the trading/investment system will be similar to those of the final product.

3.12.   Gate 3 (Chapter 24)

As with Gates 1 and 2, Gate 3 has several questions the product team must answer before proceeding to Stage 4. If the questions are answered to the satisfaction of the customer, development will be allowed to proceed.

This gate will prevent development of the trading/investment system from moving to the final stage until the required activities and deliverables have been completed in a quality manner. Furthermore, at the gate meeting, management will chart the path ahead by ensuring that plans and budgets have been made for the next stage. Approval at this gate permits full investment and trading of the system.

3.13.   Manage Portfolio and Risk (Chapter 25)

Portfolios of securities and derivatives require constant monitoring and so successful implementation of a trading/investment system necessitates that periodic reports be generated to show the performance of the working system. These reports will present the portfolio statistics and performance metrics, risk calculations, and provide documentation of the attribution of gains and losses. Traders are notorious for turning off systems right before they become profitable and leveraging up after positive statistical anomalies with strong mean reversion, which is why SPC is a critical tool. Reports should present a proper determination of the root causes of variation from the expected results, that is, nonconformance, and an action plan to deal with those variations, that is, corrective actions.

3.13.1.   Plan Performance and Risk Processes (Chapter 26)

Markets are stochastic and trading/investment system performance will be stochastic as well. Stochastic processes should be measured and monitored by tools built for the purpose. The product team, with risk management, must plan for a system of monitoring and reporting portfolio statistics, performance metrics, and risk factors. Essentially, these risk control techniques will help the team understand whether or not the system is working within specifications and in conformance with the backtest and/or a benchmark.

3.13.2.   Define Performance Controls (Chapter 27)

To monitor a working system, automated processes should keep track of the system's performance metrics. These will be valuable when reevaluating the underlying premise for the system relative to the performance experienced during backtesting.

Furthermore, every system should have a benchmark. Using a portfolio attribution system the product team can clearly identify the performance relative to the benchmark. So, to make sure that the trading/investment system consistently outperforms its benchmark the team must perform attribution analysis on the portfolio as well as on the benchmark itself.

3.13.3. Perform SPC Analysis (Chapter 28)

Risk management is effectively the same as statistical process control in manufacturing industries. Are the underlying market distributions the same as the ones that were used to generate returns for the backtest? Is the system in conformance with the backtest and the benchmark index? Or are the inputs or outputs of the process different? Risk calculations and reports will give top management a snapshot of performance, and potential losses and drawdowns both on an absolute basis and relative to the benchmark over a given time horizon. However, of course, while methods for dealing with extraordinary occurrences may be built into a trading/investment system, gaps may render them useless.

3.13.4. Determine Causes of Variation (Chapter 29)

After the attribution analysis is completed and the product team understands all of the bets the system is placing to beat the benchmark, the team must build one final set of tools. These tools are based on process control theory—namely, quality, statistics, ANOVA, and design of experiments.

The goal of these tools is to determine the causes of variation, or nonconformance, in the trading/investment system's performance. If a process goes out of control, then a cause for that condition can be found. If the team can find the cause of the process being out of control, then they can fix the process and theoretically experience less variance than the benchmark going forward.

Profitable trading/investment systems have life cycles. Eventually, the market will close the door on every trade. So, systems will need to be continuously tweaked and eventually scrapped. The goal is to quickly stop trading systems that lose their edge before they cause large losses.

3.14. Repeat the Entire Waterfall Process for Continuous Improvement (Kaizen) (Chapter 30)

Think of the steps in our methodology as a continuous, never ending spiral. Once the product team gets to the end, they start again to improve the system with new refinements or create new ideas altogether.

Top management is responsible for cultivating a professional environment that promotes continuous improvement through an ongoing effort to improve trading/investment system performance, increase efficiency, and reduce costs. Product teams should focus on continuously making small improvements to the trade selection, data cleaning, order management, and risk management processes as well as the enabling technologies, until the life cycle of the trading/investment system runs its course. A firmwide culture of sustained continuous improvement will concentrate efforts on eliminating waste in all processes of a trading organization.

Through small innovations from research and entrepreneurial activity, trading and money management firms can discover breakthrough ideas. These include, among other things, the creation of new trade selection algorithms, application of existing systems to new markets, and the implementation of new technologies for more efficient trade execution. Through continuous improvement, trading firms can extend the maturity stage of the trading/investment system life cycle.

CHAPTER • 4

Managing Design and Development

Some market watchers decry the incubator fund process of new product development. Such funds are generally owned by insiders, have very small amounts of assets, and are aggressively managed. If they hit the jackpot, they are offered to the public and aggressively marketed. If they flop, they are given a quiet burial. Firms start large numbers of incubator funds in order to "upwardly bias investors' estimates of their ability, and thereby attract additional inflows," killing them when they fail to repeat their success after they enter the real world. Nevertheless, in an industry that has come to focus on asset-gathering as its highest priority, product proliferation works. Investment management is now more about product marketing than investment management.[1] This is not necessarily a bad thing. By adopting quality, money management firms add credibility to their performance records. In a quality world, investors can safely assume that a fund's advertised rates of return are accurate, not pure illusion. Here is an example.

Returns of giant mutual funds often include the superior results they achieved when they were much smaller, returns that a fund's bloated size virtually precludes in the future. Management greed condones the marketing of funds and gathering assets beyond their ability to manage the funds effectively.[1] This is a striking conflict between the interests of the investors and that of the manager. This type of behavior is inconsistent with quality. Quality is the best marketing tool of all because it encompasses both substance and image.[2]

4.1. Trading and Money Management Firms

Development of trading/investment systems is centered on knowledge-based innovation. As such, top management and product teams must work in concert to build new revenue streams in the hopes of earning entrepreneurial reward with management's primary responsibility being to invest in new strategies that may potentially become new revenue streams and to maximize the value of the portfolio of new and existing trading/investment systems and product teams' responsibility being to maximize the value of individual systems. Financial firms do combat against other firms, where product teams are the foot soldiers and trading/investments systems are the weapons. The new Lanchester strategy for financial market is that the victors:

- Innovate to develop trading/investment strategies.
- Increase revenues by attacking competitors within range of their own core competencies.

45

- Defend their strategies through continuous improvement against competitors launching their own systems.

Financial innovation is not just inspiration or genius. It's hard work and management must be committed to its systematic practice to make it happen. To succeed, managers must identify new opportunities, assemble product teams, and oversee the process of development, with the end goal of creating more and more revenue-generating business units that junior employees can maintain and enhance. 3M's "official vision statement is to be 'The Most Innovative Enterprise in the World.' Unofficially, it seems that almost every [3M employee] has a pet project or some team activity that is focused on promoting innovation in his or her particular area."[3]

4.2. Portfolios of Trading/Investment Systems

Cooper, Edgett, and Kleinschmidt in their seminal text *Portfolio Management for New Products* report that top performing firms in other industries have:

- An explicit, established method for portfolio management.
- A management that buys into the method and supports it through action.
- A method with clear rules and procedures.
- A method that treats projects as a portfolio.
- A method that is consistently applied across all appropriate projects.
- A tendency to rely less on financial models as the dominant portfolio tool, and more on business strategy to allocate resources and make portfolio decisions.[4]

No trading/investment system, or proposed trading/investment system, exists in a vacuum. Each trading opportunity will inevitably compete with and be evaluated against other trading ideas. As a result, it is important for top management to develop portfolio evaluation methods and perform periodic portfolio reviews.

Portfolio evaluation methods are not the same as the project evaluation methods administered at the respective gates. Rather, portfolio management methods are prioritization and resource allocation tools. (It just happens that in terms of timing, portfolio evaluation processes fit well with gates.) If a particular trading/investment system under development is allowed to proceed to the next stage, management can also at that time make a decision regarding the project's priority relative to that of other projects. Effective portfolio management leads to:

- A ready willingness to kill trading system development projects.
- Focus, that is, not having too many projects and resources spread too thin.
- Rigorous review and tough decision points.
- Choosing the right projects.
- Strategic criteria for project selection.

The portfolio management process requires a strong commitment from top management and should include periodic reviews of the portfolio of all trading/investment systems. Weak portfolio management translates into a reluctance to kill new trading/investment system projects and a selection process based on emotion or politics. The end result is a lack of focus, too many projects, too few resources, and quality of execution will suffer.

4.2.1. Research on New Product Portfolio Management Methods

Portfolio management is fundamental to successful product development, and companies outside the financial industry have used portfolio management techniques for decades. After 30 years of research, both academic and real world, Cooper et al.[5] have found that many methodologies exist, including the following:

- **Financial or economic models.** These models treat project evaluation much like a conventional investment decision. They include traditional computation approaches such as: payback, breakeven analysis, return on investment, discounted cash flow methods (net present value, internal rate of return), and Productivity Index. Most often in such models, the net present value for each project is compared to cutoff criteria for gate decisions. The present value used to rank projects resources are allocated by rank. These methods also often make use of Economic Value Added (EVA) style techniques.

- **Scoring/ranking models and checklists.** These models rely less on quantified data and more on subjective assessments about strategic fit with corporate objectives, competitive advantage, and market trends.

- **Probabilistic financial models.** These models include Monte Carlo simulation, decision tree analysis, and options pricing theory. Gates are expirations on project options. Top management can choose to let the option expire worthless or exercise the options and fund continued development.

- **Behavioral approaches.** These methods include Delphi approaches, which provide a systematic way of integrating the collective wisdom of a decision-making group.

- **Optimization techniques.** This type of model searches for an optimal mix of new and existing projects, maximizing profit subject to resource constraints.

- **Decision support systems.** Such systems are mathematical models that rely on statistics, simulation, and optimization, but nevertheless permit management interaction and intervention.

- **Mapping approaches.** These models use bubble diagrams to visualize projects on a Cartesian plane, extending the stars/cash-cows/dogs/wildcats model. These diagrams typically plot potential reward against the probability of success.[5]

Research shows that portfolio management methods work. Businesses that have gone to the trouble of installing a systematic, consistent, explicit, and formal portfolio management system are clear winners. Their portfolios outperform the rest on all six performance metrics: higher-value projects, better balance, the right number of projects, a strategically aligned portfolio, and so on. The message is clear: Step 1 is to make a commitment to installing a rigorous portfolio management process in your business. Cooper et al. have found that:

- Financial models usually do not work well. Those businesses that use financial models as the dominant portfolio selection method end up with the poorest-performing portfolios. Because markets are stochastic, forecasting environments and probability distributions are difficult at best.

- Heuristic approaches are better. More strategic approaches seem to work better. Businesses that rely on strategic methods outperform the rest.
- No one model is perfect. Rather, most experts prefer a hybrid approach that permits a customized approach to portfolio management. Watch out for an over-reliance on financial methods and models for project selection.
- Scoring models are effective prioritization tools.
- Bubble diagrams work and should be a part of any model. They help firms achieve a balanced portfolio.
- Any portfolio management method is better than no method.[5]

Portfolio management is complicated by the facts that money, people, and time are limited, and that different projects, at different stages of development, may be interconnected—shared resources, strategies, technologies, or people.

4.2.2. Effective Portfolio Management

Senior management is the driver of strategy and must be closely involved in new product project selection decisions. Portfolio methods must mesh with the organization's business strategies, the decision framework of the business, as well as its core competencies. We recommend top management:

- Map out the process for determining resource allocations in strategic buckets.
- Design iterative portfolio review processes and define the key portfolio metrics.
- Name a portfolio process manager.

Because speed to market is a pivotal competitive advantage, we recommend the use of (i.e., valuing projects as real options at gate meetings using) scoring models in a Modified Delphi-style framework, unless your firm has the quantitative wherewithal to optimize a portfolio of profit centers in an EVA framework. The strengths of scoring or ranking models are that they:

- Do not overemphasize quantified, financial criteria that are likely to have doubtful reliability, especially in the early stages.
- Capture multiple goals, such as strategic importance, competitive advantage, and potential to raise investment capital.
- Reduce gate decisions and prioritization decisions to a finite number of parameters and iterations.
- Subject each trading/investment system to critical review on a complete set of criteria.
- Force managers to discuss strengths and weaknesses of each project in depth.
- In the end yield a single score which is useful for project prioritization.

Using a scoring or ranking model, management can establish consensus among panel members through repeated problem scoring, discussion, feedback and, if necessary, rescoring or reranking.

4.3. The Role of Top Management

Top management is the driving force. Leadership, commitment, and active involvement of top management are essential for developing and maintaining a commitment to quality. According to ISO 9004:2000 clause 8.5.1: "Management should continually seek to improve the effectiveness and efficiency of the processes of the organization, rather than wait for a problem to reveal opportunities for improvement. Improvements can range from small-step ongoing continual improvement to strategic breakthrough improvement projects." At many firms, this management philosophy is the rule, but at others managers obsess about working harder, not smarter, viewing quality as luxury. But, financial firms have to work smarter if they expect to uncover new and competitive business opportunities with fewer resources. Quality and continual improvement are now becoming the normal approach to doing business.

For the two processes we consider over the course of this book—the product realization process (K|V Stages 1, 2, 3) and the process of a working trading/investment system generating performance metrics (K|V Stage 4)—top management is ultimately responsible for strategic planning and execution, including:

- Building new revenue streams, starting and seeding many new strategies, and rolling out to investors the strategies that offer the best risk/reward ratios.
- Raising capital by selling shares in the firm. The firm is essentially a portfolio of uncorrelated trading/investment systems. (Portraying the firm as a high technology firm, with proprietary intellectual property that drives cash flow, will buy a much higher valuation ratio.)
- Maximizing, or optimizing, the value of the portfolio of new and existing trading/investment systems.
- Establishing quality as a firmwide initiative and setting the example.
- Overseeing trading/investment system value streams.
- Organizing product teams, defining responsibilities and assigning authority, and promoting and rewarding successful teams.
- Managing vendor relationships and partnerships.
- Assessing the need for new product-specific processes, documentation, and resources.
- Sharing best-of-breed ideas between product teams, colinking value streams, and removing the blame culture.
- Resolving disagreements between product team members and other employees.
- Creating a learning environment and encouraging all employees to become innovators.
- Tolerating setbacks to maximize individual and organizational learning.

With respect to gate meetings, management is responsible for:

- Reviewing gate meeting deliverables prior to the meeting itself.
- Attending gate meetings to review and verify the progress of trading system development projects. (Verification at gate meetings will ensure that design and development outputs of one stage have met the design and development input requirements of the coming stage.)

- Using objective criteria when making go/kill decisions.
- Committing the necessary resources to ensure project success over the following stage.
- Communicating go/kill decisions throughout the organization.
- Prioritizing individual projects within the portfolio of new and working systems.[6]

Top management also sets internal policies and controls, addresses responsibilities to investors and regulators, proposes transactional practices, and oversees business continuity planning. In accordance with the *MFA's 2005 Sound Practices for Hedge Fund Managers*, some of top managements' important responsibilities are also to:

- Oversee the investment, risk, and trading policies of the trading/investment systems under its purview.
- Impose appropriate controls over its portfolio of trading/investment systems.
- Select reliable third-party vendors on the advice of product teams including data providers, prime brokerages, risk management, and valuation providers, and monitor their performance.
- Establish firmwide practices for benchmarking third-party vendors.
- Identify regulatory filings and assure compliance with all laws and regulations that apply to the firm's products.
- Establish written compliance policies with respect to trading restrictions, confidentiality, proprietary trading, disclosures, and other issues.
- Select and monitor performance of clearing and executing brokers.
- Monitor exposures to operational risk with random spot checks, reviews, and internal controls.[7]

The first goal of strategic planning and execution in a trading/investment firm is to generate returns either by investment in profitable trading/investment systems and/or by fees paid to the firm by the fund itself. To that end, top management must assess its organizational strengths (core competencies), weaknesses, opportunities, and threats (called SWOT analysis), and optimally focus the firm's efforts around value streams, that is, processes that design and develop trading/investment systems. Once focused, only top management can authorize the expenditures of money and time necessary to make the trading/investment system realization process happen. To quote Peter Scholtes:

> Quality leadership recognizes—as Dr. Jospeh M. Juran and Dr. W. Edwards Deming have maintained since the early 1950s—that at least 85% of an organization's failures are the fault of management-controlled systems. Workers can control fewer than 15% of the problems. In quality leadership, the focus is on constant and rigorous improvement of every system, not on blaming individuals for problems.[8]

4.3.1. Assembling Product Teams

In a value-stream organization, management assembles cross-functional product teams consisting of motivated, highly skilled people in each functional area—financial engineering, trading or portfolio management, programming or IT, and marketing.

Management gives the team members the support and incentives they need, and then trusts them to get the job done. While processes and procedures are important, people make them work. As Alistair Cockburn, one of the inventors of Agile development, once said, "Process and technology are a second-order effect on the outcome of a project. The first-order effect is the people."[9] If the team does not have the minimum skills to succeed, a good process will not save a project from failure. Conversely, a bad process can make even a team of highly skilled workers fail at innovation.

Product team members can only innovate and contribute valuable improvements to quality in the right environment, where they can work without fear of failure, of having their trading ideas stolen, or even of being fired for missing short-term goals. Quality management creates such an environment, overriding the personal inhibitors of teamwork, where employees believe that the only person they can trust is themselves; where employees may be too proud or too bitter and may not be able to rely on others to help achieve their goals; or, where employees feel that cooperation is unfitting.[10] Martin Marietta's "Material Statement of Unifying Principles" sets the tone for its organization:

> In our daily activities we bear important obligations to our customers, our owners, our communities, and to one another. We carry out these obligations guided by certain unifying principles:
>
> > Our foundation is INTEGRITY.
> > Our strength is our PEOPLE.
> > Our style is TEAMWORK.
> > Our goal is EXCELLENCE.[11]

But, teams do not gel automatically or due simply to some credo. Teams can be difficult to manage. Most Six Sigma companies assign a quality facilitator whose entire job is to act as arbitrator to ensure teams work smoothly together. Also, teams tend to work best when management delegates responsibilities to team leaders and supports team members in their search for best practices to fulfill those responsibilities. In this way, the team shares design, development, and testing responsibilities and is accountable for all aspects of the project. (To reduce errors by 90%, the team should spend 30–40% of its time testing benchmarked processes.) Furthermore, teams work best when:

- They feel accountable to investors.
- They focus on overall process effectiveness rather than individual tasks.
- They are held accountable for the performance of the team.
- Both team and individual achievement are recognized and when both individuals and team performance are incentivized to do things right.
- In a setting in which management and teams work together to plan and control work.[12]

Management can only persuade a group of people to act as a team when:

- Agreement exists as to the team's mission.
- Members adhere to team ground rules.
- Fair distribution of responsibility and authority exists.
- People adapt to change.[12]

Of course, a trader or portfolio manager who works to help other team members may not have as much revenue to show for his year-end bonus as he would if he had worked alone. What is the incentive? Short-term, me-first or long-term, team-first? Teamwork is a risky business, yet it is the only way to succeed. With respect to incentivizing financial engineers and IT professionals, we recommend a three-year bonus structure, where:

- 50% of the bonus is based upon the profitability of new trading/investment systems where the individual was a product team member.
- 30% is based on the current year profitability of trading/investment systems built in the previous year.
- 20% is based on the current year profitability of trading/investment systems built two years prior.

(Many engineering firms use a similar structure to ensure that engineers and team members have a continual stake in long-term success. If something breaks, the original product team members have a strong incentive to fix the problem.)

Additionally, organizations find they must be in a constant state of learning to survive. Top management must promote ongoing training and education; process improvement correlates highest with employee training. Success in learning whets an appetite for more learning. Product team members who succeed at seminars and industry conferences are motivated to continue learning and innovating at work.

Given product teams and a commitment to quality, management's responsibility is to understand the step-by-step inputs and outputs of trading/investment system development processes (using a mapping model like K|V), identifying the processes themselves and the support resources that result in successful systems, as well as determining the necessary organizational skills. Successful organizations think lean, starting with defining value in terms of specific trading/investment strategies with specific performance attributes managed at a specific cost.

> 3 M employed a "dual ladder" approach that allowed senior, technically inclined individuals with attractive career opportunities to advance, without having to switch to top management. In addition, the company held internal showcases for products and ideas to help encourage interdepartmental cross-pollination or "bootlegging" of discoveries. As a result of these steps, 3M employees tended not to move to other companies.[13]

4.3.2.   Forecasting Team Velocity

After completing a few working systems, management will gain a feel for product team velocity and be more able to forecast future projects and how much effort each step and each timeboxed loop will actually take. Velocity measurements are significantly more accurate tools than scope-based controls, because they measure how much time it actually took to deliver a complete (and tested) trading/investment system. After only a few steps on a new project, management will have a highly reliable early prediction of project performance. (One way to visualize progress is with burn-down charts.)[14] A continuous flow of new trading/investment systems requires a reduction in variation of the design and development process through an even arrival rate of new strategies and parallel processing, that is, multiple projects and multiple teams. Managing multiple systems, both working and in development, requires a portfolio perspective and a portfolio management process.

4.4. The Role of the Product Team

Our methodology promotes team-oriented problem solving (in the style of TOPS or Ford 8D) for fact-based decision making. The product team is responsible for solving the problem posed by the Money Document—developing the market opportunity, generating the data to confirm the vision set forth in the Money Document, analyzing the technical feasibility, implementing the system, and putting in place performance monitoring processes. In the past, one person could do all of these things, the portfolio manager or trader who was the primary generator of trading profits. Today, however, the complexities are too much for one person:

- The mathematics is too complex.
- The trading strategies are too complex.
- The technology is too complex.
- The number of instruments makes trading even more complex.

A cross-functional product team consists of traders or portfolio managers, financial engineers, and programmers, who work together until the project is complete. (Each team member should write a brief autobiography so that management and/or investors can readily determine if the team contains the appropriate skill sets.) These uniquely named teams (the name describes what the team expects to accomplish) work preferably together in a single location—voice mails, emails, text messages, and instant messages generally cannot contain all of the information other team members need to know. Because good communication is usually frequent and informal, teams should have constant and direct access to everyone else to avoid wasting time. (In cases where physical proximity is not possible, or where an individual may be a member of more than one product team, good communication will be more of a challenge, and as a result, the focus of more effort.) The product team is responsible for:

- Maximizing the value of individual trading/investment systems.
- Defining the investment, execution, data cleaning, risk, and trading strategies of the trading/investment system.
- Writing the Money Document.
- Mapping trading/investment system value streams.
- Preparing and distributing performance information.
- Defining consistent and verifiable valuation policies, incorporating "fair value," for illiquid, hard-to-value instruments, and instruments with multiple official prices.
- Managing the development team of IT professionals and performing quality assurance and user acceptance testing of software.
- Recommending reliable third-party vendors/partners to top management.
- Overseeing the risk and portfolio management functions (K|V Stage 4), and reviewing performance data, risk position, and sources of variation.
- Developing and monitoring measures of leverage.
- Satisfying its double fiduciary responsibility—to provide better investment vehicles to investors and better financial results to seed capital investors.

While the product team is responsible for development of the trading strategy, it may not necessarily be responsible for ongoing operation and maintenance of the trading/investment system. If this is not the case, the operational risk increases due to having inexperienced people fixing problems. Very often, product teams move on to other design and development projects after implementing a new system. To the extent that teams may work on multiple systems, the goal is a continuous flow, or pipeline, of systems, each time increasing the velocity by improving the inputs and outputs of each step of the process. The product team should include individuals with the following skill sets and responsibilities:

TABLE 4-1

Traders or portfolio managers	Computer programmers	Financial engineers	Marketing professional
Trading	Prototype development	Quantitative research	Gather information on competing systems
Strategy development	Time lines	Backtesting	Raising investment capital
Performance testing	Performance testing	Performance testing	Performance testing
Implementation of algorithms	Object and data maps	Prototype development	Risk and portfolio attribution analysis
Risk and portfolio attribution analysis	Software design, programming, and code review	GUI and regression testing	Develop and present marketing materials

We recommend, depending on the nature and size of the project, one senior programmer and two junior programmers. (The goal is redundancy due to the risk of a single point of failure.) The lead programmer manages a software development team for Stage 3. A marketing professional should be involved in performance testing and monitoring of the trading/investment systems for suitability with the interests of the targeted investor group. Marketing a trading/investment system must interact with engineering and cannot exist separately from it, right from the outset. The product team writes the Money Document, which will clarify for all team members the business goal of the project. Clarity of purpose should eliminate problems associated with an information technology vision, a financial engineering vision, and a trader's vision that are not all the same. This should result in fewer broken promises later on.

Very important is the value stream manager, that is, team leader (who is usually also a functional team member), who directs the value-stream mapping process, approves the schedule, timeboxes (planning the schedule is best done by someone with experience using Gantt charts and critical path methods, which may very well be the lead programmer) and budget, moderates discussions, and in time of deadlock casts the deciding vote. The team leader also interacts with top management and investors, and leads presentations at gate meetings. Additionally, the team leader sets bonuses for team members, which gives the team leader equal power over a member's functional manager. Both management and the team members review the team leader once the project is complete. Normally, a financial engineer or senior IT professional makes better team leaders.

Additionally, as said, a team may have a facilitator, someone who is well versed in quality and teamwork, and helps the team interact more effectively, say, by having more productive meetings. A facilitator helps the team work smarter, but does not directly participate in the team's work or act as a rubber stamp for management. In this capacity, a facilitator keeps meetings on track, focusing discussion on gate deliverables, not hidden agendas.

In total, we recommend a product team size of between three and ten people. Smaller teams work faster and tend to produce results more quickly, while teams of greater size usually require additional advising and even subteams to operate effectively. Larger teams bring more and different knowledge and perspectives to the table, but move more slowly through the creative process (and time is usually of the essence). (Also, larger teams need heavier methodologies.) Firms may also consider using a subgroup of a few people as a design team, which reports periodically to the larger product team, as well as a software development team. Such a structure enables the design team to move quickly, while still benefiting from the peer review of the larger group.[15] Further, we of course recommend that the team manager be someone with experience managing multimillion dollar projects.

In general, a group will be more critical of its collective work than an individual.[16] A good team leader cultivates such an environment, where team members interact often and attend regular meetings. Good leaders use checklists to share ideas, to ask questions systematically, and to reformulate problems. While team members are sure to disagree, in resolving disagreements, they often do their best thinking. Nevertheless, in the end each team member is accountable to the team for finishing tasks on time. If one fails, the team as a whole fails.[17]

Importantly, management must clarify and communicate up front who owns the track record of the trading/investment system and how credit for performance will be shared, keeping in mind that retail customers prefer investment products they associate with a person instead of a firm. For retail funds, research shows that the financial media are more likely to mention funds with named managers. Since most such mentions or citations are positive, exposure leads to inflows. Despite this fact, firms today are less likely to identify managers than they were a decade ago.[18] We know of funds where the team members were not listed as managers. Rather, the named manager is a partner in the firm. This ensures that the ratings firms recognize a consistent manager.

According to Massa *et al.*, in fact, the share of funds managed not by named managers but by unnamed teams has increased by a factor of 3–4. Nevertheless, naming managers yields a significant marketing benefit and evidence also exists that naming a manager may create stronger incentives for the manager to perform well. Also found is underperformance by multimanager funds, though this is due entirely to underperformance by funds managed by anonymous teams; funds managed by multiple *named* managers perform as well as funds managed by named individuals.[18]

The research suggests that a manager (or managers) tolerates less return diversion when his (or their) name is publicly associated with the fund. Unnamed managers, it could be argued, have a higher tolerance for what we call nonconformance. Publicly giving managers or product teams credit for a fund's track record can serve as a powerful motivator. In the end, the decision to credit managers for fund performance generates a strong incentive.[18] We believe that the named manager should not be the team leader. Senior financial engineers and IT professionals should leave the trading/investment system after implementation to work on starting new systems. Keeping them with the system in an ongoing fashion will limit the long-term profitability of the firm. We recommend the named manager be either a marketing person or a trader, that is, someone who stays with the working system.

> Womack *et al.* (1990) cite the strong association of a new product's success with the career and reputation of the development team leader as a main reason Japanese new car development yielded better cars in less than half the development time compared to the US.[19]

The need to share credit in the end has tradeoffs. According to Massa *et al.*:

> Mutual fund investors as a group are known to chase past performance. Therefore, if investors associate a fund's performance with its manager rather than its family,

successful managers will enjoy significant bargaining power when they threaten to leave. As the hedge fund industry [has] boomed, so [have] outside options for successful fund managers. [Massa *et al.*] conclude that this fact—and the declining media penalty associated with offering team-managed funds—are the most likely explanations for the rise of teams in mutual fund management. Sharing credit can be in the firms' interest, but a firm needs to make certain it retains enough of the credit for itself.[20]

4.5.   The Fuzzy Front End

Product teams innovate. In the case of both bottom-up and top-down innovation, many new trading/investment system projects may be well defined while others may need additional definition before they enter the development phase.

A trading firm asked a simple question, "How do we keep the quants and the programmers under control? We know they are building stuff, but we have no idea what they are doing or when it will be done."

Poor definition is usually the result of weak predevelopment activities, where the target investor's needs are not well understood or only vaguely defined, and required trading/investment system features are fuzzy. Poorly defined projects waste considerable time seeking definition and redefinition. Better definition, through sound homework, actually speeds up the development process and reduces the odds of failure. With homework, there is a much higher likelihood of new trading/investment system success.

The term "fuzzy front end" connotes the unstructured, getting-started period of new product development, where the organization originates a trading/investment strategy and decides on whether or not to invest resources in its further development. It covers the phase between first consideration of an opportunity and when an idea conceived to exploit that opportunity is ready to enter the structured development process.[21] Relative to our methodology, the fuzzy front end includes all activities from the search for new opportunities and idea generation to the creation of a Money Document, which we collectively call K|V Stage 0), and through the design of a well-defined and documented strategy, when the strategy is no longer fuzzy, that is, through K|V Stage 1. For robust, scalable systems, just getting through Stage 2 of K|V can easily cost upwards of $1 million.

Although the fuzzy front end is the least expensive part of development, it can consume a lion's share of the time. As such, idea generation and screening is an essential part of design and development and our methodology, rather than something that happens prior to it.[22] Cooper and Kleinschmidt have found that "the greatest differences between winners and losers were found in the quality of pre-development activities."[23] The front end has the greatest potential for improvement with the least possible effort. Uncertainty, defined as the difference between the amount of information required to perform a particular task and the amount of information already possessed by the organization, can be reduced quickest and most cheaply during the front end. Systematic innovation will, down the road, reduce the number of deviations from front end specifications and increase the chances of success.[24]

Systematic innovation in trading and investment begins with an analysis of all sources of market opportunities. In business, most innovations result from a conscious and concerted pursuit of opportunity. According to Peter Drucker, seven sources of innovation exist:

1. Unexpected Occurrences
2. Incongruities
3. Process Needs
4. Industry and Market Changes
5. Demographic Changes
6. Changes in Perception
7. New Knowledge[25]

People make innovations. Now, of course, there are people who are more talented financial innovators than others, but often their talents lie in well-defined areas such as trading, quantitative or fundamental analysis, or even technology. The key is finding (or making) good innovators. According to 3M, the best inventors tend to have great technical skills, are creative, have broad interests, are problem solvers, are self-motivated, have a strong work ethic, and are resourceful.[26] However, identifying opportunities is a must. Two forms of opportunity exist:

- Market-driven, strategic trading or investment opportunities. These are found through bottom-up innovation.
- Customer demand-driven opportunities. These are found through top-down innovation.

The more complex the trading/investment strategy, the more difficult it becomes to make an early assessment of an idea, and the more complex and iterative the research and design process behind it should be. A high degree of newness makes it more difficult to reduce market and technological uncertainty. Therefore, most researchers endorse, again, the use of a cross-functional product team for idea generation and selection. Studies of other industries show that an interdisciplinary approach to idea generation and selection, more than any other front end activity, enhances communication and project success, and additionally ensures that investor and seed capital provider needs and technological capabilities are taken into sufficient consideration. Intensive front end planning helps to develop a common understanding of project tasks and milestones and therefore reduces uncertainties.

A shared team vision, a shared purpose and a shared plan of action that clarifies realistic project targets all help to create a sense of commonality. If all functions are integrated at the beginning, the team develops a common vision and goals and fewer conflicts occur later on.

4.5.1. Generating Ideas for New Trading/Investment Systems

Rapidly advancing technology, new electronic marketplaces, globalization of financial markets, and increased competition all impact the success of new trading/investment systems. Effective new trading/investment system development is emerging as the major strategic initiative for the decades ahead. One prerequisite to effective trading/investment system idea generation is having in place a new product strategy that defines areas of strategic focus relative to the organization's core competencies. For example, where market research reveals significant demand for a particular classification of risk, management develops a strategic focus on that area. In the end, though, ideas come from people, including:

- Customers
- Traders
- Programmers
- Financial engineers
- Management
- Competitors
- Reasearch journals, trade publications, the Internet
- Software and data vendors
- Sales/marketing staff
- Universities
- Research vendors.

So many new and different ideas and technologies exist these days that bringing people together often generates unexpectedly positive results. Management can foster innovation by getting traders or financial engineers from different product teams together at meetings, conferences, or committee meetings, creating an environment where employees feel free to seek out input of others from different parts of the company and where the individuals contacted are ready to share what they know.

More concretely, management can foster innovation by setting ambitious, quantifiable targets, for example, 30% of revenue must come from new trading/investment systems this year. Nor should management be afraid to deliver do-or-die ultimatums; such threats force product teams to move ideas through the process and into working systems.

Of course, not all new strategies get built. For some the timing is wrong, others are not sufficiently developed, for still others the resources simply are not available or they do not match with the company's current priorities. For this reason, some firms have set up trading/investment system idea libraries.

> *A top stock picker and portfolio manager was rumored to have in his basement nearly every article ever written on stock picking. A top options trader made it a habit to visit business schools in Chicago once or twice a year to talk with the faculty.*

A trading/investment system innovation strategy is a master plan that guides a business' new trading/investment system development efforts. It includes: the goals of the development efforts, the role of product development, areas of strategic focus including markets, processes, products, technologies, identification of core competencies, and research and development spending allocations in a portfolio framework. These plans incorporate information from trading/investment systems already in the market, systems under development, and systems planned for the future, taking into consideration product life cycles. This integration enables a longer-term view of the resource requirements of planned trading/investment systems and allows product line plans to be realistically balanced against expected development capacity.

4.6. Summary

While the number-one success factor for trading systems is the presence of unique trade selection and position management algorithms, trading/investment system innovation is still a process. For firms that convert to product teams and process management, the first visible sign will be that the time taken to turn concepts into launched systems falls dramatically. The top drivers of the process are

- Top management commitment to quality.
- The use of high quality, cross-functional trading/investment system development teams consisting of traders, financial engineers, IT professionals, and a marketing professional. Additionally, a facilitator may be used to keep the team on track.
- A high quality new trading/investment system development process, one that demands systematic approach to innovation—early product definition, tough go/kill decisions points, quality of execution, and thoroughness.
- Portfolio management processes to oversee new and existing systems that compete for scarce resources.

CHAPTER • 5

Types of Trading Systems

We classify all trading/investment systems into one of three broad categories—trigger systems, filter systems, and signal strength systems. (Our methodology is flexible so that it can be applied to any system.) Most often, of course, trading/investment systems do not fit neatly into one category. The lines are not black and white; they are varying shades of gray.

For example, an index volatility dispersion trading system could be classified under any of the three. First, trading index options against options on the constituent stocks when the valuations are different for a basket of options versus the index is what we call a trigger, or valuation, trade. Second, trading index options against a basket of stock options with implied volatility in the 80th percentile and historical volatility in the 20th percentile ahead, we call a filter trade. Third, trading the index options against an optimized basket of constituent options based upon qualitative or quantitative factors, we call a signal strength, or multifactor, trade.

The nature of any given trading/investment systems will determine the performance metrics evaluated over the course of K|V Stages 1, 2, and 3 and performance monitoring and risk management techniques employed in K|V Stage 4.

5.1. Trigger Systems

Trigger trading systems are those where an opening position is taken upon the occurrence of a trigger, and furthermore, that a closing trade is entered once another trigger occurs. A good example of a trigger trading system is one built on technical indicators. In such a system, a technical indicator signals the opening and closing trades, which are dependent only on the instrument itself, and not on other instruments, positions, or market conditions. Technical systems can range from a very simple moving average crossover system to very complex high frequency trading systems. We also consider market making systems to be trigger trading systems. Whatever the case, the concept is always thus, an event occurs and a trade or position is taken.

A portfolio of instruments could consist of many independent positions, a position in one not being influenced by a position in another. Such a portfolio may become heavily weighted in a single direction either long or short, and traders commonly place restrictions, such as a maximum VaR or a limitation on currency positions, on the portfolio risk to limit exposure. Trigger systems very often make use of high leverage.

A trigger signal is based on descriptive statistics of the inputs. To analyze and control a trigger trade, we apply statistical process control to:

- Total returns
- Winners versus losers
- Turnover per month
- Average trade length
- Number of trades over a time period.

5.2.   Filter Systems

Filter systems select positions based upon a screen, or filter. In such a system, an opening position may initially be taken based upon a trigger, say the purchase of a bond with certain duration and credit rating and in a specific industry sector. However, unlike a trigger trade, a filter trade is dependent on other instruments, positions, or market conditions to set the filter parameters. So, for example, the filter might be that a bond must yield in the top 25th percentile of the sector or the universe for a given credit grade. Even though the parameters for the trade selection appear to be trigger trades, what is different is that in this case one bond or 30 bonds may be purchased depending on the number that meet the criteria.

The second step in a filter trade is portfolio management, from basic risk restrictions to attribution analysis. A filter system holds the instruments in portfolio until they no longer meet the initial selection criteria or until they pass some other filter. (There could be one filter to enter the position and another to exit the position.) Statistical process control for a filter trade applies to the percentage of stocks that pass or meet filter requirements.

A filter is really a hypothesis test between two mean returns, the mean of the sample selected and the mean of the sample not selected. The normal outputs of a signal trade to be analyzed and controlled using statistical process control are

- Returns, excess returns versus the universe, excess returns versus the benchmark.
- Volatility of the portfolio for the entire period and rolling periods versus the universe and benchmark.
- Risk return measures such as Sortino and Sharpe ratios.
- Cumulative returns and annualized effective returns.
- Drawdowns.
- Correlation to the benchmark.

5.3.   Signal Strength Systems

A signal strength, or multifactor, system ranks instruments based on factors or indicators, such as P/E, P/S, or relative strength. Ranking stratifies the instruments into quartiles, deciles, or percentiles, and may be calculated relative to the investable universe or a subset of it. For example, high tech stocks generally have high P/E ratios given the perception of high growth rates, whereas basic materials stocks, where demand is relatively flat, are perceived as having low growth, and therefore have low P/Es. Ranking all stocks together by P/E, would effectively create a first decile consisting of all high tech stocks. To ensure a diversity in selection, algorithms should rank instruments within their sectors first. A blended P/E rank, weighted between the sector rank and the universe rank, produces a more robust signal. For price momentum signals, we normally recommend sticking with the universe rank, since the goal of a price momentum signal is to find instruments that are increasing in value the fastest.

Ranked signals should be tested individually, independent of each other, using statistics to determine their predictive ability. Individual signals are often grouped to form a single overall signal for position selection. Grouped signals should also be tested. The goal is to find a linear relationship between both the individual indicators and the group indicator, and returns using the Spearman correlation. (The correlation value is normally referred to as the information coefficient.) Sophisticated money managers mine data in this fashion to find anomalies and inefficiencies.

A multifactor system is effectively an ANOVA/regression test. The normal outputs of a signal strength trade to be analyzed and controlled using statistical process control are

- Ranks and returns by quantile, including cumulative active returns chart (fan chart).
- Standard deviations by quantile.
- Scorecard performance cart (i.e., growth of $10,000 versus benchmark).
- Sortino and Sharpe ratios by quantile.
- Statistical tests to determine if the means are different and the variances are homogeneous between quantiles.
- Drawdowns.
- Information coefficient.
- Number of weeks the top ranks have outperformed the bottom ranks.
- Correlation of the algorithms return to the benchmark. (Preferably zero.)

5.4. Example Trigger System: Statistical Arbitrage

In the trading industry, statistical arbitrage of stocks within a particular industry sector is popular because of their convergence characteristics. Statistical arbitrage is based on fundamental analysis. On a fundamental basis, the companies in the pair are very similar. This is the foundation of all pairs trades. Statistical arbitrage is a bet that the relationship between the prices of two stocks will diverge and then revert back to some predetermined mean ratio, since the market tends to price the two similarly. Therefore, short-term deviations from the mean will eventually correct itself for two fundamentally similar companies. Instead of correlation analysis, which does not work that well, this book will focus on looking for absolute return performance as opposed to performance relative to an index or peer group.

So, our trading system seeks out pairs of stocks that are in the same sector and have similar fundamentals. This similarity produces a relatively stable ratio between the prices of the two stocks. Our trading system monitors this ratio and uses it to generate trading signals as the ratio diverges or converges.

To create a more stable value for the ratio, our system uses a 30-day moving average of the end of the day stock price of each company. Observed spread prices around this 30-day moving average are essentially noise and not a true reflection of the value of the company. The goal of a statistical arbitrage trading system is to exploit this noise. Our system compares the observed market price of the spread to the more stable value, the 30-day moving average. To normalize the difference between the observed price and the 30-day moving average, our system uses a simple z-transform method:[1]

$$\Delta_{norm} = \frac{\Delta - MA_{30}(\Delta)}{\sigma_{30}(\Delta)}$$

- Where Δ is the observed price of the spread and the normalized prices, Δ_{norm}, expresses the normally distributed price in terms of standard deviation from the mean.
- The mean prices, $MA_{30}(\Delta)$, is defined as the 30-day spread-price moving average.

Assumptions of the strategy:

- A long position in the spread is defined as short Stock A and long Stock B.
- A short position then is defined as long Stock A and short Stock B.
- Same holding horizons of 20 trading days to measure the strength of the signal. (An alternative method is to have a signal to close the position, as well.)
- We assume that all opening trades are executed at the closing price on the day the signal is received and closing trades executed at the closing price n days hence.
- Dollar amounts assume that long positions are paid for in full and a margin of 50% is assessed on short trades.

The strategy is to monitor the spread price and calculate the normalized price. When Δ_{norm} exceeds 2, we consider this a bearish signal as we expect a reversion of the spread price down to the mean, 0, and take a hypothetical short position in the spread. Alternatively, when Δ_{norm} is less than -2, we consider this a bullish signal as we expect to see a reversion of the spread price up the mean. In this case the system simulates a long position in the spread. The system holds positions for five trading days, at which time positions are closed.

5.5.   Example Filter System: Buy Write

Filtering an investable universe to select securities that should outperform a benchmark is a standard methodology. The key research in the validation of filters was done by Fama and French in 1992, who showed the effects of fundamental classifications on predictions of stock returns. A second application of filtering can add covered call positions to increase the return. This strategy was developed by Whaley for the Chicago Board Options Exchange and is even a tradable index (BXM). Each strategy in and of itself is designed to outperform a benchmark index. By combining the two, we hope to create a portfolio that will outperform the index with lower volatility.

The filter trading strategy incorporates these two filters combined into a single system. The first filter selects the basket of stocks; the second selects the moneyness of the call options to be sold. Stock selection starts with the S&P 500 as the investable universe.

Then, the system filters stocks based on price-to-book and market capitalization criteria and a momentum indicator. The system buys the top 50 stocks according to the filter and holds them for one month.

We then attempt to enhance the portfolio return through a second filter that selects index options to sell. The system calculates the portfolio beta versus the S&P 500 and sells the appropriate value of index call options based on a minimum call away return. The filter selects call options to sell based upon their moneyness.

We will benchmark this trading system against the S&P 500 index and/or the CBOE Buy Write Index. By selecting better stocks and enhancing the returns through covered call writing, we will produce a portfolio with better performance characteristics than the index.

5.6. Example Signal Strength System: Multifactor Long–Short

Beginning with the combined S&P 500 and Nasdaq 100 as the investable universe (to ensure shortability), our multifactor system ranks stocks on a grouped factor, consisting of the individual factors' relative strength, P/E, P/S, and earnings growth rate. (These factors are widely believed to have predictive ability in the finance literature.) Each individual factor is demeaned and ranked by sector and universe. The stocks are then ranked by percentile and those percentiles are turned into deciles.

The deciles by individual factors will then be combined into an overall universe score by placing optimized weights on different factors. We will then again rank the overall score by percentile and again turn them into deciles. In the end, we have ten baskets ideally with the same number of stocks, from which we can calculate a basket return and a basket volatility. The strategy is to sell the bottom decile and purchase the top decile, a standard long/short strategy.

5.7. Conclusion

In reality few trading systems fit neatly into a single category. Most consist of complex trade selection, portfolio creation, and risk management strategies that may include concepts from all three categories. While these systems can be complex, the basic building blocks of the K|V methodology apply to all systems—define, backtest, implement, manage. Adherence to a methodology will maximize the value of the firm's portfolio of trading/investment systems. The only limitation on the K|V methodology is the user's ability to create the quantitative trading algorithms and performance measurement methods during the design and development stages.

CHAPTER ◆ 6

STAGE 0: The Money Document

The trading and money management industry is highly entrepreneurial. Individuals who start new trading/investment systems (in any legal form) are confronted with traditional activities related to entrepreneurship—raising seed capital, product development, marketing. Trading/investment system start-ups are distinguished from other new business ventures, however, by the need to develop the investment/trading strategy concurrent with the business strategy. Put another way, before any trading can begin, trading/investment system entrepreneurs must consider two sources of capital:

- Seed capital to fund design and development of the trading strategy and the enabling technologies.
- Investment capital used for trading.

The main costs of starting and running a new trading/investment system are hardware and software, data, and people. And none of these comes cheap. To raise seed capital to cover start-up costs, we propose a formalized model we call the Money Document. From a design perspective, the Money Document is the highest level abstraction of a trading/investment system.

The purpose of the Money Document is to provide an overview of a proposed trading/investment system in order to raise seed capital to fund the research stage (K|V Stage 1) of trading/investment system design and development. Subsequent to successful completion of the research phase, additional funds will be released to continue to the backtesting and implementation stages. Although created by the product team, a Money Document should be written in simple enough terms (i.e., not mathematically advanced language) so potential seed capital providers can grasp the nature of and prospects for the proposed system. The Money Document should reference specific competitive analysis and market data to justify the capital expenditure of building a new product.

In the business literature, several studies show that well-defined deliverables and procedures during the fuzzy front end reduce deviations and foster project success. (We consider the Money Document essentially to be Stage 0 of the K|V methodology.) The most successful firms review each new trading/investment strategy in a consistent and logical manner. A Money Document develops a business case for a new trading system founded on estimates of market trends, investor demand, capital requirements, competitive analysis, and project uncertainty. Further, the Money Document allows firms to review quickly new ideas so that seed capital allocation becomes an objective process. Provision of seed capital should be based on the merits of a strategy, not political power. The Money Document forces consistency of purpose for the product team: building a new profit center for the firm.

A benefit of a Money Document is that it ensures consensus between management and the product team regarding the mission, goals, opportunities, challenges, development costs, maintenance costs, ROI, time to market, and constraints of the project. Also, it provides a foundation upon which to develop the remainder of the requirements specifications (i.e., while a Money Document is at a high level of abstraction, it can nevertheless be viewed as a primitive incarnation of a Software Requirements Specification.)

Because trading/investment systems are housed largely in software applications and tools, we sought inspiration for the structure of the Money Document in traditional software documentation. From software development, the Vision and Scope Document formalizes business requirements. As such, it generally contains a list of specific capabilities of the proposed software that will satisfy customer demands. In the case of automated trading software, however, the saleable benefits are not those of the software itself, but rather of the quantifiable performance of the trading/investment system it embodies. So, we have also borrowed from the traditional Market Requirements Document which goes into much greater detail about target markets, competitive advantages, and other issues that pertain more directly to commercial success. A combination of these two applied to trading/investment systems form the backbone of the Money Document, which in the end should answer the fundamental question: is this a business worth investing seed capital in? To wit:

1. How is the trading/investment strategy going to make money?
2. Who wants the risk, that is, is there a demand for this trading/investment system?
3. What will be the competitive advantage this system will have over the competition?
4. How much money will be required to design and develop the system?
5. How much profit will be generated?
6. How much investment capital will the working system require and is it scalable?

(A Money Document is especially necessary for bottom-up innovations, where product teams must sell their ideas to management or external seed capital providers. For top-down innovations, a management order for a particular type of system may come with money attached. However, teams should still complete a Money Document for purposes of clarity.)

As with all of the processes described in this text, we expect development of a Money Document to be evolutionary. Even after the initial seed capital is granted, the Money Document will continue to evolve since, at some point, it may be used for marketing or to raise additional capital. A Money Document consists of three sections—the business description, market analysis, and because it is after all a sales document, a request for seed capital:

I. Business description
   A. Introduction
   B. Description of the trading/investment system
      1. Overview
      2. Preliminary research

6.1. Business Description

6.1.1. Introduction

By way of introduction, the Money Document will include three names: the name of the trading system (preferably one that is descriptive of the goal of the system), the name of the firm, and the name of the product team. These names will clarify communications and focus all stakeholders on a singular project and purpose. (When naming these three, we recommend keeping in mind the key buying motivations the project is targeting.)

The introduction should also provide an executive summary as to why seed capital providers should consider seeding the proposed trading/investment system development project. For example, the new system may accomplish market or strategy diversification, product line expansion, or take advantage of new opportunities from regulatory changes or a shifting economic environment.

6.1.2. Description of the Trading System

The description section of the Money Document should describe in layman's terms the trading/investment strategy, again without using overly complex mathematical or technological terms. Nevertheless, creating the perception of scientific rigor is an important sales tool. Investors prefer quantitative research and methods over fundamental logic because of the greater objectivity. This objectivity allows the product team to describe the design, research, and development as scientific, where fundamental methods would otherwise be questioned.[5]

In the business world, seed capital investors absolutely require clearly defined business goals prior to contributing capital. During the design stage, goals can drift and scope can creep if not bounded by written and well-understood documentation. In the trading world, this is often not the case when evaluating new, proprietary ideas. Often, simple Excel models are used to prove strategies without ever writing a business plan. While this may be a quick and dirty route to launching a hedge fund, it is not a foundation for building a long-term, sustainable, scalable business. If we cannot present a clear, concise overview of the trading system, it is doubtful we will ever be able to build it.

6.1.2.1. Overview

The overview should list the type of trading/investment system (i.e., trigger, filter, multi-factor), products to be traded, the time horizon of the trades (i.e., intraday, daily, weekly, monthly, yearly, or to expirations/maturity), minimum and maximum projected investment capital required, and expected source of investment capital (i.e., proprietary trading, pension/mutual funds, and/or retail investors).

6.1.2.2. Preliminary Research

A preliminary survey of research should discuss similar trading strategies, well-known research from journals, books, and online resources and show examples of performance indicators. For example, assuming a product team is proposing a growth at reasonable price strategy (GARP), this section could include a graph of indicators like average P/E ratio for GARP funds versus returns. A review of research already done will increase the credibility of the team.

6.1.2.3. Competitive Advantage

This section should convey the expected competitive advantage(s) of the proposed system relative to competitors and an index benchmark, which should also increase confidence in the team's ability to deliver a successful system. This section should describe how the trading system provides better performance by way of higher returns, lower risk, lower expenses, fewer drawdowns, greater scalability, wider distribution, or even faster technology. Discussion should also convey, for example, how the team expects to arrive at a more precise set of factors, or how it will perform the attribution analysis to ensure the algorithms are adding value. Such discussion will convey a clear understanding of the strategy's performance and its long-term survivability.

6.1.2.4. Performance Forecasts

Preliminary performance forecasts must be realistic, based on, to the extent possible, annual returns for comparable strategies. If it is a completely new strategy, then conservative estimates based on what known knowledge does exist are reasonable.

Frank discussion and graphical presentation of investment risk is also warranted, including expected standard deviations of returns, Sharpe and Sortino ratios, maximum gains and losses, as well as a display of drawdowns showing the amount of money investors using similar strategies have lost over, say, a six-month window.

6.1.3. The Product Team

The product team writes the Money Document (or at a minimum is heavily involved in the process). Marketing a new trading/investment system must be an interactive process;

it cannot exist separately from engineering. This has the advantage that team members will be more closely involved in the initial design and that there will be fewer broken promises later on.

The highest priority of the product team is to satisfy seed capital and investment capital providers through delivery of profitable trading/investment systems. To the extent that teams may work on multiple systems, the goal is a continuous pipeline of such systems.

Each member (or proposed member) of the product team should write a brief autobiography so that management and investors reading the Money Document can immediately determine if the team has the requisite skills not only to build the trading system but also to market it in an ongoing fashion. A team filled with only quantitative analysts doubtfully will have the skill to program software tools or the time to successfully perform high quality customer presentations. The goal is to achieve a proper, multifunctional balance across the team.

Product teams should be focused, with an experienced team leader and clear team objectives. Beyond that, it is also appropriate to discuss the team's design and development methodology (like the one proposed in this book). Such discussion will also increase seed capital providers' confidence in the team's ability to successfully complete the project.

6.2. Market Analysis

The goal of market analysis is to determine if there is a viable investor demand for the trading/investment system prior to seeding development. The market analysis and its constituent sections should contain at least the following information:

- The amount of money invested in this type of money management or trading style.
- Average returns per group and index benchmark for this type of strategy.
- Average lifetime of funds in this type of strategy.
- Number of competitors in this sector and who the leaders are.
- Money inflows and outflows into this type of strategy and investment cycle.

6.2.1. Target Market

The Money Document will describe who the expected investment capital providers are. Furthermore, it is desirable to discuss the size of the target market. If possible, we recommend teams utilize credible numbers from sources rather than broad generalizations. Of course, these will be rough estimates especially until the team can more closely research competitors' market shares. The analysis of the target market includes:

- Who wants this type of system?
- How big is the market?
- Why is the system of value to the investor?
- How much will they invest?
- What are the growth estimates for this market?

6.2.2.   Distribution and Marketing Channels

Unless the product team works at a proprietary trading firm, they will need to raise investment capital in order generate sufficient fee income to operate the system continuously. Costs associated with designing and developing new trading systems are very high. Gone are the days of placing $50,000 in a trading account, leasing a seat on a trading floor, and becoming a millionaire. Today, management expenses for servers, high-speed leased lines, back office accounting software, personnel, and data alone can easily exceed $500,000 annually.

In a very short amount of time, financial markets have evolved from a world where very simple business models could generate exceptional returns on capital, to a world where high hurdle rates exist just to generate positive cash flow. The idea of using a small amount of seed capital and generating enough investment return or management fees to support the infrastructure is becoming outdated. So, for most trading/investment systems there is a minimum, or threshold, sum of capital that the product team must raise prior to launch. For all business structures (i.e., mutual funds, hedge funds, proprietary trading groups), the bear minimum to support a very small operation might roughly be $500,000 in fixed costs.

An analysis of ongoing expenses will in part drive analyses of potential distribution channels and how best to market the trading investment system. For example, the system may be distributed as an open-end mutual fund, where brokers market shares to the general public, or as a closed-end fund. The trading system could be packaged as an Exchange Traded Fund (ETF) so it would need to be marketed to and through an exchange. The system could also be marketed as a hedge fund or as part of a fund of funds. The choice of distribution channel will impact how the product team will build the trading/investment system, some strategies such as the use of leverage may not be available for different structures. Choice of distribution channel also impacts time-to-market, and time-to-market affects cash flow and profitability.

Here is a brief analysis of cash flow under typical fee structures for mutual funds, hedge funds, and proprietary trading firms. For start-up mutual funds that might receive 75 basis points annually, investment capital of at least $66,666,667 is required to break even. This is certainly not a trivial amount of money.

TABLE 6-1

Capital	$66,666,667
Fees	.75%
Cash flow	$500,000

For a new hedge fund to break even with fees of 1% on assets under management plus 10% of the excess returns over and above its benchmark, the assets required are somewhat lower. Let's assume that a hedge fund returns 20%, while its benchmark returns 15%. The assets to break even under this scenario are $33,333,333. Lower than that for the mutual fund, but still not an insignificant amount.

Working at a proprietary trading house, where management invests in start-up trading systems, is the most direct avenue of raising investment capital, but a high hurdle rate very often makes it difficult to build a consistent track record and a scalable trading system. In large proprietary trading firms, fixed costs are usually shared among multiple

TABLE 6-2

Capital	$33,333,333
Fees	1%
Performance incentive	10%
Cash flow	$500,000

trading groups, but in small firms the costs are borne directly by traders. With $2.5 million in trading capital, a 50/50 split with the trading house, and $10,000 in expenses per month, a trading team would need to return 50% annually to generate just a little over the $500,000 cash flow. While $2.5 million is not a lot of capital, the 50% rate of return will not likely be sustainable, nor would it likely be scalable should the management or other investors be interested in investing $25 or $100 million.

TABLE 6-3

Capital	$2,500,000
Return	50.0%
Profit split	0.5
Expenses/month	$10,000
Cash flow	$505,000

So, with the large amount of investment capital needed, the product team must plan for how they intend to generate such an amount prior to obtaining seed capital. If the team cannot raise the capital itself, then they will need to find someone who can, and sell that person on the strategy.

Once a primary distribution channel is chosen, we recommend the product team decide on a second choice channel. The product team can then design the system and create a marketing plan to offer the system through two channels. For example, a system that implements a long–short strategy intended as a hedge fund could be designed for easy conversion to a long-only strategy and marketed through a mutual fund distribution network. Consideration of an alternative distribution channel also mitigates personal risk, where the loss of, say, a primary sales contact or other avenues of access to an investment pool would otherwise negatively impact success.

Lastly, while business people in other industries (namely technology) think about how best to sell out their businesses to larger firms, very few in financial markets think about the opportunities to sell their trading/investment strategies and systems to other firms. Larger firms often wait until trading/investment systems are in the growth or maturity stage before they buy smaller businesses. The product team considers targeting external buyers of the business in addition to external sources of investment capital.

6.2.3. History of Investment Cycles

Styles of trading and portfolio management come and go as market conditions change. The growth versus value research is an example of changing investment cycles. Launching a fund or trading system of a particular style when that style is losing or is out of favor can lead to failure. Launching a large cap growth fund, one of the oldest and most consistent strategies, in 2000 would have been extremely difficult, regardless of the merits of the strategy itself. Investors were just not interested in large cap growth in 2000. By reviewing investment cycles, the product team should be able to gain insight into the demand for the particular type of risk and, furthermore, the amount of time it has to launch in order to ensure a favorable environment. If a system will take a year to design, test, and build and the market cycle is three years into what is expected to be a four or five year trend, the product team must consider the potential of launching in a bad environment, making it much harder to raise investment capital.

As a rule of thumb, we caution against launching a trading/investment system at a time when the rolling cumulative returns for the benchmark over the past 12 months are down. You will likely be fighting against the odds for investment capital. Under these conditions, a strategy will likely have a difficult time generating a year-to-year track record of positive absolute returns. Investment advisors, pension fund boards, brokers, and trading firm managers have nothing to gain by placing money into new strategies in underperforming asset classes or strategies.

An analysis of the history of investment cycles should at a minimum include a graph of the returns for the past five years, the track records of comparable systems including drawdowns, and if possible the number of competing systems and how many have started and closed in each of the past five years.

6.2.4. Competition

In this section, the product team will list all known competitors with an overview of their individual strengths and weaknesses, and moreover, how its own trading/investment strategy will beat the competition. A discussion of major competitors can include the amount of capital allocated to competitors, long-term return history, the growth or reduction in the number of competitors, reference materials such as marketing documents, research reports, Morningstar reports, and the like.

6.3. Request Seed Capital

This section may be the most important piece of the Money Document. A request for seed capital must clearly articulate the purpose of the proposed business, along with the initial amount of seed capital the product team requires to enter Stage 1 of our development methodology. Key points are

- Proposed initial funding to build a prototype.
- Proposed time to build a prototype.
- Minimum/maximum amount of money to manage.
- Deliverables for the next step.

All trading/investment system design and development projects that expect to receive seed capital must have clearly defined goals that will be reviewed by a management or investor committee. A review committee will make sure that the product team has completed a proper Money Document and that the proposed trading strategy is understood, at least at a high level, and scoped prior to initial seeding. A seed capital provider will not allocate capital both to well-planned strategies and to vague ideas. Such an inconsistency would create a disincentive to document properly. Most traders or money managers tend to dislike processes and if left to their own devices more than likely do the minimum amount of work to get their trading system approved. Consistently applied standards for a Money Document greatly increase the chances of the success of the trading/investment strategy as well as successful completion of the development project.

6.3.1. Projected Revenues

In the Money Document, the product team must represent projected revenues and expenses honestly, even if they are abstract at best. The formulas for revenue estimates may be, for example, 1% on assets under management plus 20% of the excess returns over and above some benchmark. The revenue projections go forward quarterly for at least the first year with annual projections over the ensuing four years. The same can be said for projected expenses based on the increased capacity in technological infrastructure and personnel over the five years. We recommend product teams use a Delphi method for arriving at estimates for revenues, expenses and time lines.

6.3.2. Estimated Development Costs

In this section, the product team provides an estimate of how much it will cost to get up and running and how much it will cost to maintain the trading/investment system on an ongoing basis. The estimate will include the development costs and year-by-year fixed costs for management, as the project is not yet well defined. No specifications will be defined until seed capital providers are confident of a return on investment. We recommend the team communicate clearly the rough nature of revenue and expense estimates, and the expectation that expenses will become clearer as the team progresses through the design and development process. Management can expect firmer estimates at gate meetings.

6.3.3. Data and Technological Infrastructure Requirements

This section of the Money Document will present an overview of the technological infrastructure necessary to implement the trading/investment system, as well as address its technological feasibility. Furthermore, if the technology itself will be a competitive advantage, this is the place to describe how the team will accomplish this. Such discussion should remove doubt as to whether or not the trading system development team will in fact be able to get the system up and running. An overview of the technological infrastructure should include discussion of the following items:

- Markets to be traded and the connectivity required for real-time data feeds and order execution, including clearing firm connections.
- Available third-party software vendors and their respective application programming interfaces.
- Necessary data and databases.

- Hardware and network architecture.
- Trading system speed and its impact on trading system performance.
- Availability of an appropriate test environment.

A side benefit of this type of analysis is that forcing a survey of new technologies may foster unknown improvements or uncover technological trends that may make existing trading systems obsolete.

6.3.4.   Preliminary Time Line

Seed capital providers will of course want to know how long it will take to get the proposed trading/investment system up and running. All projects, to be successful, need time lines and milestones. A lack of documented project management processes at many trading firms often leads to many good strategies withering away, due to a lack of firm deliverables and firm delivery dates. These projects are often killed because it was taking longer than expected and because the people responsible for its development failed to provide any details of project progression. Many times such systems gain new life at new firms, where the project is restarted and quickly completed. (The second-build of a system usually goes smoother and with a higher probability of profitability since the initial problems were solved utilizing the original firm's capital.)

A preliminary time line with defined gate reviews at stated intervals ensures the product team will either complete the project on time or that it will notify management of changes in the time line due to unforeseen problems. It is not necessarily fatal to be behind schedule, as long the team is making measurable progress according to the original plan.

Sometimes development of a trading system gets behind schedule when backtesting shows poor performance results. This is certainly acceptable. Proving that a system does not work and understanding why it does not work can be valuable knowledge. If, for example, the investment cycle has changed, then the firm will know to shelve the strategy and wait for a new cycle. Checking the performance of the system will prevent additional time and resources from being spent on unprofitable projects. Only by having a time line with clean deliverables can you tell the difference between a project gone awry and a project that is just more complex than initially estimated.

6.3.5.   Risks, Constraints, and Assumptions

Acknowledging risks up front will enhance the credibility of the product team in the eyes of seed capital providers. In this section, the product team should describe the weaknesses of a proposed trading system and threats to its completion and successful operation. Such discussion should address the potential for new competition, new technologies, new regulations, new trading environments, or new products that may adversely affect the success of the system.

The U.S. government forced the options industry to list option contracts on multiple exchanges, which led to the creation of a new exchange, the International Securities Exchange (ISE). The option market making industry quickly moved from a single floor-based exchange to the ISE's electronic market. The traditional source of revenue for option traders, the bid/ask spread, collapsed by 50% in short order. Many small option trading firms closed their doors soon after.

Electronic markets, leased lines, and high-speed computers have made high frequency, algorithmic trading possible. Some trading firms have not successfully coped with rapid changes in technology that enable new competitors to remove their advantage. New regulations can give rise to new trades and new trading firms that specialize in automated strategies that can kill firms that are slow to react. Products are continually being added to the financial markets and there is an opportunity risk that a firm may miss the chance to take advantage of new products. Following a development methodology, like the one we propose in this text, will mitigate these risks. Teams that follow the K|V methodology are able to quickly modify existing software and trading/investment strategies to take advantage of technologies, new regulations, and new products.

6.4. Conclusion

Trading/investment systems are small businesses and starting such a business requires entrepreneurial effort. Product teams face unique challenges including the concurrent development of a business strategy and a trading strategy; a hybrid of activities combining concepts from software development and trading firm start-up; and two groups of investor, seed capital providers and investment capital providers. As a result, product teams must raise two pools of capital, seed capital for development of the trading strategy data/software and investment capital for trading or investment.

Creating a Money Document enables product teams to clarify the fuzzy front end of new product innovation, including:

- Standardizing the communication protocol to clarify the legal and business structure of the organization, and the investment strategy of the fund.
- Naming a product team containing the required skill sets.
- An analysis of the demand for a proposed strategy and a discussion of the distribution system, providing an understanding of investment cycles and the issues a marketing plan should address.
- Starting a description of the trading system, which will evolve and grow as the product team flows through the stages of development.

STAGE • I

Design and Document Trading/ Investment Strategy

CHAPTER • 7

STAGE 1: Overview

The spiral stage structure of K|V begs two perspectives—one, that of the loops; and two, that of the steps. One can look at the four steps that comprise a single loop, or the three loops that comprise each step. We will do both. This chapter will present an overview of the three loops. The following four chapters will examine each of the four steps and each pass over each step. The number of loops is not by any means fixed. (We decided that three iterations were sufficient to cover the commonly encountered substeps.)

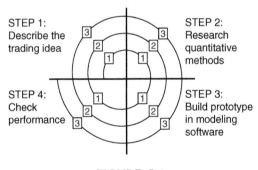

FIGURE 7-1

"Quality must be built in at the design stage," according to W. Edwards Deming. Stage 1 is design and analysis, that is, problem solving, a process of gathering requirements for the implementation of the trading/investment system, and testing and managing changes to the design. The requirements gathered will be the solutions to the design problems presented by the project's vision and scope, the Money Document. At the start of Stage 1, the product team has a complete Money Document (approved by the seed capital investor, be it management or an outside entity) and has been provided with sufficient capital to complete the stage. Stage 1 is also opportunity analysis, translating opportunities into well-defined business logic over several iterations (the duration of each loop should be no more than a few weeks). Design should focus on high-level strategies, such as the quantitative methods and how they will work together, as well as some lower-level designs, such as how individual components will work, the graphical user interface design, and data design. During this stage, the product team defines the specifications of the implementation software, developed in later stages.

A survey of more than 8000 projects found that the top three reasons that projects were delivered late, over budget, and with less functionality than desired all had to do with requirements-management practices: lack of user input, incomplete requirements, and changing requirements.[1]

Steve McConnell in his text *Rapid Development* points out that design serves as the foundation for construction, project scheduling, project tracking, and project control, and as such effective design is essential to achieving maximum development speed.[2]

Early and often delivery of prototypes, which enable feedback from interested parties, is a key factor to project success and of our methodology. Over the course of Stage 1, product teams design and document in as much detail as possible the new trading/investment system's functionalities. Over each loop, the team should consider different algorithms and build prototypes of components of the trading/investment system. Prototypes in Loop 1 are usually scaled down, and represent approximations based on research into competing systems. Subsequent loops investigate new quantitative methods and produce new prototypes. Team members evaluate prototypes and their strengths, weaknesses, and risks, iterating through the spiral until the refined prototypes collectively represent the final trading/investment strategy. Lastly, these refined prototypes are assembled into a consolidated prototype, which should be thoroughly evaluated and tested.

Planning prior to entry into K|V Stage 1 should determine what resources will be needed for the design and development effort. The product team should be sure to obtain a sign-off in advance of the Stage 1 as to the timing, duration, money, and personnel issues that will impact the team's ability to successfully complete its work. We recommend these forecasts be made using a Delphi approach (described in Chapter 2). Prior to entering the development process, the product team and top management must agree on:

- The steps necessary for the trading system's design and development.
- The review, verification, and validation appropriate for each of the steps in Stage 1.
- The responsibilities and authorities necessary for the design and development processes.

As design and development will usually involve contact with personnel external to the product team, top management must understand and exercise its obligation to manage the interfaces between the product team and different departments the team will encounter during design and development to ensure communication and establish clear lines of responsibility.

As the design and development process moves forward, changes to the original plan may be necessary and even desirable. Should that be the case, the organization must update the plans. Top management and the product must determine the design and development inputs relating to product requirements:

- Functional requirements, that is, what is the product supposed to do?
- Performance requirements, that is, how does it do it?
- Performance metrics.
- Applicable regulatory requirements and laws.
- Information derived from previous similar designs where applicable.
- Any other requirements essential to the design and development.

- Review these inputs to assure they are complete and not conflicting.
- Time-to-market, cost, materials, reuse of appropriate designs, and compatibility issues with existing systems.

Stage 1 design and development outputs must:

- Meet the backtesting stage input requirements.
- Provide information needed for purchasing data, building the system.
- Either contain or make reference to trading system acceptance criteria.
- Specify characteristics necessary for safe implementation including software attributes and requirements.
- Design and development outputs must be in a form that allows verification against the inputs.

In order to proceed, the team leader must assign tasks to the various members of the team (division of labor is key to success). In general, the trader defines trading rules and logic, the financial engineers research quantitative methods, and programmers (with financial engineers) prototype models as necessary. This way, the existing technology platform, or technology stack, becomes a part of the context in which requirements are formulated.

The marketing professional will primarily investigate competing systems. All team members are responsible for performance testing. In the end, the team is responsible for all tasks. Tasks are given and finished parts assembled after completion of each iteration. Then, new knowledge is added to a written description.

The description step encompasses the planning and management of each loop. The iterative process of researching, prototyping, testing, and the documentation of results and new knowledge will allow all team members to educate themselves on all parts of the system. The first encounter with the first stage starts where the Money Document left off. (The Money Document is the input into Stage 1.) The description of the trading system from the Money Document serves as the launching point for entry into the entire K|V model. From there the product team loops until they arrive back at the first step, Describe the Trading Idea. Each time through the spiral, the team adds new knowledge to the written description and plans the scope of the activities for the next loop. Each time they encounter the Research Quantitative Methods step, they will gather new information and new knowledge, which they will incorporate into a new prototype, which will then be tested, and so on.

Over the course of Stage 1, the team defines and documents order selection algorithms, order execution algorithms, and base-level performance and risk management metrics. Upon completion of Stage 1, the description will have evolved to contain all of the quantitative methods and all of the business logic of the trading/investment system. Further, the team will have completed its research into strategies and quantitative methods and created working, fully tested prototypes. The team will present the documentation of their activities at the Gate 1 meeting. The description, references, and prototypes developed in Stage 1 will gradually evolve into a software requirements specification document for Stage 3.

7.1. LOOP 1: Analyze Competing Strategies

STEP 1: Review Money Document Description
STEP 2: Research Similar/Competing Systems
STEP 3: Prototype Known Calculations
STEP 4: Perform White Box Test of Formulas

The first loop is competitor analysis, an attempt to gain as much knowledge as possible about competitors' products and trading/investment strategies. The competition for the particular strategy is firms offering the same or similar trading/investment products either now or in the future, or firms that could remove the competitive advantage a trading/investment system has. By knowing competitors, firms may be able to predict the competition's next move, exploit their weaknesses, and undermine their strengths. Benchmarking quantitative methods starts with a competitive intelligence program. As Sun Tzu, the great Chinese military strategist, wrote in *Art of War* around 500 BC:

> *If you are ignorant of both your enemy and yourself, then you are a fool and certain to be defeated in every battle . . . If you know yourself, but not your enemy, for every battle won, you will suffer a loss . . . If you know your enemy and yourself, you will win every battle.*

No trading or investment company is an island. Quantitative finance electronic trading promotes the clustering of researchers in financial centers to facilitate the sharing of innovations between firms, "because we can learn what our competitors are up to and share ideas about new applications of quantitative modes with colleagues—what might work, what doesn't, go to seminars about new ideas."[3] Effectively, businesses fight to gain competitive advantage and the attention of investors. Like war, successful firms understand the competition and the strategies employed by their competition, including:

- How the competition thinks.
- What their core competencies are, that is, their strengths and weaknesses.
- What competitive advantage they exercise.
- Where the competition can and cannot be overcome.

7.2. LOOP 2: Develop New Strategies

STEP 1:   Review Knowledge and Plan New Research
STEP 2:   Research New Methods
STEP 3:   Prototype New Calculations
STEP 4:   Perform Gray Box Testing with Inputs and Outputs

The second loop (and, if your implementation of the K|V methodology consists of more than three loops, all loops prior to the final one) refines the broad output requirements set forth in the Money Document through empirical research into quantitative methods. Benchmarking continues with a research survey and new formulas, an application of known and unknown knowledge to an unknown problem.

7.3. LOOP 3: Consolidate Trading/ Investment System Design

STEP 1:   Consolidate Trading System Details (All Equations and Logic Rules)
STEP 2:   Research Performance Metrics and Reporting Methods
STEP 3:   Build Consolidated Prototype
STEP 4:   Perform Black Box Testing, Documenting Results using Inputs and Outputs

The final loop of Stage 1 consolidates all component descriptions into a single document with all of the trading rules and a single prototype and performance run. A final, consolidation loop will address the main drawback of the spiral design model—endless loops.

7.4. Outputs/Deliverables

At the completion of Stage 1, the project will encounter the first gate, a management meeting. At this meeting management will expect several deliverables, including:

- Full description of the trading system, including a Business Rules Catalog, a detailed discussion of the quantitative methods and business logic.
- Referenced white papers or research papers that describe benchmarked methodologies.
- Trading system performance metrics, software quality attributes and requirements.
- Complete consolidated prototype built in Excel or other modeling software.
- Complete performance test results appropriate to the type of trading system including graphs, etc.
- Estimated time line and commitments for the backtesting stage.
- Estimated data and software expenses for the backtesting stage.

The gate meeting will allow management to review the trading/investment system, as well as the development process itself and the portfolio of competing systems. The team should also go to the meeting armed with a recommendation on the prospects for the strategy and a plan for moving forward to Stage 2.

7.5. Summary

The requirements analysis and design stage of the development process yields specifications used for the implementation of the software tools of the trading/investment system. Over the course of Stage 1, the product team will engage in evolutionary, test-driven development, where every benchmarked method will have a prototype and tests that verify its operation. It is well understood that the less functional the initial delivery, the higher the quality of the final delivery. And, the more frequent the deliveries, the higher is the final quality.[4]

CHAPTER ◆ 8

Describe Trading/Investment Idea

When people think, they make errors. Human thought processes are inherently bad. (Research shows convergence of error rates in all human cognitive activities.) In all stages, our methodology attempts to force thinking, and to test that thinking to find and prevent errors. Before research can begin, planning of the research and knowledge management strategies will speed the path to successful strategies and root out errors. (The step following this one, Research Quantitative Methods (K|V 1.2), will fulfill research goals by surveying and benchmarking quantitative methods and business rules.) Now, while most financial engineers, traders, and portfolio managers (i.e., inventors) are conceptual thinkers, trading systems are linear constructs, and planning, documenting, and communicating trading system details must be done linearly. As a result, good researchers plan and conduct their work only with the help of writing, and writing they do right from the start; they do not wait until after they have gathered all their sources and data. Documenting research forces clarity and understanding with the purpose of communicating specific ideas linearly. Documenting, and doing it well for all of the documents produced over the course of design and development, is important because it:

- Forces clarity, linearity, and objectivity between members of a cross-functional team.
- Demands that researchers think logically and exposes faults.

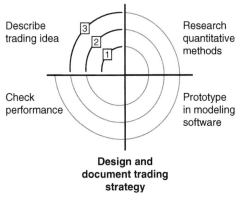

FIGURE 8-1

- Begets new learning.
- Facilitates self-criticism and peer review.
- Eases the organization of ideas and makes possible the organized storing of knowledge.
- Helps researchers remember.
- Allows researchers to find larger patterns and interrelationships among otherwise disparate concepts.
- Facilitates transparency, enabling product teams to easily communicate with investors or regulators regarding the objectives, strategies, and risk factors of the trading/investment system.

Engineers spend 50 to 70% of their time communicating, but as the President's Science Advisory Committee expressed years ago "many American scientists and technologists can neither write nor speak effective English."[1] If you cannot communicate well, you will not get investors, and you will have product team members (from different functional areas) with different understandings of key concepts (sometimes the same problem can be viewed from two completely different perspectives), spiraling out of control. (The famous old woman/young woman illusion shows how two people can look at the same thing in different ways.) The team leader must also communicate clearly verbally and in written form as to what each team member is responsible for over the ensuing loop.

FIGURE 8-2

Beginning with the Money Document as the project's initial scope and vision, new additions to this core document (the original Money Document should not be discarded) will define the visions and scope for each loop through Stage 1. Market opportunity originally drove the description and the evolving description will guide iterative research into quantitative methods and business rules that will satisfy that opportunity. In this way, the product team can assess the nature, scale, and complexity of the work to come. The vision and scope should clarify the objectives and boundaries of the loop, including what and what not to research and build. By Stage 3, this evolving description will in the end fully articulate the trading/investment system in all of its mathematical and technological complexity.

Although one could argue that time spent documenting trading/investment system specifications reduces the time available for discussion and further research, it improves the quality of discussion and research.[2] For technical writing, the focus is on content (in this and all other kinds of technical writing), which can lure researchers into viewing documentation as a purely mechanical task, a churning out of dull reports to satisfy policy. But, technical writing as a term focuses too little attention on the process of fully describing a trading/investment system. Without written words, research and market experience is only a fuzzy, subjective flow of impressions, adages, disparate spreadsheets, and data. Words, equations, diagrams, and other forms of documentation make knowledge objective. Documentation reduces research and experience into facts product teams can remember and criticize. Describing a trading strategy in writing forces the logic and order of sequential thought.

A component of building new strategies is starting with fresh new perspectives on old strategies or research, deconstructing preconceived ideas about quantitative finance and how to study markets (i.e., to focus on science and not scientism).[3] Often faults in old strategies become apparent only when product team members reassess the mathematical and technological ideas that in the past supported the conclusions. Documenting new thinking is particularly useful because it requires the team to reveal its thought processes, providing a snapshot in time of the team's understanding of a trading/investment strategy, permitting them to identify and evaluate problems and helping them resolve those problems. Through repeated efforts to articulate logic on paper, team members transform their knowledge of specific strategies and of relationships between disparate strategies into an analytic process, subject to peer review.

Team leaders and managers who read descriptions learn about the team's thought processes, their points of view, insights, and difficulties. Without realizing it, traders and financial engineers often create semantic noise (in communications theory, superfluous information is called "noise"), leading to confusion about details of system design.[4] But, managers can critically review written descriptions:

- Showing teams precisely where thinking is unclear or noisy.
- Posing questions designed to shed light on problems underlying their unclear thinking.
- Providing feedback for communicating complex financial and technological analysis more clearly.

Documenting specifics of a trading/investment strategy goes beyond what has already been learned to what the team learns as they write. In this regard, documenting enables product teams to continue to learn about trading and strategy development, that is, writing begets new learning. Researching quantitative methods can be largely a process of acquiring facts and isolated equations, and the process of documenting (at the level of the average reader) helps define and clarify what the product team knows and does not know about a strategy. This is crucial because successful learning is engaged and interpersonal. New knowledge and new discoveries of interrelationships among existing knowledge that teams uncover on their own tends to be more innovative than knowledge they simply reference. Furthermore, documenting effectively involves the team in the formulation of abstract ideas and self-criticism. Serious technical writing forces focus, organization, and structure, all of which are essential elements in the acquisition of new knowledge.[5]

Over the course of their research, successful product teams do more than just photocopy source documents, including:

- Writing up what they find. What you do not write down, you are likely to forget, or worse, misremember.
- Keeping notes, outlines, summaries, commentary, critiques, and questions.

- Maintaining a catalog of documentings and sources. We recommend you build a consolidated knowledge database with references, and, even better, employ a wiki-style tool.

Writing supports thinking, not just by helping you understand better what you have found, but by helping you find in it larger patterns of meaning.

One purpose of researching a trading or investment strategy is to increase the store of knowledge, and so even the very best work is useless if the firm cannot store it, retrieve it, and effectively communicate it to the rest of the firm. Building and maintaining a proprietary library of unique quantitative methods is a key to long-term success.

In summary, writing is important. Cognitive processes involved in writing, from making simple flowcharts to analyses of complex financial data, shape all aspects of trading/investment system design and development. Notes and documents evolve into written descriptions and deliverable documents. Describing trading strategies in written form, though, is difficult, primarily because the process is not a one-for-one, step-by-step march through the logical processes undertaken during research. Rather, the process of describing trading/investment system details is an attempt to guide the logical processes of the team leader, top management, investors, and even potential regulators to an understanding and acceptance of the team's conclusions. In the end, descriptions are read by others and writing for others demands more than writing for ourselves.[6] From the perspective of these readers, there is a clear connection between the quality of documentation and the quality of the underlying research.

8.1. Writing Descriptions Effectively

Documenting is worth doing, and if it's worth doing, it's worth doing well. A well-structured description of a trading/investment system should begin with the high-level overview of the strategy from the Money Document. From there, the body of the description should detail specific equations and business logic necessary to implement the strategy. While the high-level overview remains fixed, the specifics of the implementation, described in the body, will evolve as the team spirals through Stage 1. Teams should organize the content thoughtfully, not starting with a mass of details and citations and photocopies, hoping that readers will somehow devine relevant parts.

For each subsection of the description, we recommend writing a brief introduction that describes its organization and what is in each part. It need not be a Ph.D.-level dissertation; the readers may often be less sophisticated quantitatively, either junior-level analysts, managers, or lay investors. Sections should include:

- Trade selection algorithms for both position opening and closing.
- Trade execution algorithms.
- Position and risk management logic.
- Base-level performance statistics and metrics.

Subsections may be as short as a sentence. Also, readers have not spent as much time with the paper's structure and content as the team has, so helping to orient them is always beneficial. We recommend:

- Be brief, but be complete. Try to use shorter, more direct phrases whenever possible. Give facts in the form of:
  - Bullet points.
  - Short paragraphs to provide overviews and link subjects.

  - Screen shots and drawing with captions.
  - Prototypes (e.g., sample spreadsheets) with embedded documentation.
  - Logic flow diagrams.
  - Mathematical equations with legends.

- List discarded alternatives to chosen quantitative methods at the end, with only short descriptions as to why they were discarded. We gain knowledge from failure and all failures should be cataloged and stored, but the strategy description is not the place for it. The readers are interested in what works, not in what does not.

- Avoid using the passive voice. In trading system descriptions, the passive voice obscures who the actor is, which event caused what to occur, and when it happened.

- Avoid words like "easily," "obviously," or "clearly," as in "the rest of the calculation follows easily." Also, avoid anthropomorphizing equations or computers, as in "the calculation acts up when..." or "the software thinks that...."

- Choose singular over plural number. For example, if you say that "data sequences induce time series analyses," it is not clear whether data and analyses are in one-to-one correspondence, or the set of data collectively induces a set of analyses. "Each sequence of data induces an analysis of the time series" avoids confusion.

- Use terms consistently. If you are trading bonds, use one term, say, bond. There is no need to intermingle "fixed income," "instrument," or "debt security," unless the use of synonyms distinguishes unrelated concepts. For example, we use the synonyms "stage" and "step," and "loop" to identify specific phases of our methodology.

- For clarity, give unique, descriptive names to concepts.[7] For example, you may name a certain model, say, an execution algorithm as something unique, like "The Extended VWAP Model." Using an acronym like "XVWAPMod" is confusing. A good name gives team members a shorthand way to refer to a package of related procedures and aids in reuse.

Some of the suggestions in this document are about good writing, and that might seem secondary to the research. But documenting clearly helps teams think and plan more clearly and often reveals flaws or ideas that had previously been invisible. Giving examples also helps clarify concepts. Examples make concrete in the reader's mind what a specific technique does. A running example over the course of the description may help illustrate how algorithms work and work in sequence.

Now, one may (and should be) concerned about getting hung up in the pursuit of documentation instead of the pursuit of working trading systems. Documents can easily become cumbersome in a highly dynamic, research-oriented field of new trading/investment system design. But, at the same time, teams should recognize that verbal communication is rarely consistent and that only written information is clear and constant.

8.2.   Logic Leaks

Logic rules give rise to leaks, and logic leaks can occur in any type of trading/investment system. To illustrate, however, we will use as an example a simple moving average crossover system. According to our hypothetical system, when the fast moving average crosses over the long moving average to the upside, this is a bullish signal. When the fast moving average crosses over to the downside, this is a bearish signal. Now, let's examine the logic implications. Every time our trading system receives a price update from the market, it must recalculate the moving averages and understand the new state. From lowest value to highest, these states are

1. Price, short MA, long MA
2. Price, long MA, short MA
3. Long MA, price, short MA
4. Long MA, short MA, price
5. Short MA, price, long MA
6. Short MA, long MA, price.

Now consider also that such a system, fully automated, may or may not have a position on long or short. So, multiply these six states by 3—long, short, flat—for 18 possible total states. Also, our system must be able to identify crossovers. If the previous state was that the short MA was above the long MA, but upon recalculation, the short MA is now below the long MA we have to raise a flag indicating a bearish (or alternatively, a bullish) signal. Remember, MAs are one thing, but our system trades on prices, and when it takes a position, it may bracket the position with a target price and a stop price. But not just any stop price, a trailing stop price. And one last thing, what happens if a partial fill is received and the state changes? Should the system cancel the remaining quantity?

This is a lot of logic, a lot of "if" statements. The number of possible combinations grows exponentially as the number of logic statements grows. Trading logic like this can quickly turn into a spaghetti bowl of logical comparisons; if any potential state is unaccounted for, the trading system may go out of control. Logic leaks are dangerous. Putting pen to paper forces a product team to think through all logical outcomes. A clear logic map or logic flow diagram will enable them to plan for and prove all logical outcomes.

We recommend that you map all of your logic before you start prototyping. Any change to the logic must first be changed in your logic map, because changes will have unthought of implications in other places. You must be sure that all states are accounted for, that all logical outcomes are handled. Once you have started coding, it is too late; you will not be able to figure it out on the fly.

8.3.   STEP 1, LOOP 1: Review Money Document Description

The K|V methodology begins with a review of the input, the trading/investment strategy description from the Money Document, and a plan for research.

> *We know of cases where the research drives the development of new trading systems. In K|V, the Money Document, a sales tool, provides the impetus for research and development.*

In the step following this one, K|V 1.2, team members will benchmark the quantitative methods and business rules that comprise the trading/investment system's strategy. Disciplined research will ensure that teams produce proper specifications, establishing a common understanding of what the different parts of the trading system will do and, furthermore, facilitating testing of prototypes since testers can check whether the prototype results agree with the written specifications. While prototypes flow from inputs to quantitative methods to outputs, the process of specification should run the other way around; the results, that is, the objectives of the model, are most important and should determine the model's structure.[8] Researching quantitative methods is an iterative search for best practices, benchmarking five things:

1. Trade selection algorithms.
2. Trade execution algorithms and trade cost analysis calculations.
3. Cash management procedures.
4. Risk algorithms.
5. Performance monitoring and reporting.

The plan for the first loop is competitor analysis. Reputations on the street mean investors know the differences between companies. They may know that a particular firm has strong quantitative research, while another firm is strong technologically. One firm may be big in fixed income, while another may be focused on equity options. The competition has secrets that can be the difference between success and failure. Identifying these secrets to the extent possible may thus be crucial for survival. There are four stages in monitoring competitors:

- Collecting information.
- Converting information into intelligence by cataloging it and integrating it with other information, and analyzing it.
- Communicating intelligence.
- Countering competitor actions that may cause special variation in the trading/investment system.

One mistake many firms make is to start collecting information with no plan on how to use it. If it cannot be used as a driver of the firm's strategy then the effort spent collecting information is wasted. If a firm is planning a new trading/investment system, information on what the competition is doing in the same area will aid decision-making processes for the new system. Alternatively, a firm may be looking at how the financial industry will evolve over the next five or ten years. Successful firms identify key areas of concern. Other information is ignored or stored for later use. Such study should be focused and planned, and aimed at answering intelligence requirements relevant to the strategy under development.

Prescott and Gibbons advocate an ongoing competitive intelligence program, "a formalized, yet continuously evolving process by which the management team assesses the evolution of its industry and the capabilities and behavior of its current and potential competitors to assist in maintaining or developing a competitive advantage."[9] At a minimum, we recommend the product team create a file for each competitor and their competing system. Any marketing pieces, regulatory filings, prospectuses, information, or ideas from industry contacts or news articles should be reviewed and filed.

8.4. STEP 1, LOOP 2: Review Knowledge and Plan New Research

The second loop through this step assumes that the descriptions are inclusive of the equations researched in the previous loop. In the end, the description will lay out the business logic that will lead to entering into and exiting from positions in the markets. For example, the description will include all the indicators and what actions will be taken based upon their differing values. Also, we will want to understand what, if any, dynamic inputs will be part of the system. That is, will the user be able to change any parameters, say stop limits, or optimization constraints. Of course, the nature of the trading rules will be different for different kinds of systems, for example, market making versus market taking systems. Nonetheless, common to all systems will be an explanation of why a particular instrument will be bought or sold, or rather why a bid or offer will be entered on a particular instrument.

Successful product teams approach quantitative research, the search for best practices, in a methodical manner. The goal over the course of the following research step, K|V 1.2.2, may be to assemble, say, 20–50 references. A research survey of this size requires planning. In the end, though, the team may only select and prototype a small subset of the total research found; the full complement of references become part of the firm's library.

8.5.   STEP 1, LOOP 3: Consolidate Trading System Details (All Equations and Logic Rules)

The final loop consolidates all component descriptions into a single document with all of the trading rules. A consolidation loop will prevent endless looping. Never-ending looping through the design stage is a serious issue in trading/investment system development; researchers almost always aspire to optimal solutions. Very often, however, the perfect solution takes too long. The goal must be to deliver profitable, working strategies in the short term, with the goal to continuously improve working systems over the longer term.

Consolidation should not occur without planning. Stitching together disparate prototypes requires forethought on data formats and conversions and merging graphical user interfaces. Furthermore, problems during consolidation may corrupt component prototypes. We recommend backing up all prototypes beforehand and documenting graphically the architecture of the final prototype before any work begins. The final prototype will form the basis for the software requirements documents in Stage 3.

After consolidation, our methodology assumes that all quantitative methods and business rules are fixed, except for optimization of parameters, which can occur over the course of Stage 2.

8.6.   Summary

In summary, documenting reveals aspects of the process trading strategy research that may not be apparent from general communication. The ways in which product teams organize discussions of quantitative, qualitative, and technological issues may reveal gaps in logic or unchallenged assumptions. Product team members should follow a standard model for organizing discussions of trading system design and development. A standard way of presenting financial research, such as certain topics first followed by solutions, is to present the pieces of the analysis in an expected order, then use inductive reasoning to structure discussions. Revising the organization of a discussion clarifies thinking and promotes clear writing; and clear writing in turn promotes clear thinking.

The necessity of documenting, and documenting well, with accountability to team leaders and top management, forces product teams to do better research.

8.6.1. Best Practices

- Document all aspects of the trading/investment system.
- Diagram logical paths using logic maps.
- Develop a standardized protocol for presenting research results.
- Create a research plan for each loop.
- Develop a common language for communicating ideas within the product team.

CHAPTER • 9

Research Quantitative Methods

Research is the driving sector of the financial markets. Those who cannot reliably do market research, in any of its forms, or evaluate the research of others will find themselves on the sidelines in an industry that increasingly depends on innovations based on good data and produced by sound research.[1] While Stages 1 and 2 of K|V can be thought of as an empirical research methodology, concerned with the process of research, they are together better thought of as a process to manage ideas and combine innovations into working systems. This step, K|V 1.2, addresses the process of research most specifically. Each encounter with the previous step, K|V 1.1, should have defined a clear goal for the research step.

We recommend that, at the start of each loop through the research step, the product team defines the problem by restating the research goal as a question. For example, "what is the best way to price options?" This will help form well-defined boundaries for research. In general:

- Define the research problem.
- Gather information and models.
- Fit the problem to the models.
- Select the model that best solves the problem.

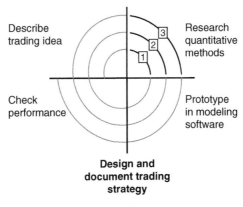

FIGURE 9-1

97

9.1.   Benchmarking Quantitative Methods

Benchmarking is a comparative process. To be specific, over the course of this step, researchers compare and benchmark the following:

1. Trade selection algorithms
    (a) Valuation and forecasting calculations
    (b) Optimization routines
    (c) Entry characteristics
        (i) Signal definition (position rationale)
        (ii) Quantity
        (iii) Order type
        (iv) Entry price
    (d) Exit characteristics
        (i) Profit targets
        (ii) Trailing stops
        (iii) Time till exit
        (iv) Rebalancing exit
2. Trade execution and trade cost analysis calculations
3. Cash management procedures
4. Risk algorithms
    (a) Risk calculations
    (b) Hedging algorithms
    (c) Drawdown procedures
    (d) Cash and borrowing procedures
    (e) Credit risk exposures
5. Performance monitoring and reporting
    (a) Performance metrics
    (b) Simple metric calculations
    (c) Shutdown triggers.

The drive to uncover best practices will reveal what really works, including the conditions under which it works. Successful teams work from the general to the specific, understanding the entire strategy prior to modeling the pieces. Most complex trades can be broken down into simple concepts that should be understood before research starts.

In cases where many practices exist, researchers must be able to recognize the best practice, the one that will, either on its own, in collaboration with other methods, or through extension of the theory with proprietary calculations, produce a better, more stable trading/investment system. According to Robert C. Camp the best practice is one where:[2]

- Performance is clearly superior. For example, a comparison of several forecasting methods may indicate that one clearly proves better than others.

- The quantified opportunity is large. For example, one strategy for exiting positions may prove to be more profitable than others.

- Endorsed by expert judgment. For example, financial engineers, either internal or external, may widely agree that one method is superior.
- The same practice recurs. For example, a survey may find that one method is used by all firms.
- Leadership position has been attained. For example, one execution algorithm may prove time and time again to provide superior performance relative to a VWAP, arrival price, or implementation shortfall, or pretrade, benchmark.

The research step permits the product team to survey all the relevant mathematical and logical models. The goal of the research process is to speed the path to the design or application of the best practice algorithms. Any quantitative method will fall into one of four categories:

1. Usable in a production system.
2. Usable only in the absence of a better model.
3. Totally unusable.
4. Model in inventory. Maybe not appropriate for the problem at hand, but worthy of further research for other, later problems.

Benchmarking trading/investment strategy processes is a proactive search for superior performance that includes gaining a concrete understanding of the competition as well as trying out new ideas and proven practices and technology. Process benchmarking should be approached on the basis of investigating industry practices first.[3] Capability maturity advances when proven best practices are incorporated in trade selection, order management algorithms, and risk management algorithms.

9.2. STEP 2, LOOP 1: Research Similar/ Competing Systems

The first loop of research begins to refine requirements into defined inputs the trading system will receive, actions taken by it, and defined outputs it will produce. Rarely, though, do firms dream up completely new trading/investment strategies. More often, they build on ideas of the past or of others, adding a twist or two here or there to enhance performance; many trading ideas are simply copies of ones that were successful in the past. The goal of a new system may in the first year be to simply imitate a competitor or index benchmark, matching its performance. Down the road, in successive years, the goal could be to improve on the results and outperform the benchmark. At some firms, the goal is to make each new trading system or product team cash flow positive within some timeframe. After that, algorithms are refined. Finally, the steady-state goal may be to consistently perform in the top 10% of the peer group.

The SEC's general push toward increased disclosure of holdings by mutual funds (and inevitably hedge funds) allows one fund manager to mimic another. Such funds are called copycats. In fact, research by Mary Margaret Frank *et al.* suggests that copycatters can even outperform the copycattees. The study found that hypothetical funds copycatting the 100 largest equity mutual funds in the United States, updating the portfolios semiannually based on publicly available information, generated returns "statistically indistinguishable, and possibly higher" than the returns of the copycatted funds. The disadvantage is that copycats' access to information is delayed. The advantage is that copycats pay lower research costs.[4] Information can be gleaned by:

- Observing positions that the competitions' trading/investment system takes.
- Gathering information about the strategies and technologies the competitor uses.
- Searching for quantitative methods that replicate the competitor's performance.
- Comparing the performance of a copycat system to the performance of the competitor's system.

Information will come from within the organization and external to it. Traders, quants, programmers, and even human resource and sales and marketing professionals deal on a daily basis with vendors, news media, other traders, professional associations, patent attorneys, and academics and will hear about impending competitive pressures. Mutual funds publicly disclose their portfolio holdings periodically, revealing which stocks or bonds the fund manager believes are undervalued. That is useful information to competitors. Also, public pensions regularly hold meetings where money managers compete for investment dollars. Fund overseers usually grill managers about strategies and expenses at these meetings, which are often by law open to the public. Attending these meetings can reveal a lot about what your competition is doing and how they sell.

> *The Vanguard Group stopped reporting information about the net cash flows into its funds because third parties were apparently using this information to trade ahead of Vanguard funds, thereby raising Vanguard's effective cost of executing stock transactions.*[5]

Though not as simple, information can sometimes be had on the Internet, at trade shows and conferences, and by interviewing industry experts, even by talking to or interviewing the competitions' customers and employees (for some firms this is part of their routine), and by reading marketing materials and prospectuses. Sometimes vendors will brag about how your competitors use their system. Whatever the case, information can be filed on paper or in a database so that when new information comes along, it can be quickly linked to similar information that had previously been found.

9.2.1. Reverse Engineering

Reverse engineering is the process of capturing the specifications of existing trading/investment systems and then using the information as a foundation for designing a new system. The new design could be a replica of the original or an entirely new adaptation of its underlying strategy. Reverse engineering can be viewed as the process of analyzing a system to:

- Identify the system's components and their interrelationships.
- Create prototype models of the system in another form or a higher level of abstraction.
- Create the technological implementation of that system.

Reverse engineering includes any activity a product team may engage in to determine how a trading/investment system works, or to understand the strategies and technologies that make it run. Given, for example, a competitor's returns, the product teams perform regression and principal component analysis to understand the system. Reverse engineering is a systematic approach for analyzing the design of existing trading/investment systems.

Most trading and investment firms are highly secretive, protecting proprietary methods. Even identifying the best competitors can be difficult. Nonetheless, information should be pursued. (Although it is tempting to use illegal or unethical ways of gaining an advantage, quality and its customer-focus prohibit such short-term thinking.[6]) Consider the following ethical uses involved in reverse engineering:

- Do not reverse engineer components of a trading system if a licensing contract prohibits it.
- Remember to perform reverse engineering using only information that is not proprietary to the firm you are scoping.

If you intend to perform reverse engineering, be sure that:

- The firm does not have access to proprietary information.
- The firm does not obtain information from disgruntled employees who work or very recently worked for the competing firm and/or who are under contractual obligation to refrain from releasing proprietary information. (Employees at firms that use quality money management should not be disgruntled!)
- The firm maintains complete documentation of each component it reverse engineers so there is a record that will stand as proof in court that it performed its reverse engineering lawfully.

Reverse engineering initiates the redesign process, wherein a product is observed, tracked, analyzed, and tested in terms of its performance characteristics. The intent of the reverse engineering process is to fully understand and model the current instance of a trading strategy in order to compress the new product development time.

9.3. STEP 2, LOOP 2: Research New Methods

Because the best practice is in fact unknown (and theoretically unknowable), benchmarking is really a misnomer. We are not simply copying a competitor's system deemed to be "best practice" and implementing it in-house. Product teams use a benchmark as a reference point against which to compare its own proprietary calculations. Without a reference point, the team cannot know if its calculations are in the top rank of its peer group or not.

Over the course of their research, financial engineers investigate mathematical models and logical constructs according to best practices, taking notes, writing up, and critiquing what they find, comparing alternative methods in an attempt to best describe the interaction between data and the desired outcome. Successful researchers calibrate their methods by first applying them using known inputs and outputs and documenting the results before applying the methods to unknown inputs. In practice, the accumulation of evidence for or against any particular quantitative method involves a planned research design for the collection of empirical data. The best method is algorithm benchmarking, which will increase the probability of success.

We recommend the team keeps research independent of data and testing (our methodology forces this separation). This will help avoid, among other things, spurious correlations. Best practice also requires that teams separate the process of specifying the formulas from building the prototypes (in the following step, K|V 1.3). In this step, team members should document the logic behind the trading/investment system in an unambiguous statement of how prototypes will calculate the results. Clarify a quantitative method first; replicate second.

Researching quantitative methods means doing some leg work. Team members assigned this task, namely, the financial engineers, will either derive some proprietary algorithms or more likely go to the library and Internet, find white papers, published papers, working papers, and books, and assemble resources and articles. All of the resources, information, and articles should be organized into folders and the folders cataloged by title, concept, and author. (Building an organized library of quantitative methods is a key to the long-term success of the firm.)

We recommend that researchers standardize the formats of equations. Beta in one paper may not mean the same thing as beta in another. Some notation conversion must take place to standardize all the equations into a common format. Also, calculations should be labeled with journal names and page numbers. These documents should each have a cover sheet and be placed in bibliographical order.

We recommend product teams do a complete survey and identify all appropriate methods in order to exhaust all of the information that may exist in the research data, including intercorrelations and potentially all of the relevant projections. This process will start with empirical research, followed by an attempt to improve results with additional, theoretical research. (Research is often an imitation, or replication or corroboration, of the research of others, done with little understanding of what lies beneath the surface or consideration to the process of discovery. The search for better, though not perfect, performance must be the ultimate objective of research.)

We know a major trading firm that uses a model for a common tradable instrument that is known to be incorrect. We figure if they had performed a full survey of the body of knowledge, they would be making even more money. One day the market will punish them.

All equations and algorithms used in trading/investment will inevitably fall into one of four categories:

1. The model will be used successfully in a production environment.
2. It will be used in desperation for lack of or inability to implement a better model that will invariably cause losses and additional cost of rework sometime down the road.
3. It will be totally unusable and discarded.
4. It will be placed into an inventory of models for future research.

9.4.   STEP 2, LOOP 3: Consolidate Trading/ Investment System Design

The final loop of system specification is to assemble the component quantified methods and business rules and fully define the outputs that the trading system will produce. Also in this final pass over Step 2, team members must agree on what information team members and management will require in the form of GUI and reports to oversee the fully operating trading system, that is, in Stage 4, including what is the purpose of each report and what will be the appropriate level of detail.

The final loop through this step should also define what the appropriate risk tools will be. A discussion of these tools should then be added to the description. This will prepare us for Stage 4, Step 1—Monitor Portfolio and Statistics as well as Stage 4, Step 2—Document Profit and Loss Attribution.

> *Very few firms pay attention to defining what will constitute abnormal or nonstable performance relative to a benchmark or peer group once they implement a system. Those that do will have a competitive advantage once certain indicators lose relevance.*

9.5. Summary

The world of trading and investment has changed from one of place and time to one of algorithms and computer speed. Good research is no longer a luxury; it is a necessity. Simply adding more analysts to produce more standard research does not work. It takes too long. Ideas must be generated and vetted quickly. Nevertheless, clean, well-documented trading/investment rules lead to better automation of trading processes and scalable systems. To speed up research the firm should consider building or buying automated research and/or strategy evaluation tools. Research is applied, not theoretical, and our spiral methodology followed by a gate meeting should focus researchers on business deliverables instead of elegant equations. The advantages of doing research properly are many and cannot be overstated. Good research forms the foundation of a scalable trading/investment business.

9.5.1. Best Practices

- Before each loop through this research step, the team should form a hypothesis as to what they expect the research to accomplish. Be sure to have well-defined boundaries.
- Work from the general to the specific.
- Keep research independent of data and testing (our methodology forces this separation). Likewise, separate the process of specifying the formulas from building the prototypes.
- Keep records of research as you go. Translate notation into a common format as you proceed.
- Identify several potential solutions and evaluate them, as well as their respective sources carefully, and review your work weekly.

CHAPTER ◆ 10

Prototype in Modeling Software

Trading/investment strategy development processes should strive to deliver small, rudimentary component, or unit, prototypes and systems early and often, within the first few weeks of the start of the project, then continue to deliver systems of increasing functionality. Converting mathematical models into prototype models leads to quick decisions and, furthermore, produces a defect-removal strategy with the greatest efficacy. The goal of the iterative process is to deliver working prototypes frequently.

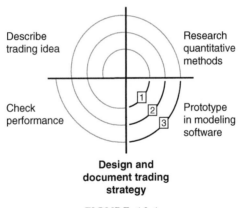

FIGURE 10-1

> *Before there is a prototype, the idea exists in abstract form only. It is described in words and leaves scope for misunderstanding. It is hard for the originator to convey exactly what he or she has in mind, and it is easy for people to get hold of the wrong end of the stick. Once the prototype exists then people can see and touch and feel the idea. Comments for improvement will flow thick and fast. Whether the prototype is a model in cardboard and string or a software application consisting of a few skeleton screens with nothing behind them, it presents a framework for refinement and extension of the idea.[1]*

This step is where prototype development and testing takes place, that is, development and testing go hand in hand (although we will discuss additional testing concepts in the following step). A good rule of thumb is that development and testing should consume the same amount of time.[2] Prototypes will vary in scope and complexity from a small

105

experiment to a final, consolidated version of the trading/investment system. Whatever the case, prototypes allow product teams to:

- Clarify calculations and expose inconsistencies in specifications.
- Rapidly evaluate alternative methods.
- Deliver intermediate, working versions to end users and other interest parties for feedback.

Furthermore, prototyping leads to:

- Improved morale because progress is visible.
- Early feedback on whether the final trading system will be acceptable.
- Decreased overall code length due to better designs.
- Lower defect rates because of better requirements definition.
- Smoother effort curves, reducing the deadline effect.

10.1.   Rapid Development

The term "rapid development language" (RDL) refers to any programming language that offers speedier implementation than do traditional third-generation languages such as C++. RDLs produce their savings by reducing the amount of construction needed to build a product. Shorter cycles make incremental development methods, such as evolutionary prototyping, practical.

> *Studies have shown that early introduction of software products is the dominant factor in long-term profitability for many, though not all, products. This holds true for trading/investment systems as well. Early and often delivery of potentially tradable prototypes is imperative.*

Software developed in RDLs is generally better suited to the development of in-house software, with more limited distribution than systems software. Widely used RDLs in finance, however, such as Excel, Resolver, and MATLAB, require many fewer lines per function point relative to other languages. Function points, a language-independent measure of program size based on a weighted sum of the number of inputs, outputs, inquiries, and files, allow developers to think about program size in a language-independent way, easing comparison between languages. A low-level language, like Assembler, requires many more lines of code to implement a function point than does a higher-level language such as C++. A language's level is the number of Assembler statements needed to replace one statement in the higher-level language. Here are the levels of some different languages:

TABLE 10-1

Language	Level	Statements per function point
Assembler	1	320
C	2.5	125
C++	6.5	50
Excel	c. 50	6
C#	12	27
SAS, SPSS	10	30
Java	6.5	50

Suppose a trading system was thought to consist of about 1000 function points. It would take about 125,000 lines of C code to implement the trading system, 50,000 lines of C++ code, or 6000 lines of Excel code. When developing evolutionary prototypes of trading systems, where time-to-market is paramount, this translates into a significant saving of time over each loop. Where an iteration using C might take two months, it might take two days using Excel. For maximum development speed, trading firms generally use the language with the highest level. Excel and MATLAB, however, usually lack adequate performance for full-scale trading systems, constrain flexibility, and are limited by quality-related problems. We recommend product teams use these RDLs as prototyping platforms.[3,4,5]

10.2. Prototyping Components

Prototyping is an exploratory, iterative process. System components should evolve toward a complete prototype as the product team loops through Stage 1. In later stages, the full trading system will be built and implemented in a traditional programming language, using nonprototyping approaches. In this stage, though, developers should not give prototypes a robustness they do not need, nor should they waste time working on prototypes with no clear direction—the direction is a complete, consolidated trading system prototype. Prototypes should generally be designed to handle only the nominal cases, not all cases or exceptional ones. Prototypes enable developers to explore design alternatives allowing them to learn lessons the cheap way. Prototyping provides for:

1. **Clear definitions of algorithms.** Building a prototype forces the team to clearly define and formulate calculations. If the team cannot explain the system well enough to build a prototype, then there is little chance that they will be able to build the working tools. Also, prototypes are needed before implementation for verification.

2. **Clear definition of data requirements.** Prototypes will bring into focus what data inputs are needed for implementation and what outputs a working system will produce.

3. **Requirements for graphical user interfaces.** This forces discussion about how humans will interact with the software components of the trading/investment system. The purpose of UI prototyping is to ensure that the operator can change dynamic inputs and states, shut down, turn on/off, and select instruments or exchanges.

4. **Development of a working application for regression testing against at least one product.** This is very important for programming teams since words can be misunderstood.

As we have said, Excel, Resolver, and MATLAB are excellent tools for prototyping component algorithms and trading systems. A component prototype is a unit or portion of a complete system. Developers should keep in mind, though, that prototypes in Excel and MATLAB should be programmed with an eye toward later conversion into object-oriented, programming code, like C++ or C#. So, Excel and VBA functions and algorithms should be fully documented and functions should be C-style and procedural in nature and neither static nor instance methods as classes defined at this stage, which may conflict with a more preferable architecture at a later development stage.

Spreadsheet risk management is a new area of research aimed at creating patches for problems that arise from use of the wrong tool. Using a hammer to drive screws creates problems. Patching holes and replacing stripped screws is not a solution. Using the right tools for implementation and quality management prevents problems from arising.

The primary reason for creating a prototype is to resolve uncertainties early in the process—can the system make money? And, is it feasible, can it be built? A prototype is useful for revealing and resolving ambiguity and incompleteness in the requirements. The presence of unclarified portions of requirements may create an expectation gap between the management's vision and the developers' understanding. Prototyping makes software requirements tangible by bringing use cases to life and closes gaps in a team's understanding of requirements. (Financial engineers may be the only ones able to understand the equations and symbols. Prototyping helps explain complex calculations to less quantitative team members.) Early feedback on prototypes of GUIs, reports, and business logic helps the stakeholders arrive at a shared understanding of the system's requirements and performance, which reduces the risk of dissatisfaction.

Prototypes of GUIs and report generation modules are generally called horizontal prototypes. These do not include details of the inner workings of the system, but rather depict a portion of the user interface, and let a product team explore behaviors and refine requirements. Horizontal prototypes often use facades of UIs and permit navigation, but with no real functionality behind it. The information that appears will be faked and report contents will be hardcoded. Vertical prototypes, on the other hand, implement slices of application functionality from the GUI through to business rules. Vertical prototypes are used for optimizing algorithms, evaluating database schema, or testing critical performance requirements, though such prototypes may not be able to produce real-time responses.

10.2.1.   Prototyping Tips

Prototype modeling is a combination of investigating and demonstrating the essential components of the proposed trading system. The outcome is a definitive requirements specification. Later, the prototype models will act as the basis for the development of production software. Here are some tips toward effective prototyping:

- Include internal or external documentation, consisting of:
  - A brief description of the model and who built it.
  - The version number and location of the master copy.
  - Details about the input data used in the model.
  - Summary of model change requests, that is, a model change control document.
  - Summary of logical assumptions.[6]
- For all members of the product team, use the same style conventions, for example, font, color coding, size. These conventions are part of the internal language of the product team.
- Make prototype tracking and control a priority.
- While financial engineers and programmers will be involved in prototype development. The process must include and, furthermore, should be overseen by someone trained in software testing.

- Focus initial prototyping efforts on poorly understood or risky areas. Furthermore, since prototyping quantitative methods consists of scientific experiments, be sure to carefully monitor and control them.

- Consider performance in prototype design. Do not develop quick and dirty code for the prototype. Risk rises when the prototype has significantly different performance from the final working system. Prototyping is not an alternative to good design.

- Be sure management and the team leader understand the difference between a limited prototype and a full-scale, working product. Miscommunication can lead to a risk of underbudgeting prototyping projects.

- Avoid digressions. Do not put too much work into prototyping and evolving any piece of the trading system puzzle until you are certain it is going to remain part of the production system.

Visible work may be done quickly; other less visible work is what often takes time. Low visibility work includes database access, maintenance of database integrity, security, networking, and data conversion. The biggest risk is that a stakeholder will see a running prototype and conclude that the product is nearly completed. The purpose of building a prototype is to prove design aspects as early as possible, before resources are committed to full-scale development. Proving can be iterative as well. We recommend the team look for feedback through intrateam peer review and refine the prototype until everyone agrees it is correct. They can be for:

- User interfaces
- Interactive performance
- Real-time timing constraints
- Data sizing
- Proof of concept aspects.

10.2.2. Throwaway Prototypes

In most cases, we recommend throwaway prototypes. In throwaway prototyping, the product team develops code to explore factors critical to the system's success, and then that code is thrown away. Prototyping, both horizontal and vertical, uses tools such as Excel or MATLAB; programming languages and development practices are much faster compared to the implementation language and practices. When used as a requirements specification aid, throwaway prototyping accelerates project development.[7]

Throwaway prototyping delivers speed due to its ability to explore individual requirements, design, and implementation options quickly. The product team should employ throwaway prototyping anytime where clarification of requirements is needed, to decide on an architectural issue, to compare design or implementation options, or to test performance optimization. One of the key problems in developing throwaway prototypes is that the prototype might not get thrown away.

Throwaway prototypes must be discarded. Delivering an Excel prototype, for example, will likely result in poor performance, poor maintainability, and poor design. Because prototypes emphasize quick implementation at the expense of robustness, reliability, performance, and long-term maintainability, we recommend that spreadsheets and code be segregated and prevented from becoming a production system in all but the most immediate of circumstances. Product teams must resist the temptation (and often management pressure) to add more implementation capabilities to prototypes. The team cannot successfully turn the intentional low quality of a prototype into the maintainable robustness that a production system demands. Prototyping facilitates rapid iteration and iteration is the key success factor in testing and evaluating new trading ideas, but in the end prototypes should be discarded.

10.2.3.   Evolutionary Prototypes

Evolutionary prototyping is a development approach in which the product team prototypes selected parts of a system first, and then evolves the rest of the system from those parts. Unlike throwaway prototyping, in evolutionary prototyping, the team does not discard the prototype code; rather they evolve the code into the production application that they will ultimately use in the implementation, that is, the prototype evolves into the production software. Evolutionary prototypes provide a solid foundation for building a trading system's software tools incrementally as the requirements through iteration become clearer. These prototypes must be built with production-quality code from the outset and must incorporate good architecture and solid design principles. There's no room for shortcuts in evolutionary prototypes.

Evolutionary prototyping supports rapid development by addressing risks early. The product team starts development of the riskiest areas first. If obstacles prove too difficult, the team can cancel the project without having spent any more seed capital or time than necessary. Because of the risks, initial planning should identify the biggest obstacles. The first loop of an evolutionary prototype is generally a pilot release that implements whatever requirements are well understood and stable. Lessons learned from user testing and performance evaluation of the prototype as well as new research into quantitative methods will lead to modification in the following loop. The working system, in the end, is the end product of a series of evolutionary prototypes. These work well for trading systems that grow with each iteration and gradually integrate various data sources and external systems.[8]

Sometimes, S-Plus, SAS, MATLAB, and even Excel and Resolver prototypes may not be thrown away. Over the last decade, there has been tremendous growth in the number and types of software applications appropriate for modeling financial instruments and trading strategies. Some of these applications compile production code (in .dlls) from prototypes built in the software itself. (For example, MathWorks offers a unique set of tools that lets you convert MATLAB code into C++ or .NET code automatically. Ultimately, MATLAB lets you develop prototypes and convert them into usable software more quickly.) This trend is sure to continue. These new tools enable evolutionary prototyping although the performance in production may yet fall short. While we generally prefer throwaway prototyping, we recognize that evolutionary prototyping may very well be the future.

Evolutionary prototyping may, however, create unfulfillable expectations about the overall trading system development schedule. When end users, seed capital providers, managers, or marketers see rapid progress on a prototype, they sometimes make unrealistic assumptions about how quickly the team will finish. Additionally, with evolutionary prototyping, the team cannot know at the outset of the project how many loops it will take to create an acceptable product. The team cannot know how long each iteration will last. For this reason, we strongly recommend a minimum of three loops, and a maximum of five, followed by a gate meeting. If the project is spiraling out of control due to fuzzy specifications, management can kill the project or reconstitute the product team.

10.3. Spreadsheet Modeling

According to the European Spreadsheet Risk Interest Group (EuSpRIG):

> Research has repeatedly shown that an alarming proportion of corporate spreadsheet models are not tested to the extent necessary to support Directors' fiduciary, reporting and compliance obligations. Uncontrolled and untested spreadsheet models therefore pose significant business risks. These risks include: lost revenue & profits, mispricing and poor decision making due to prevalent but undetected errors, fraud due to malicious tampering [and] difficulties in demonstrating fiduciary and regulatory compliance. These risks are ignored due to a widespread failure to inventory (keep records of), test, document, backup, archive and control the legions of spreadsheets that support critical corporate infrastructure.[9]

In some ways, Microsoft's Excel spreadsheet is the crack cocaine of financial markets—it is cheap, easy to obtain, and creates the illusion of speed. The many financial modeling books have gotten traders and financial engineers hooked by teaching the construction of hybrid Excel and VBA applications with essentially no consideration of planning or software design.

A Canadian company took a $24 million charge to earnings after a spreadsheet that contained mismatched bids caused them to buy more U.S. power transmission hedging contracts than they needed and at higher prices than they wanted to pay.[10]

Too often graduate-level courses in financial engineering focus solely on algorithm development and not on the process of building robust trading/investment or risk management systems. Students design systems in Excel that should otherwise be properly implemented as object-oriented applications using C# or C++.

Nevertheless, Excel will never go away. Spreadsheets are more pervasive than ever due to the increasing pace of change. Excel has a well-developed network of suppliers that provide myriad add-ins, and Excel projects are understandably additive; traders and financial engineers can quickly add new spreadsheets and new calculations to existing systems. But Excel's place should more often be as a prototyping tool, not an implementation tool, especially when constructing real-time trading/investment systems. Using Excel to prototype software implies a subsequent conversion to programming code, which often becomes a reverse engineering project by programmers that may or may not understand the spreadsheet's underlying context—the financial mathematics or trading strategy.

Excel is a programming environment where the idea-makers, rarely versed in software development and testing processes, are the developers. "The ranks of 'sorcerer's apprentice' user-programmers will also swell rapidly, giving many who have little training or expertise in how to avoid or detect high-risk defects tremendous power to create high-risk defects."[11] The problem is software development methodologies are rigorous and difficult to implement.

Spreadsheets are an excellent platform for creating prototype models because, among other reasons, spreadsheets allow the user to easily manipulate data, reducing the time it takes to set up and modify models. Furthermore, spreadsheets include efficient graphing and good report generating functionalities.[12] However, Grossman and Ozluk point out that "spreadsheet programming currently resembles a bag of tricks rather than a well-organized, coherent toolbox."[13] Through experience and hard knocks, individual firms have generally organized their design techniques relative to their business context. Nevertheless, some best practices exist. The six golden rules of spreadsheet design:[14]

- Separate inputs, calculations and results. Place inputs in a separate part of the worksheet from calculations. Outputs should be in another part still.
- Use one formula per row or column.
- Refer to the above and to the left.
- Use multiple worksheets for ease of expansion and for repeatable blocks.
- Use each column for the same purpose throughout the model.
- Include a documentation sheet that identifies key formulas.

Grossman and Ozluk add the following:

- Keep formulas simple to enable check of intermediate calculations.
- Use named cells and ranges.
- Enter each input once.
- Use absolute references.
- Use cell-protection to prevent accidental or unauthorized modification of formulas.
- Make the spreadsheet file read-only to prevent accidental overwriting.[15]

Also, we recommend enhancing the look of the spreadsheet with bold fonts, borders, shading, and graphs when displaying results. This will make the spreadsheet easier to read.

10.4.   STEP 3, LOOP 1: Prototype Known Calculations

After researching similar and competing systems, the product team should convert all known calculations and logical algorithms to a common, standardized format. The team members charged with the prototyping task, namely, the financial engineers and programmers, can take the standardized equations and build component prototypes from them.

> *We know a firm that used Excel's standard functions to average the volatility between historical volatilities. That is, given several standard deviations for several stocks, they calculated the portfolio volatility as the average of the constituents. Of course, standard deviations are not additive, but no one caught it for several years. How much money do you suppose they lost because their programmers used standard Excel functions in unexpected ways?*

In prototyping, the difficult step is taking known knowledge and applying it to an unknown problem. (Our methodology teaches how to perform research by also teaching how to apply unknown knowledge to unknown problems.) As stated previously, we believe in risk-driven iterative development. As such, the team should consider which components they believe will be the most difficult to build. These components must be the first ones built into prototype models. There are multiple reasons for this approach:

- Time spent on the easy tasks will be wasted if the harder portions end up not working.
- Objectives could radically shift based upon the conclusions formed after building the most difficult pieces. For example, calculating a model for an entire volatility

surface and related prices could turn out to take several minutes. Hedge funds have solved this problem using strategies ranging from solid-state drives to building a function that stores all of the prices for fast retrieval. Solving the problem required large amounts of up front work prior to building the system.

- Agreement to build the hardest parts first focuses the team on the true goal of the software, rather than the goals of the individual components.

- Once the hard work is done, team members will find it much easier to break the system into components since everyone will understand core relationships between the pieces.

- Killing a project that has only one failed component is easy. Projects where many simple components (such as user interfaces, reports, and calculations) are already built are hard to kill. By the time the project reaches the most difficult stage, team members may feel compelled to force them to "work" even though the core engine does not function properly.

10.5. STEP 3, LOOP 2: Prototype New Calculations

In the previous step, financial engineers should have documented the logic behind the trading/investment system in an unambiguous statement of how prototypes should calculate the results. Furthermore, financial engineers will have assembled research articles and highlighted equations and algorithms that may apply to the trading system. All of the resources and information and articles should be organized in folders and the folders cataloged by title, concept, and author.

Once financial engineers have laid out all the methods and valuation equations, developers can prototype them one by one in an organized fashion.

> *A full prototype should include test data and user interface mock-ups for all dynamic inputs. One trading firm realized too late that real market scenarios including price jumps would cause big losses in their system. They could have tested for big jumps earlier and saved thousands of dollars in programming costs.*

We recommend keeping a single folder with subfolders to contain all of the files of component prototypes for a particular system. Prototyping trading rules will also require development of time series data so that all possible scenarios of changes in prices of the respective instruments can be investigated and modeled. Data files should be saved within a documented file structure as well.

10.6. STEP 3, LOOP 3: Build Consolidated Prototype

The final loop of Stage 1 requires that the product team consolidate the prototypes into a single model, with one set of code. This consolidated model should be fully labeled, with code fully documented and all calculations clearly shown.

> Among other things, a consolidated prototype will alert programmers to thread-safety issues down the road. The trading industry is littered with failed real-time software projects.

The final pass through this step should construct a single prototype with the chosen, benchmarked methods for the trade selection algorithms, trade execution and trade cost analysis calculations, cash management procedures, risk algorithms, and performance metrics. The consolidated prototype will be the primary input into the technology specification requirements documents for Stage 3.

10.7.   Summary

The advantage of prototyping (either in Excel, Resolver, MATLAB, Zack's, Mathematica, SAS, and/or in other software) is to allow the team the ability to quickly prove complex mathematics and trading strategies in code.

- Transferring from math to code allows everyone to understand the math.
- The spiral method with firm deliverables focuses financial engineers on deliverables and not elegant mathematics.
- Prototypes force data issues early in the development cycle.
- Excel is an excellent prototyping language due to its ability to model quickly.
- Prototypes are the deliverable of the first stage since the prototypes will be used as a foundation input into later stages.
- Prototypes should be throwaways. They are not implementation mechanisms. Teams should discard prototypes and build proper algorithms in code over the course of Stages 2 and 3.
- Prototype the hardest parts first.

Managers can avoid the problem of not throwing away throwaway prototypes by maintaining a firm commitment to whatever prototyping paradigm was initially chosen. Developers can do their part by fully defining and communicating a prototype's scope and purpose.[16]

Spreadsheet testing is important, because the spreadsheet becomes the oracle for later stages of development in K|V. For the remainder of the book we will use "well defined" to mean that a trading system has been fully prototyped.

10.7.1.   Best Practices

We have touched on many low-level best practices over the course of the chapter, but to summarize here are more high-level recommendations.

- Prototype the hardest parts first and test component prototypes as you build them.
- Use team-oriented testing and inspection. Do not rely on standardized functions in Excel and third-party software. Understand first how they work.
- For spreadsheet prototypes, follow the six golden rules as well as the additions by Grossman and Ozluk.
- Specify and communicate to users beforehand whether a prototype is throwaway or evolutionary.
- Document prototypes internally.

CHAPTER • 11

Check Performance

As we have said, there are three types of trading systems—trigger systems, filter systems, multifactor systems—and systems of each type should have their own unique method and mechanism for testing performance. Since systems rarely fall neatly into one of the types, product teams must develop a unique testing process for each new system. Checking performance includes not only determining whether or not the trading system makes money, but also checking the performance of design and development processes through quality assurance testing. This is the step where a team tests the validity of the proposed trading system in addition to another review of the correctness of the units. Outputs of this step will control the evolution of the trading/investment system either through the following loop through Stage 1 or through Stage 2.

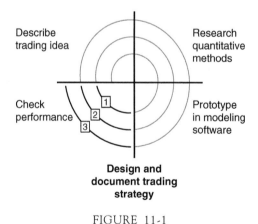

FIGURE 11-1

11.1. Walkthroughs and Inspections

Some product teams skimp on time allotted to quality assurance practices, such as design reviews, walkthroughs, and inspections, while others try to make up for lost time by compressing the testing schedule. A decision to ignore techniques that find defects is tantamount to a conscious decision to postpone corrections until later stages when they are more expensive and time-consuming. That is not smart, especially when time-to-market is important. Fast track projects are particularly vulnerable to shorting quality assurance, even though poor quality is one of the most common reasons for finishing late.[1]

Preventing or detecting and removing defects early allows product teams to realize significant schedule benefits in later stages. Reworking defective trading/investment system requirements and design can consume nearly 50% of the total cost of development. As a rule of thumb, every hour spent on defect prevention in Stage 1 will reduce repair time anywhere from three to ten hours later in Stage 3 or 4 of K|V.[2]

Design walkthroughs are useful for rapid development because teams can use them to detect defects before backtesting begins in Stage 3. The earliest time that testing can detect a requirements defect is after the requirement has been specified, designed, and prototyped, that is, a walkthrough can detect a requirements defect at a specification time.[3] Furthermore, research shows that walkthroughs can find between 30 and 70% of the errors in a software program. We expect that results would be similar for trading system development.

Inspections are a kind of formal technical review that has proven to be extremely effective in detecting defects throughout a project. During inspections, product team members use checklists to systematically review trading/investment system design components, each person identifying defects in logic, data, mathematics, prototypes, or design as they go. Throughout the inspection, team members should gather data on the number of defects, hours spent correcting those defects, and hours spent on the inspection process, so that later management and teams can analyze and improve the velocity of trading system design and development.[4] Again, ample amounts of research show that inspections find from 60 to 90% of defects and reduce schedules by 10 to 30%. Rather than slowing things down, quality assurance speeds things up and speed is vitally important.

Detection of defects in trading system design early on, when they are easy to find and fix, will relieve the need for time-consuming and expensive rework and redesign down the road. Just as unit tests serve as compilable documentation for the internals of the system, acceptance tests and performance runs serve as compilable documentation of the performance of the trading/investment system.

11.2.   Spreadsheet Testing

As Dr. Ray Panko points out:

> consistent with research on human error rates in other cognitive tasks, laboratory studies and field examinations of real-world spreadsheets have confirmed that developers make uncorrected errors in 2–5% of all formulas ... Consequently, nearly all large spreadsheets are wrong and in fact have multiple errors ... Spreadsheet error rates are very similar to those in traditional programming. However, while programmers spend [25]–40% of their development time in testing, testing among spreadsheet developers in industry is extremely rare ... [but] the only proven way to reduce errors dramatically is testing.[5]

To programmers, "testing" means what Panko calls execution testing. In execution testing the tester tries several input values to see if they produce correct results. However, how does the developer know when a result is correct? Developers refer to this as the oracle problem. An oracle is a way of knowing when results are correct.

For spreadsheets, there seldom are obvious oracles. Runtime errors do not happen. Rather, logic errors result in incorrect calculations. Team testers must compare results with known calculated values. In some cases, however, there may be no known comparable calculation. In nearly all spreadsheets, calculations are extended well beyond what has been done previously with manual calculations. In such cases, there is no oracle other than the spreadsheet calculations themselves. This lack of a readily available oracle is the most serious problem in spreadsheet execution testing. Without a strong and easy-to-apply oracle, execution testing simply makes no sense for error-reduction testing. A major problem in finance is that much of the research is correct only for the limited sample data presented and may be incorrect over larger, real-world samples. Also, many papers deliberately withhold full documentation of equations to keep proprietary information secret. In such cases, the team has no choice but to build its own test cases and oracles.

Regression testing is attractive for spreadsheet execution testing. Regression testing is undertaken after modification to a spreadsheet to ensure that the spreadsheet still works properly in parts where no changes were made. In a regression test, suites of input values previously used in the model are reentered and the bottom-line, output figures are compared to the values experienced before the spreadsheet was changed. In regression testing, the fact that the only realistic oracle is the spreadsheet itself is not a problem. Spreadsheet testing is important, because the spreadsheet (or model in other software) becomes the oracle for later stages of development in K|V.

In a spreadsheet logic inspection, team members examine all formula cells. In contrast to auditing, which frequently focuses only on the parts of the spreadsheet that seem risky, logic inspection is comprehensive. Logic inspection at the prototyping stage, before conversion to code begins in later stages, allows errors to be detected again when the cost of fixing them is small. In software development, Fagan[6,7] developed the code inspection methodology for IBM.

Although there are several variants, we will discuss Fagan inspection as a basic model for spreadsheet logic inspection. Fagan mandates team inspection rather than individual inspection, because in several laboratory experiments, individuals typically catch fewer than half of all errors. Having multiple inspectors raises this detection rate substantially. Fagan's inspection process has seven steps:

- **Planning.** Preparing materials, obtaining participants, and scheduling meetings.
- **Overview meeting.** Introduces the software, lays out roles, and describes the process.
- **Preparation.** Inspectors, working alone, examine the spreadsheet. The goal is not to identify errors but to understand the software module.
- **Inspection meeting.** The goal is to detect errors. There should not be discussions beyond those needed to identify and clarify errors. Should be limited to no more than two hours to prevent loss of diligence.
- **Process improvement.** The inspection also should provide feedback to the firm's inspection process guidelines. Each inspection must generate statistics on time spent, errors found, and error severity.
- **Rework.** Fixing the software is done after the meeting.
- **Follow-up.** To ensure that changes are made appropriately.

The need for team logic in spreadsheet testing has also been demonstrated in the laboratory. Panko shows that gains from team inspection are unsurprising in view of teamwork's long-proven ability to reduce errors more than individual work.[8]

Code inspection does not entirely eliminate errors; error-reduction methods never eliminate all errors. Typically, a round of team-oriented logic inspection is likely to eliminate 60–80% of all errors. That is why we condone iterative development. The more passes over the K|V Stage 1 spiral, the more opportunities there are for errors to be removed. For code inspection, team size is usually three or four. We recommend the team:

- Create a policy requiring comprehensive prototype testing. Testing should consume 25–40% of prototype development time.
- If pretesting is done, look over spreadsheets for errors and sees that error checking programs are good but should not be used in lieu of comprehensive testing.
- Only use execution testing for regression testing unless the user training and oracle problem can be overcome.
- Use logic testing for comprehensive testing.

For team testing we recommend the following roles be divided among the team:

- **Author.** Developer of the spreadsheet.
- **Moderator.** Inspection leader.
- **Reader,** who paraphrases the spreadsheet logic being discussed.
- **Recorder,** who records spreadsheet errors found during the inspection meeting.
- **User.** Either a trader, who will use the spreadsheet, or a programmer who will convert the spreadsheet to code in later stages.

11.3.   STEP 4, LOOP 1: White Box Test Formulas

As mentioned, all team members are responsible for performance testing. All team members should review the formulas and test them against proven journal reference results and unit test all prototyped calculations against known inputs and known outputs.

Coding is fun. Testing is boring. There is real money at stake, so you had better make sure $4.72 is the correct theoretical price of the option.

White box testing, also known as glass box, structural, clear box, or open box testing, is a software testing technique whereby testers have explicit knowledge of and access to the internal workings of the model being tested as well as the test data. Unit tests are white box tests that verify the individual mechanisms, or components, of the system. In a white box test, the tester first analyzes the code and then derives test cases, targeting specific logical paths so as to achieve broad coverage, including boundary conditions.

Experienced programmers often perform scenario tests (a form of white box testing) with large numbers of combinations of inputs. While this is a good testing technique, we believe complete scenario testing is not feasible for most trading/investment systems. Scenario testing is slow and cumbersome, requiring a huge effort to produce and document exhaustive coverage of possible scenarios. We recommend the product team test only known scenarios and move on.

The advantages of white box testing are that testers can quickly uncover programming errors and examine potential error handling techniques, dependencies, and logic flow. Furthermore, such tests are a check on design decisions and mathematical formulas and may point the way to more robust designs. However, because white box tests require such intimate knowledge of the system, they generally do not scale well to large applications with thousands of lines of code or spreadsheet cells. Also, white box testing will not account for errors caused by omission.

Despite its shortcomings, white box testing is critical as it allows skilled team members to develop test cases. Test case data should be inputs and outputs against which future regression tests can be run for the life of the development project. The more test cases, the higher is the quality of the prototypes, and eventually the implementation software, and in the end the overall quality of the trading system. Any changes to the prototypes or fully functional software must be tested to ensure "fixed" versions generate the same output values as the white box test cases.

White box testing is also good for team development since it is normally accomplished by having a programmer and financial engineer sit at a single computer and walk through the code in debug mode to test calculations and outputs. This type of close testing builds trust between team members; when the team encounters complex problems down the road, they will have working relationships to solve problems. Everyone is equal on a team and white box testing can be an effective management tool for preventing cultural problems. Early testing helps avoid the blame culture before it becomes a major issue in the later stages of development, where the team cannot afford to have isolated members who believe their way is the only way.

In the end, white box testing is only the start. For a complete examination, gray box and black box tests are also required.

11.4. STEP 4, LOOP 2: Perform Gray Box Testing with Inputs and Outputs

All team members should test the performance of the trading system. At this point, however, the model code may very well be sufficiently complex so as to require not white box, but gray box testing. Gray box testing is a software testing technique where testers have limited knowledge of the internals or source code of the system, relying instead on architecture diagrams, state-based models, interface definitions, and functional specifications. Based on what knowledge they do have, testers can derive intelligent test cases. Of course, without knowledge of the code, the tester must deduce test cases.

For trading system gray box testing, we recommend both the trader and marketer sit with the financial engineer and/or programmers and perform unit testing using examples selected by the trader or marketer. This type of testing builds teamwork and understanding of the system along with finding errors. Traders tend to test extreme events, such as gap moves and highly volatile instruments. (Every trader remembers that extreme day where they lost or made a lot of money.) Marketers also tend to test extreme cases. In many ways, this is actually the start of value at risk testing of the system.

11.5. STEP 4, LOOP 3: Perform Black Box Testing, Documenting Results Using Inputs and Outputs

Black box testing, also known as functional testing, is a software testing technique whereby the internal workings of the software are unknown to the testers. For example, in a black box test on a software design the testers only know the inputs and what the expected out-comes should be and not how the program arrives at those outputs. The testers do not ever examine the programming code and do not need any further knowledge of the program other than its specifications. A black box tester typically interacts with the prototype soft-ware through a locked-down user interface, providing inputs and examining outputs for cor-rectness. For consolidated trading system prototypes, black box testing will almost certainly be the only appropriate type of testing. The advantages of this type of testing include:

- The tests are unbiased because the tester's perspective is independent from that of the developer.
- The testers do not need knowledge of any specific programming languages.
- Test cases can be designed as soon as the specifications are complete.
- Moderately skilled testers with no knowledge of hardware, software, or quantitative finance can perform tests.

A disadvantage of black box testing is that many possible scenarios are unrealistic because it would take an inordinate amount of time; therefore, many logical program paths may go untested.

In the end, acceptance tests are black box tests that verify that the requirements set forth in the Money Document and the evolving description and documentation of the trad-ing/investment system are met. Acceptance tests are written by folks who do not know the internal mechanism of the system, that is, not the quant and not the programmer and most likely the trader and marketer or testers external to the team.

The final loop through this step double checks all of the calculations, verifying that the consolidated prototype is working properly. Also, during this final pass we will generate all of the charts and supporting documentation. The results of this acceptance, black box test will form the baseline or gold standard, the trusted results of the trading/ investment system performance, against which backtesting results, in the next stage, will be compared, using a regression test. If the results in backtesting differ from the gold standard, an error condition will exist. How else would the team know if everything is running right?

11.6.   Trading the Prototype

After acceptance, we acknowledge that, in theory, traders and/or seed capital providers could demand to begin trading the system using the consolidated prototype. After all, the highest priority is to satisfy the seed capital investors through early and continuous deliv-ery of working trading system prototypes. However, we strongly caution that trading be delayed at a bare minimum until after the Gate 1 meeting where top management can approve its use. Nevertheless, the product team must communicate clearly that trading of a prototype assumes no automation of order entry, no risk or algorithm monitoring with SPC, and no portfolio management, so results will vary greatly.

The primary purpose of trading the prototype should be only to fully understand the performance monitoring tools that will be required in the later stages. Be aware, though, that the performance of the system in probationary trading at this point will not be indica-tive of the performance of the completed system. Trading may occur for a limited period of time and with a small amount of capital in order to more fully understand the behav-ior of the system and as mentioned to understand what tools will be needed to manage the risk of the system and the market. As before, checking the performance of the system will prevent additional time and resources from being spent on unprofitable projects. The team may need to loop back to the initial research stage and reassess the quantitative methods and algorithms after the onset of trading.

If trading does occur, we recommend that for systems consisting of spreadsheet prototypes the product team at a minimum employ Tom Grossman's six application development features:

- Protect source code from user changes.
- Prevent user customization.
- Restrict linking user spreadsheets into the application.
- Prevent users from sharing the application.
- Provide easy control of protection features using a well-designed user interface.
- Prevent user tampering with protection features by employing passwords.[9]

Following these guidelines will at least make it very difficult for users to mess around with the code and introduce errors or untested modifications.

11.7. Performance Runs and Control

Performing multiple test runs of a trading/investment system can lead to confusion about which versions generated which results, and which conclusions depended upon which assumptions. Normally, programmers use a tool, such as Microsoft SourceSafe, to control versioning. However, when using prototyping languages, the team cannot easily use these types of tools, so the team must control versioning itself. Over the successive tests, product teams should generate individual run packs, computer folders with unique names for each run. Included in the run pack should be a copy of the prototype software and data used to generate the run, and a run control document, containing:

- The unique run number and date/time.
- A summary of run pack contents, signed off on by all team members.
- Reports, graphs, tables of trading system performance results.
- Details of key assumptions.
- Recommendations for further development.

11.8. Summary

K|V delivers rudimentary unit prototypes of the trading system within the first few weeks and then strives to continue to deliver systems of increasing functionality. Traders or seed capital providers may in theory choose to put these systems into production if they think they are worthy. Research shows that skimping on testing leads to errors and failure. The goal of the iterative process is to deliver tested, working prototypes for use as oracles, gold standards, and run packs for regression testing of later implementations.

Prototypes will indicate what data to collect. Teams collect that data and analyze it to validate the continued suitability and effectiveness of the trade selection algorithms, position management, and risk management logic compared against known results generated during backtesting. Proper testing will ensure the correctness of new systems and increase the probability of success.

11.8.1.   Best Practices

- Use walkthroughs and inspections to ensure quality.
- Conduct unit tests to ensure pieces of the system are correct.
- Document the need for performance monitoring tools necessary for implementation.
- Document procedures for white, gray, and black box testing and acceptance test run packs, the gold standard results for backtesting in the next stage.
- Use a team approach to testing.

CHAPTER ◆ 12

Gate 1

As with most services, trading/investment systems are candidates for external review to evaluate the prospects of the product itself and to ensure the product team is following proper procedures. Such a review, either by management or a peer group, should in total take no more than a week or two, not a month or two. As Dunham suggests, review, in the form of a gate meeting, "done right ... can help teams move more quickly as they enter the next development phase."[1]

According to Cooper, Edgett, and Kleinschmidt in their seminal text *Portfolio Management for New Products*, gates are quality control checkpoints. Gate meetings are a forum for making decisions about incremental investments in new trading/investment system development projects. Good decision-making requires a process for the exchange of information between the product team and management (or product review board, or peer group), who understand the portfolio context of the trading/investment system under consideration. Management (as seed capital provider) decides whether or not the project will continue to the backtesting stage. Alternatively, management may also instruct the product team to return to the previous stage with instructions to rework components of the system before meeting again to make a final decision. Management may also provide focus, direction, and conditions for the following stage if the project is allowed to proceed; for example, the team may need to resolve a specific problem as a first priority.[2] Specifically, gates serve to:

- Control the burn rate of seed capital.
- Cut off the burn rate. In this way, seed capital commitments have optionality to them.
- Make sure that all ideas are properly vetted, discussed, and approved or rejected with everyone's input.
- Provide a forum to formally add and remove new trading systems to the list of priorities and to communicate why and what those priorities are.

System verification, that is, proving via demonstration, evidence, and testimony at gate meetings will ensure that design and development outputs of the prior stage have met the design and development input requirements of the following one. Verification requires that the input requirements have been tested and that the results have been documented. Effectively, by Gate 1, concept risk should have been removed. That is, management should be able to make a well-informed decision as to whether the concept, the well-defined trading/investment strategy, is worth investing in. The Research and Document Calculations stage, K|V Stage 1, outputs must:

- Meet the design and development input requirements of the backtest stage.
- Provide information needed for purchasing data, including cost estimates, and backtesting the system.
- Either contain or make reference to trading/investment system acceptance criteria.
- Specify trading system characteristics necessary for proper implementation.
- Be in a form that allows verification against the inputs of the Money Document. The information is typically in the form of specifications, drawings, instructions, verification and test methodology, and acceptance criteria.

The product team should arrive at the gate meeting with its deliverables and a recommendation supported by data. A recommendation to proceed to the backtesting stage must of course be accompanied by a request for additional resources. At the meeting, management will review the recommendation and decide what course to take.[3] In order to pass through Gate 1, several questions must be answered.

- Is the trading/investment system well defined (i.e., has it been fully prototyped)?
- Has the product team delivered the required documents?
- Is the product on time and on budget?
- Does the trading/investment system have a competitive advantage?
- Does the project show a good probability of successful implementation?
- Is the project technically feasible? What are the software quality attributes?
- Are the resources requested for continued development acceptable?
- Is there a plan for moving ahead through the backtest stage?
- Is the team functioning as a team or does top management need to reform it?

This gate will prevent development of the trading/investment system from moving to the backtesting stage until the required activities and deliverables have been completed in a quality manner. Furthermore, this gate will chart the path ahead by ensuring that plans and budgets have been made for the next stage.

Gate meetings also provide an opportunity to reexamine project forecasts and modify them and those of others where appropriate. Although some information needed for planning may at this point in time be difficult to forecast, overall uncertainties are reduced by learning from experience and reassessing processes that move projects from development to launch.

12.1.   Running a Successful Gate Meeting

Gate meetings are critical in any industry where time-to-market is key to success. Anything that unnecessarily delays a trading/investment system's time-to-market may hurt its profitability and therefore the profitability of the firm. If management meets and agrees that a new trading/investment system should be funded and development restarted immediately, that system's time-to-market will be reduced. If management stops development of a trading/investment system, it can quickly reallocate resources to other more promising projects. For active firms, we recommend that gate meetings happen once every month or so, or at least as often as necessary to set and reset priorities.

The objective of a gate meeting is to obtain development approval and allocate resources, so everyone who has a say in these matters should be invited, including all the members of the product team and top management and any external seed capital providers. At some firms, a cross-functional product approval committee fulfills the management function at gate meetings. At others a peer group fulfills the role. With respect to gate meetings, responsibilities of the product team represented by the team leader are to:

- Provide deliverable materials to management at least a few days before the meeting.
- Keep the presentation brief and to the point. We recommend 15 to 20 minutes followed by 30 to 45 minutes of discussion.
- Use document and presentation templates so management understands the structure of the presentation.
- Make the recommendation and supporting data the core of the presentation.
- Be specific about resources required and how they will be used.
- Articulate clearly what help the product team will need from management to eliminate project risks.[4]

Responsibilities of top management with respect to gate meetings are to:

- Be prepared. Read presentation materials before the meeting. Start on time.
- Only ask clarifying questions during the presentation.
- Stay on target with the discussion. Only ask questions relevant to the stage and that the development team is able to answer.
- Make sure every decision-maker is heard from and their position made clear.
- Make sure that back-door decisions do not circumvent the meeting process.[5]

The rules of the gate meetings are that top management cannot request information beyond that specified in the deliverables and must make their decision based on the criteria for that gate. At the gate meeting, the product team should ask management (or seed capital investor) to sign off on the Stage 1 results as well as the interpretation of those results.

12.1.1. Meeting Format

Gate meetings are systematic reviews of design and development performed in accordance with planned arrangements to evaluate the ability of the results of the trading/investment system to meet requirements and to identify any problems and propose necessary actions. This is intended to prevent design and development from being done in an unstructured, uncontrolled fashion.

Well in advance of the meeting, management should notify all interested parties about which trading/investment systems will be discussed. This allows everyone to give their input well in advance. The objective is not to spring new trading/investment ideas in the meeting, but to give people time to think about them.

As a prelude to a successful gate meeting, management should provide an overview of the economic environment, financial markets, and significant changes since the last gate meeting, and review the portfolio of current trading systems as well as those under development. At the meeting the audience should first address the current environment to ensure that there is consensus as to the feasibility of proposed new systems in the current environment. If current projects are slipping, it makes no sense to add new projects without removing others. The audience should understand, then, how time and seed capital are already being allocated. Then, they can review the appropriateness of these allocations in the current economic environment. From there, the discussion can move on to new proposals and changes to existing projects. We recommend review of no more than four or five products in a single meeting.

Well-run gate meetings end with another review of all trading systems currently under development, including new decisions, approvals, and prioritizations made at the meeting. Gate meeting minutes should be published immediately; written confirmation of decisions and priorities will clarify objectives. As discussed, decisions regarding under-development systems fall into one of five categories—Go, Kill, Hold, Return, and, potentially, Trade.

- **Go.** If it is added to the list of approved systems, the next stage is started.
- **Kill.** If there is not sufficient justification to continue development, or it no longer fits into the organization's strategy, then it should be canceled and removed from the list of priorities.
- **Hold.** At times a system may need to be tabled for what ever reason. In such a case, whatever additional activities should be performed and the project should be discussed at the next gate meeting. For example, if the system fits into the company strategy, but additional resources are unavailable, we may put it on hold until some future time.
- **Return.** Return to a previous stage for additional research or testing.
- **Trade.** Trade the existing prototype. (Only for short-lived strategies, e.g., tax trading algorithms.)

Additionally, decisions may take into account the following criteria:

- Does the project fit into the organization's long-term competitive strategy?
- Does the market opportunity for the project align with the company strategy?
- Will there be sufficient revenue from the product to justify the work required?
- If there is not sufficient revenue, are there other highly compelling reasons to justify the work?
- Are there resources available to do the work?
- If the resources are not available, should this project take priority over other projects?

Beyond the basic format of presentation, allotting significant time for discussion of risks to the project can facilitate alignment between the product team and management. Product teams naturally want to start by pointing out the merits of the trading/investment strategy they are pursuing and what impressive progress they are making. But, teams also need to engage in an open dialog about risks and risk management techniques. Risk factors might involve development cost overruns, operating-cost miscalculation, technical feasibility issues, performance issues, or any other factor that could result in a less-than-satisfactory final product. If both the product team and management make project risk management a priority, discussion will be more fruitful. Product team members may feel threatened by conversation that shines light on issues they might have missed or assumptions they should reconsider. But, teams that avoid a defensive posture learn faster, their projects will move forward faster, and their credibility will rise in the eyes of seed capital providers.[6]

At the point of the Gate 1 meeting, the design must be ready for full-scale backtesting, and a freeze is typically applied on the quantitative methods and business/trading rules, apart from optimization routines that will be run as part of the backtesting stage. After this, quantitative methods may be changed only through a change control process and a return to Stage 1 for review, testing, and verification, including an evaluation of the change's effect on other parts of the trading/investment system. Management must review all design change proposals at gate meetings to ensure that the change is required, and that the change will likely accomplish the intended result.

12.2. Inputs/Deliverables

At the gate meeting, management can expect the following deliverables:

- Full description of the trading system, including detailed discussion of the quantitative methods and business logic along with a recommendation from the product team as to how to proceed.
- Referenced research papers and documented business rules.
- Complete consolidated prototype built in Excel or other modeling software.
- Complete performance test results appropriate to the type of trading system, including graphs, etc.
- Estimated time line and commitments for the backtesting stage.
- Estimated data and software expenses for the backtesting stage.

12.3. Summary

The benefit of gate meetings is tighter planning, leading to greater speed to market, and ultimately to a higher probability of success for the trading/investment system.[7] Both the product team and seed capital providers (presumably top management) should come the gate meeting prepared to discuss the relevant issues and make go/kill decisions. As we will discuss in the chapters on Gates 2 and 3, gate meetings are also good opportunities to reflect on the stage just completed and to review the portfolio of new and existing trading systems and reprioritize projects.

STAGE • II

Backtest

CHAPTER • 13

STAGE 2: Overview

The spiral stage structure of K|V begs two perspectives—one, that of the loops; and two, that of the steps. One can look at the four steps that comprise a single loop, or the three loops that comprise each step. We will do both. This chapter will present an overview of the three loops. The following four chapters will examine each of the four steps and each pass over each step. The number of loops is not by any means fixed. (We decided that three iterations were sufficient to cover the commonly encountered substeps.)

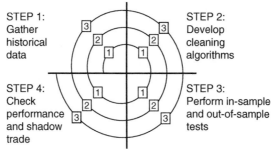

STEP 1:
Gather
historical
data

STEP 2:
Develop
cleaning
algorithms

STEP 4:
Check
performance
and shadow
trade

STEP 3:
Perform in-sample
and out-of-sample
tests

FIGURE 13-1

Successful trading/investment system design necessitates research into past market movements as a way to analyze, optimize, and validate a system—a process called backtesting. A backtest is a simulation and statistical analysis of a trading/investment system's inputs and outputs against historical data, taking into account factors such as transaction costs and slippage in execution. Proper optimization of the system and backtesting will not only confirm the validity and accuracy of a system's algorithms, but also its performance and process variation. That is, backtesting will assess the trading/investment system's ability to satisfy the requirements of investors.

All trading/investment systems product performance metrics vary, and that variation can be analyzed using statistical methods. If the trading/investment system is not in statistical control due to unknown factors, there can be no way of understanding its ability to satisfy investor requirements with any degree of precision.[1]

Because backtests have multiple objective functions, the process leaves the field of pure mathematics, where environmental factors must be static, and enters what we call the "field of NASCAR," where a team attempts to fine-tune the machine for optimal performance in the current environment in order to beat the competition. Quality should not be understood as an attempt to hit a performance target. Quality is not mathematics or an optimization routine. Instead, the product team uses quality techniques to minimize variation in the process, and optimization to maximize returns. Our methodology blends these two ideas together, using heuristics and design of experiments (DoE), to understand the interactions between multiple factors and the environment and the effects of those interactions on the stability of the trading/investment machine. The goals of backtesting are to:

- Determine the likely profitability of the trading/investment system.
- Understand the risks of the system.
- Understand the common variation inherent in the system, that is, the stability of the system.
- Measure the effects of economic cycles on the trading/investment algorithms.

As Reiner Bohlen reports, "Effective backtesting requires use of many resources, including data streams, data vendors, software vendors, application developers, hardware platforms, and personnel . . . Instead of requiring a human pilot to manually manipulate data and optimize every month of a backtest, organizations create integrated software environments that reflect their unique business processes and technology."[2]

While backtesting will reveal the performance characteristics of the system, the primary issue at hand is the need to accurately produce multiple trials that, time and again, perform exactly the same, or very nearly so. Backtests should be executed ideally in a high-level, backtesting language which often will be provided by a third-party vendor (MarketQA language, Zack's Backtest, Quantifi, Sungard's FAME, Factset, etc.). Excel, Resolver, MATLAB, and SAS can also be used to backtest effectively; however, the team should take care to lock down scripts and workbooks for zero user-input or command line entry.

In some instances, the product team may be able to or be required to convert and compile all of the calculations in C++, Java, or .NET code objects that can be used in the production system. By coding algorithms, the team can be sure they will be identical in future tests. Human interaction at this stage, where team members can and do alter the internal structure of the system for each test, promotes errors. It must be avoided and the system must be rigid, which is why we recommend producing an investable universe. Where algorithms are converted to code, the team should not spend extra time and resources on programming at this stage, while being careful not expand the scope of programming beyond that of components absolutely necessary for backtesting.

Resolver software is a particularly powerful tool because it allows developers to easily create spreadsheets that integrate databases, Python code, and external components such as real-time data APIs. A Resolver application is at the same time a spreadsheet and a Python computer program. Spreadsheet algorithms are coded automatically in Python, which makes the conversion step, at least into Python, irrelevant.

13.1. Converting Prototypes to Coded Models

Relative to the Research and Document Calculations stage, K|V Stage 1, backtesting may require a tool change from prototypes (in Excel, Resolver, MATLAB, SAS, etc.) to coded implementation of trading algorithms. In such cases, regression testing is key to achieving successful and reliable development of the software that implements the trading/investment strategy and will ensure that tool changes and additions do not alter the algorithms. Furthermore, regression testing will control project time lines, budget overruns, and software errors that may affect the performance of the system. The absence of a well-defined and implemented regression testing policy for tool conversion can doom a development project.

Regression testing against prototypes developed in Stage 1 can identify when codified implementations of benchmarked and prototyped algorithms fail, allowing product teams to catch errors as soon as they arise. Tool changes can have unexpected side effects that might break previously tested functionalities. Regression testing will detect hard-to-spot errors, especially those that occur because a programmer did not fully understand the mathematical or logical constructs or the internal connections between algorithms of the trading/investment system. Every time code is converted from one implementation (say, an Excel cell formulas prototype) to a new one (say, a C++ .dll add-in), or is modified, regression testing should be used to check the code's integrity. Ideally, the product team will perform regression testing regularly to ensure that errors are detected and fixed as soon as they arise.

Given that the product team converts prototype models into code, our methodology assumes that regression testing is built from the successful white, gray, and black box test cases used during testing of prototypes (K|V 1.4). These test cases, which in the past verified components of the trading/investment system and its overall functionality, can be rerun regularly as regression tests against coded implementations developed in this stage. During regression testing, known inputs generate outcomes that can be compared to known, correct outcomes from Stage 1.

Lastly, the product team will document the architecture of the final working software that implements the trading/investment strategy. While this documentation is normally an output of K|V Stage 3, to the extent that conversion to code occurs in this stage, the team should begin preparing the relevant content for the architecture document at this point.

13.2. Information Management and Database Design

The backtest stage also addresses the information management task. Information management consists of gathering, processing, structuring, and distributing data. This includes the design and management of data and databases for working trading/investment systems. As its name implies, a database design document should present the design of all data sources that will be part of a trading/investment system. The typical objective of a database design document is to formally document the logical and physical design of all databases to ensure that:

- Persistent data is correctly and efficiently stored.
- Data is identified consistently in documents, objects, and data sources.
- Installation, configuration, and maintenance of the databases is as simple and consistent as possible.
- Developers can easily integrate code with databases.

The typical contents of a database design document according to the OPEN Process Framework[3] are:

1. Database Overview:
   (a) Name
   (b) Objectives in terms of contents and usage

    (c) Type (e.g., XML, object, relational, network, hierarchical, flat file)

    (d) Vendor (e.g., Oracle, SQL Server, LIM, Access, Excel)

    (e) Deployment (e.g., database server).

2. Characteristics:

    (a) Legacy or newly developed

    (b) Internal or external to the trading/investment system

    (c) Location

    (d) Expected size and access rate

    (e) Source of data (e.g., data entry, existing database, external data feed).

3. Logical Data Model (i.e., Logical Database Schema):

    (a) Relational Model (e.g., relationship diagrams, table definitions, stored procedures)

    (b) Object Model (e.g., class diagrams, class specifications).

4. Approach to maintenance, backup, and disaster recovery.

Anything that holds persistent data for the trading/investment system software should be documented in the database design document, including databases, flat files, registry entries, XML files, and others. The database design document will as usual require iteration as the product team discovers new information and/or new technologies. Normally, development of a database design document and architecture documents iterate in parallel because database requirements impact the architecture and the architecture impacts the capabilities of the database. Where coded components are being developed, the architecture documents should be started in this stage. The database design document should reference the relevant documentation of any COTS database. Furthermore, the database design document should include discussion of any changes made to COTS products to enhance its abilities.

    A data dictionary contains definitions and representations of data elements and a data map will show the flow of data into and out of the system. Both of these will be expected at the Gate 2 meeting as well.

    The purpose of all this documentation is to provide a detailed data flow description, proposed normalized structures for results, and to facilitate linking to accounting, risk, and execution software. This needs to be completed now so in Stage 3 integration into the existing technological environment will be well understood.

13.3. LOOP 1: Quality Assurance Testing

STEP 1:   Survey Data Needs and Vendors
STEP 2:   Identify Required Cleaning Activities and Algorithms
STEP 3:   Define Testing Methodology
STEP 4:   Perform Regression Test to Validate Algorithms and Benchmark

Loop 1 is a full-scale experiment design in the production environment. This is similar to industrial process design where a product from the research laboratory is scaled up to a prototyped production facility. The product team will build sample inputs and outputs for the full-scale experiment. The goal is to create a stable test environment, defined as a system where all assignable causes are removed. Also, the team will remove known errors, and produce the data cleaning algorithms.

13.4. LOOP 2: Optimize Signals

STEP 1:   Purchase Data
STEP 2:   Clean and Adjust for Known Issues
STEP 3:   Perform In-Sample Test for Large Sample
STEP 4:   Perform Regression Test of In-Sample Results against Prototype

Loop 2 is the actual full-scale experiment. From an industrial viewpoint in a research laboratory, the team has produced a working new process in Stage 1. Now, the team has also designed in the first loop of this stage a prototype production facility. Over the course of Loop 2, the team operates the prototype production facility to ensure that the initial research is correct and scalable. The reason for producing a full-scale production facility is the same between manufacturing and finance; it is to ensure our initial findings can be turned into a profitable, working system. Loop 2 is also optimizing signals, including what mix of indicators gives the highest performance, using a subset of the data and multiple objective functions:

- Returns, excess returns, and volatility.
- Portfolio tradability (average holding period, percentage of float and total volume, number of trades, turnover, etc.).
- Sharpe and Sortino ratios.
- Stability of the system.

13.5. LOOP 3: Generate Simulated Track Record

STEP 1:   Document Data Maps, Result Tables, and Hardware Requirements
STEP 2:   Document Cleaning Algorithms
STEP 3:   Perform Out-of-Sample Test
STEP 4:   Perform Regression Test of OS Test Results against IS Results and SPC Outputs and Shadow Trade

Loop 3 is the final out-of-sample test of the process. This is done to measure and validate how the design process will actually perform in production. The outputs of this stage should be considered proxies of the actual outputs of the finalized system. This loop is critical to ensure that the previous loops have not produced a system that has been optimized for a specific set of data or economic conditions that may or may not occur in the future. This problem is called overfitting the data, which is very common in time series analysis, neural networking, and optimization where algorithms routinely predict 95% of a processes variation historically and 0% in the future, which is only discovered by performing out-of-sample testing. Over each backtest, the product team should again create individual run packs, computer folders with unique names for each run. Included in the run pack should be a copy of the prototype software and data used to generate the run, and a run control document, containing:

- The unique run number and date/time.
- A summary of run pack contents, signed off on by all team members.
- Reports, graphs, tables of trading system performance results (probably in Excel for ease of statistical analysis).
- Details of key assumptions.
- Excel spreadsheet with trade selections for backtests and shadow trades.

13.6.   Outputs/Deliverables

At the completion of Stage 2, we will encounter the second gate and, as a result, a gate meeting. At this meeting management will expect several deliverables, including:

- Full description of the database and real-time data feeds, including comparison of alternative data sources.
- Full investment policy outlining the investable universe.
- Complete definition of the data cleaning rules and optimization methodologies. This may be included in an updated version of a business rules catalog.
- A data dictionary, data and data flow maps, and a database design document.
- Documentation outlining the in-sample/out-of-sample tests with performance metrics, including mocked-up reports, SPC charts, and user interfaces.
- Full prototype, including proof of concept, trade selection charts for shadow trades, including results of regression tests versus prototypes delivered at the completion of Stage 1.
- Identification of software quality metrics.

(For best practices regarding writing stage deliverables, refer to Chapter 8.)

13.7.   Summary

Backtesting is essentially the make or break stage of the trading/system design and development project. Either the system generates acceptable performance or it does not. If the system does not, then the project will be killed or sent back to Stage 1. This spiral also contains the highest risk as testing migrates from a very small sample data set used to prove components in Stage 1 to a real set of data and all of the issues that go along with real data. The initial test data could be an anomaly versus real data that does not prove the concept. Product teams often try to force the system to work with the real data, attempting to find anomalous data where it proves successful. But, the structure of our methodology prevents endless testing and modification; product teams report progress and cannot go back. The monitoring and formalized reporting of results of K|V is an important benefit over most other software development methodologies. After this loop, the building of the system will be a straightforward process since only the interfaces and algorithm control (SPC and risk management) system will be left to complete. These methods and software components that implement them are well defined and documented in the finance industry.

Key points to recognize regarding Stage 2:

- Stage 2 is the make or break spiral. Either the math works or it does not.
- K|V's required deliverables for Gate 2 keep the team on track. To change the math the team will have to go back to Stage 1 and again through Gate 1.
- Data makes or breaks a trading/investment system. Selecting, cleaning, and filtering out bad data is the key stage in the development cycle and will be important for risk management in Stage 4 as well.
- Performance of the system at the end of this stage will be the performance of the working system.
- Design of experiments is very useful in tuning the algorithms. It was designed to allow scientists to tune multifactor machine processes. Optimization utilizes standard math such as principal component analysis and genetic algorithms that tend to overfit the data.

CHAPTER • 14

Gather Historical Data

Once the initial prototype has shown a system worthy of further investment of time and resources, the real make-or-break task of backtesting begins, where the team truly tests the ability of the trading/investment system to meet the specifications set forth in the Money Document. Prior to building and implementing the system, a product team tests it over a large sample of historical data, and in many cases for a large sample of instruments. Backtesting should reveal if the performance results experienced in Stage 1 are real and scalable or due simply to overfitting the original data sample. Backtesting requires lots of data versus the Stage 1 tests, which used small sets of data. Product teams purchase customized databases of past data and purchase software systems that facilitate the backtesting process, which in itself can create problems due to known and unknown errors in the data and software that may cause variation not seen in the sample data. While in theory buying data and software appears simple, properly integrating systems is complex and time-consuming due in part to a lack of understanding of how to build a scaled prototype test environment.

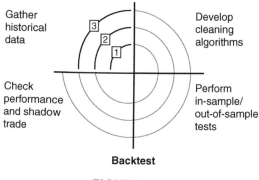

Backtest

FIGURE 14-1

Since the necessary data may either not exist at all or may be prohibitively expensive based upon the prospective returns of the trading/investment system, investigating the availability and price of data ahead of time is a very important first step.

14.1.   Purchasing Data from Vendors

Quality data for backtesting results from a comparison between what is required and what data vendors are able to supply, and they usually will promise whatever is asked for. The product team must judge data quality independent of the assurances of the data provider. To the extent possible, the product team:

- Establishes vendor selection criteria.
- Maintains records of data vendor evaluation results.
- Ensures that vendor-supplied data conforms to requirements to the extent possible.
- Establishes data vendor controls proportionate to the effect the data can have on backtesting processes and the finished trading/investment system.

This correlates, in manufacturing, to properly selecting and controlling the raw inputs into the process and performing machine run-off tests to ensure the purchased materials or machines meet the agreed upon quality specifications. When purchasing data, the product team should:

- Identify the need for data and the specifications of data available for purchase.
- Evaluate of the cost of data, taking into account price, delivery, and performance.
- Assess vendors' differing criteria for verifying data (i.e., how forthcoming are they about assumptions in the data).
- Read and evaluate vendor's documentation.
- Consider the experience of the vendor.
- Compare each vendor's performance relative to competitors, including:
  - Data quality and the vendors ability to satisfy requirements
  - Delivery performance, support, and responsiveness to problems
  - References of past customers
  - Financial viability
  - Compliance

14.2.   STEP 1, LOOP 1: Survey Data Needs and Vendors

As with Step 1 in all four stages of K|V, this step involves planning. Where prototypes completed in Stage 1 used few instruments and limited data, backtesting will require lots of data. The questions are the following: what data does the team need and where can they get it? Assessing the need for data and surveying potential providers takes planning. Specific questions to be answered are

- What environment will be used to store the data? Excel, database server, or a proprietary or third-party system?
- Where will the results be stored?
- Does the firm need to own the data or can it simply buy only the results? (Which begs another question: where will the calculations be run? With some vendors, the team may not be able or allowed to move the raw data without risking a contract

violation. The data and results may have to remain with the vendor and cannot be moved to a local server.)

- Which data vendor should we choose and why?

The answers to all of these questions should be defined in a data requirements document.

We know of trading system projects that failed because certain data for testing, both historical and real time for simulated execution, did not exist. The only way to test the models was to let the system run loose and enter live trades. They lost over $2,000 in less than a minute, not to mention over 300 hours of lost development time. Because they did not properly design the test plan, which could have had the system enter opposite orders immediately and pay the spread as the cost of data, they will never know if they killed a good system.

Sophisticated trading/investment systems may potentially incorporate several different types of data. For clarity, we define five types of data.

14.2.1. Price Data

Price data consists of the real bid/ask, trade, and volume data for securities and derivatives. For different instruments, different complications arise:

- **Stock data.** Stock price data is complicated by cross-listing and activity on ECNs. For example, consider the end-of-day price for a listed stock. Quite simply, there is no single such price anymore. Different trading venues may potentially show different last-trade prices. Also, most ECNs do not have closing prices per se; trading may continue till 5 or 6 p.m., or even overnight. To get clean prices, teams must benchmark methods for dealing with data from multiple exchanges and different times, and for averaging bids and offers.

For tick data on stocks (actually all listed instruments), getting every tick may not be feasible or even possible. Data vendors often use standard time intervals, for example, one tick per second. For seconds, or even minutes, without ticks (although the bid and ask may be moving) vendors sometimes make assumptions as to the price for that interval. Also, vendors may not include ticks from all exchanges. Some claim to provide every tick, but whether that is for all markets, or a single exchange, can be difficult to discern. Also, the exchange may not publish every tick when volume exceeds an exchange's limit, so historical tick data may be different than what you would be able to receive in real time. Whatever the case, you may not be getting every tick, which means calculations like VWAP may in real time be different than backtested values.

For high frequency trading systems, flat ticks (i.e., multiple trades going off at the same price) reflect neither changes to the bid and ask prices nor the likelihood of a new limit order getting filled, especially for contracts that use a FIFO order queue. When testing a high frequency trading system, historical volume data and order book queue data, in addition to price data, is essential in order to estimate queue position and estimate fills.

- **Option data.** For stock option data, all the above issues again are relevant. However, a more difficult issue comes up. Since options are quoted in implied volatility space, and then converted to dollars, the primary question is the following: what is the proper way to calculate implied volatility? Should it be done per exchange, per option and then a blend, or should you blend prices? Because we believe in put/call parity, call and put volatilities should be equal. Many market participants and data vendors do not really believe in put/call parity and calculate separate volatilities for puts and calls. These vendors' data shows the put volatility below and call volatility above the at-the-money volatility.

When we convert from put and call option prices to implied volatilities, we try to calculate a single value for implied volatility. This can only be done by incorporating multiple interest rates depending upon the delta of the position, hard to borrow rules, earnings information, boundary conditions, splits, and other data to properly adjust the call and put model inputs. As a final step, we smooth the final difference, which is normally less than half a volatility point, by delta-weighting the values.

The firms that do not follow put/call parity prefer instead to allow call and put volatilities to be different, and simply average the two volatilities to price OTC options.

> *Incorrect pricing models that incorporate incorrect implied volatilities have caused several blow-ups. The firms used incorrect volatilities and proprietary models to mark-to-model their positions. The symptoms are always the same: on paper the system is making a lot of money, but when the positions are marked-to-market by third-party bids and offers, the system is losing money. The response is always the same: "Our theoretical edge is growing so pay us our bonus."*

At the end of the day either your implied volatility calculation is right and your mark-to-model and mark-to-market values are very close, or you are wrong and go bankrupt.

Financial engineers sometimes forget that you need to sell to make money. The financial engineers use the same incorrect model and volatility surface in both the front office and back office at large firms since the desk quants mainly come from the back office at large firms so they convince the back office quants in their logic. We believe the gold standard in implied volatility is where put/call parity holds for the entire surface.

- **Fixed income data.** Several firms sell fixed income data, although sometimes it is not readily apparent whether the prices are observed transactions or theoretical values. The major data vendors provide both. On days where there is no activity, they will calculate a theoretical price for the fixed income securities and derivatives. This theoretical price appears to reduce the volatility of the price as it could be the same for several days in a row. Of course, no dealer is obligated to buy or sell at a theoretical value.
- **Futures data.** In general, futures data is very clean. Standardized contracts with well-defined pricing, and generally little cross-listing are the reasons volume is so large in electronically traded contracts. However, on days where contracts do not trade, that is, when the contract's lock limit is up or down, exchanges publish no price data. Regardless, OTC contracts for the underlying may still trade.

14.2.2. Valuation Data

Valuation data is different from price data. For bonds, swaps, and all OTC derivatives, no historical trade price data exists, or if it does, it is a highly guarded secret. For all these, valuation data is all there is, that is, the "price" exists only in theory, and, furthermore, is not a firm bid or offer that any market maker is obliged to honor. As one can imagine, then, during market meltdowns, valuations are basically meaningless since brokers have no obligation to trade; they have no incentive to add liquidity in these markets (whereas on organized exchanges, market makers must do so). The implication for backtesting is that the trading/investment system should show returns at least 5–10% above what the team believes is the hurdle rate for acceptance.

Also, valuation data requires the team to mark-to-model the system's positions. We strongly recommend that a combination of the simplest industry model be used along with whatever high-level proprietary model is being tested. Backtests should feed both models whatever cleaned data is available at the time of trade execution, and measure value and performance metrics using both the simple model and the high-level theoretical model. The difference between the two measures can be called the theoretical edge. The goal is to turn the backtested edge into real performance. A bad sign is when the edge keeps growing in the backtest since it can mean the theoretical edge can never be captured.

14.2.3. Fundamental, or Financial Statement, Data

Fundamental data consists of everything that is disclosed in 10-Q quarterly and 10-K annual reports, including key business items, such as earnings, sales, inventories, and rents. These facts are certified by the company itself. Of course, not all companies follow the same accounting principles. In fact, every company does it differently. Analysis of financial statement is a well-developed and important area of research.

Fundamental data should be updated almost continuously to fully reflect the new data of the corporations. Updates include inserting data on newly listed companies, mergers, new financial data, etc. Now, if the trading/investment system acquires real-time, streaming data and translates it into a usable representation, then the entire update process would be truly continuous. (Of course, automated tools cannot analyze most nonquantified information.)[1]

Fundamental data should be normalized across the entire universe. Normalization reconstructs fundamental data according to identical accounting rules. So, EBITDA for one steel company will be calculated exactly the same way as all other steel companies, and almost all other companies. Normalization is time-consuming since it forces analysts to read footnotes and make adjustments. Normalization is the real service you pay a data vendor for.

14.2.4. Calculated Data

Given fundamental data, the next question is the following: should the team purchase calculated data (ROE, price to book, and beta, forecasted dividends, free cash flow, etc.) or should they calculate this data in-house? Whatever the case, we recommend that all calculations first be prototyped in Excel to allow for proper cleaning and normalization of the numbers. This way the team can agree or disagree with the method the data provider uses.

One data vendor we know rounds EPS data to two decimal places—simple and intuitive enough. But, let us assume that the stock has an EPS of $.05. Then there is a stock split. So, EPS is now $.025 rounded to $.03. Then there is another. $.015 is rounded to $.02. Then there is another split—$.01. And yet another split. This time the vendor made the assumption that .005 will always be rounded up to $.01. Under these types of assumptions, MSFT had no EPS growth through the decade of the 1990s. But, the vendor will not likely point this out.

14.2.5.   Economic Data

Economic data, such as CPI and GDP, are key indicators and can alert the product team as to when a trading/investment style is or is no longer working. For example, some strategies, say small cap value, tends to work quite well coming out of a recession, because small companies are hard to value. In a recession, properly valuing small companies can generate large returns. Large cap momentum strategies tend to work very poorly, because you tend to buy companies that have outperformed the index the most, which tends to be lagging stocks. The lagging stocks tend to be the next group to decrease in price. Economic data is primarily for trading/investment systems that:

- Make country selections or bets on currencies.
- Select sectors or capitalizations.
- Calculate a value/growth mixture.
- Build Bayesian-style indicators to shift weights to those that perform better under particular economic conditions.

Broad economic factors can be used to shut down trading/investment systems when the economics no longer justify the strategy. When the economic cycle shifts and depending upon the nature of the trading/investment system, the product team may stop trading, or close the fund, as opposed to continuing to trade and losing money in a bad environment.

SPC will raise a flag when something has fundamentally shifted. (We use economic data for design of experiments, to look for assignable causes, except for currency trading systems where the main signals are economic data.) By using SPC to analyze the outputs of the trading algorithms, the product team can detect a shift in the underlying stochastic process. Once detected in a backtest, the team can then perform root cause analysis to determine what caused the shift. The first step of root cause analysis should be an analysis of economic cycle data around the time the algorithm stopped working (e.g., did our growth algorithm stop working three months before a recession?).

14.3.   STEP 1, LOOP 2: Purchase Data

What a trading/investment firm buys from a data vendor is not just raw data; it buys engineering and capability. Once the data requirements are firmly established over the course of the previous loop. To get correct data, the team should produce a request for quotation. A quotation from a data vendor should answer several questions in addition to the cost.

1. How do we get the data? Streaming, real-time data feed via API or Excel DDE Link? FTP open or closed?
2. How much responsibility does the vendor take for the data?
    (a) Who does the splits?
    (b) Who synchronizes the data?
    (c) Who stores the historical data?
    (d) Who normalizes the data?
3. Which frequency do we use? It should be in the frequency we expect to trade in.
    (a) Trade-by-trade tick data?
    (b) Time intervals or bars?

4. Who provides the interface?

5. How timely will the data be? When will it arrive?

No data source can do everything, but the trading/investment firm that waits for delivery of data only to learn later what they have bought is wrong deserves what they get. Given competing vendors, we recommend buying from the vendor whose data integrates best with your architecture regardless of cost.

> *A trading firm refused to pay a data vendor for historical data. It was too expensive. Instead they used it without permission in violation of their contract. They then complained about the fact the data was not properly split adjusted. Their historical volatility was regularly wrong and caused bad trades. The money lost on bad trades would have paid for the data. However, the CIO would not pay for data; in his mind it should be free and clean. Eventually, the traders complained and forced the CIO out. Now the firm pays for clean data.*

With respect to price data, we recommend you pick a data vendor based on the following questions:

- How do you calculate what you believe the closing bid/ask is?
- Can I pick the exchange?
- How do you handle uneven volume at the close?
- Can I get an off-close final price that I can use with my options?
- Can I synchronize my option closing price with my stock closing price?
- Do you use CUSIP or your own unique identifier?
- How do you handle mergers and spin-offs?

We recommend that ideally you get the price at the time you want, with a unique identifier that is consistent between the stock, the underlying of options, and the underlying of the corporation's bonds; ones that do not change with expirations, mergers, or spin-offs. The nonofficial closing prices can be considerably cleaner since block trades and end-of-day anomalies are not in the data. In currencies, there are multiple closes so traders can select a time they believe gives the cleanest price. Why cannot traders in other markets (that are now becoming 24 hour markets) select times?

The best data is the data where you understand its errors and issues, and works properly with your other software systems. For example, an algorithmic risk engine may be integrated with data from a third-party provider using unique IDs. It would be foolish not to buy data from the vendor since it is already integrated into your risk management and backtesting engine.

When you look for fundamental data, we recommend buying it all from the same data provider to ensure calculations have been consistently applied.

> *We know a data vendor that offers their data through four different wholesale products. Believe it or not, the values that are in the data may or may not be the same for the four. How do you know which numbers are correct? The vendor claims that it comes from the same source, yet we can show where the data is different. Legacy code must be making changes behind the scenes. To further complicate the problem, the wholesale products have their own cleaning algorithms that further change the data. The scariest part is that the vendor cannot solve the problem!*

We recommend you buy fundamental data from a single vendor and single wholesale product and that you do not mix between wholesale products. If you need to mix, our recommendation is to initially purchase a software product whose sole purpose is to consolidate data for backtesting, such as Factset, FAME, or MarketQA. After the system is up and running and successful, we strongly recommend the building of your own proprietary database and consolidation engine, allowing you the ability to create your own custom calculations and data into your backtester.

14.4. STEP 1, LOOP 3: Document Data Maps and Results Tables

By this loop the in-sample test is done and the team should be preparing for the gate meeting. The goal is to complete a data definition document and a data map. Within the context of a database management system, a data dictionary begins as a simple collection of column names and their definitions and data types, but should evolve to include in-memory representation of data elements such as integer, string, and date formats as well as data structures and a Rosetta Stone. The goal of a data dictionary is consistency between data items across different databases and different tables.

Data mapping is the process of laying out data elements and conversions between disparate data models, between data sources and destinations. Here is an example of what we mean. A real-time API we have worked with gives data as a string with no decimals. Of course, in order to use this data for calculations, it must be converted and conversion rules and techniques must be documented.

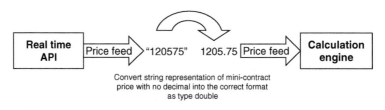

Convert string representation of mini-contract price with no decimal into the correct format as type double

FIGURE 14-2

A data flow map will show the flow of data into and out of the system, how it is cleaned, and how it is being stored. For example, a data map will show what data flows into and out of the calculation engine, the risk engine, and the accounting engine. These documents will eventually be used by programmers for implementation in Stage 3. The documents should be appended to include the cleaning algorithms.

> *Multiple databases, data vendors, and data formats can really create problems. Documenting formats early will save countless hours of debugging later on.*

14.5. Summary

A backtest is a test of the ability of the trading/investment system to meet the specifications set forth in the Money Document. Backtesting requires lots of data, which may not be available and is certainly not free. Sophisticated systems often incorporate several different types of data—price, valuation, fundamental, calculated, and economic data. To facilitate incorporating data and databases in a working system, the product team should complete a data dictionary and a data map. These documents will eventually be used by database programmers for Stage 3, the programming of the full working system.

14.5.1. Best Practices

- Know your data and buy your data. The best data is data whose errors you understand. Also, do not try to get free data from the Internet, because you will have no control over when the data changes and what the numbers mean.
- Use one consistent source for fundamental data if at all possible.
- Establish data requirements long before making a purchase.
- Complete a data dictionary and data maps.
- Do not bet the firm on the assurances of the data vendor.

CHAPTER ◆ 15

Develop Cleaning Algorithms

Good inputs are the key to success in financial modeling, and forecasting, as well as risk management, requires good, clean data for successful testing and simulation. Over the course of backtesting, the use of a large amount of in-sample data will produce a more stable model and reduce the danger of curve-fitting, thereby increasing the probability of out-of-sample success. Virtually no data, however, is perfect and financial engineers spend large amounts of time cleaning errors and resolving issues in data sets, sometimes called preprocessing the data. It is very easy and very common to underestimate the amount of time preprocessing will take. Most financial engineers can recall wasting countless hours spent backtesting only to have drawn bad conclusions because of bad data. Easily half the time required for high quality backtesting can be spent cleaning data.

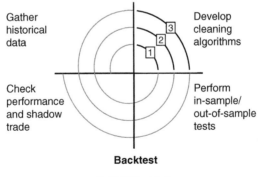

FIGURE 15-1

The problem is that nobody wants to clean. Everyone is too busy to clean, but failing to adequately consider the impact of bad data can lead to bad models or worse: systems that pass the backtest stage but lose millions in actual trading. The quality of data purchased from vendors can range from very clean to very dirty; usually there is a positive correlation between the price and quality of data. Using high quality, more expensive data almost always pays off in the long run, though even high quality data will have problems. Whatever the case, time spent finding good data and giving it a good once over is worth the time and effort. However, this is rarely done in the industry.

149

All data should be cleaned before use. In K|V, the product team preprocesses data up front, so as to have good clean data for backtesting in this stage as well as for risk processes in Stage 4. Serious data cleaning involves more than just visually scanning data and updating bad records with better data. Rather, it requires that the product team decomposes and reassembles the data. And this takes time.

In this step, the product team investigates alternative data cleaning methods to arrive at benchmark processes, the ones that generate the best performance. Benchmarking data cleaning processes focuses the product team on improving the performance of the trading/ investment system. A best practice for one system, though, may not be a best practice for every trading/investment system, because each will have its own unique input data. In the end, cleaning data will remove variation from the process, so the team can get a good clean look at the process, the common variation and the potential of the system.

As with any process, it pays to plan ahead before cleaning data. First, identify and categorize all the types of problems you expect to encounter in your data; then survey the available techniques to address those different types of errors; and finally develop methods to identify and resolve the problems. Data problems fall into one of four categories:

- Bad, or incorrect, data.
- Formatting problems.
- Outliers, which skew results.
- Point-in-time data problems.

It may seem like an oxymoron, but not all data is the same, even if it is the same data. If you run a backtest with historical data from one vendor and then run the same backtest with data from another, you will likely end up with different results and different conclusions. This is because while some databases offer snapshots of data known at a certain time, others restate historical data to enable comparison over time. You see, the issues are complex.

Now, data cleaning (if it is done at all) is usually assigned to a low-level person with, more often than not, few, if any, tools to do the job right. High-level people often believe cleaning data is beneath them, so they assign the task to interns. In manufacturing, however, senior-level engineers are assigned to teams that perform full-scale experiment design in the production environment. These engineers ensure that the inputs meet the quality specifications and that both inputs and outputs of the experiments are properly captured. This task in manufacturing would never be assigned to junior-level engineers, since an error at this stage would be too costly. Trading firms need to have senior-level people design Data Transformation Management Systems, the tools and processes to clean data, just like in manufacturing. These tools should be automated, to the extent possible to allow junior-level financial engineers to investigate errors and outliers graphically, using scatterplots, SPC charts, and histograms, just like in manufacturing where quality personnel use similar tools. This is consistent with quality engineering where most tools are graphical, so management can train nontechnical people quickly to identify problems.

15.1. STEP 2, LOOP 1: Identify Required Cleaning Activities and Algorithms

In the first loop in this step, the product team should identify what data problems may exist and alternative methods to handle them. As with quantitative methods and trading algorithms, data cleaning algorithms should be benchmarked and documented using the research and documentation methods described in K|V 1.2.

All data, both real-time and historical, contains errors and issues, and the nature of the trading/investment system dictates what types of problems the team will likely encounter. For example, data issues for high frequency systems will center more on clean tick data, whereas those for systems with longer-term holding periods will focus more on, say, dividends and releases of and revisions to financial statements.

15.1.1. Bad Data and Reformatting

In all cases cleaning of bad data is a process that consists first of detection, then classification of the root cause of the error, and then correction of the error—bad quotes, missing data, bad dates, column shifted data, file corruption, differing data formats. If we assume for a minute that there are 100,000 stocks and options that trade in the United States, on any given day there will be somewhere in the neighborhood of 250 bad end-of-day prints alone, based on our experience. That is a lot of bad data. Historical data with these errors, however, may have already been cleaned (at least according to the vendor). This may or may not be a good thing depending on the timeliness and repeatability of the process. Here are some common types of bad data.

TABLE 15-1

Type of bad data	Example
Bad quotes	Tick of 23.54, should be 83.54
Missing data	Blank field or data coded as "9999," "NA," or "0"
Bad dates	2/14/12997
Column shift-data	Value printed in an adjacent column
File corruption	CD or floppy disk errors
Different data formats	Data from different vendors may come in different formats or table schemas
Missing fundamental data	The company may have changed the release cycle

Cleaning of real-time data means including quality control measures. For example, bad quotes and network failures can lead to bad trades. Systems developed with quality in mind elegantly handle problems, such as bad data, exchange shutdowns, and incorrect third-party calculations (think incorrect index prices). When benchmarking data cleaning algorithms, the product team should be sure to address error handling and system shutoff/down procedures in the event of externally generated exceptions.

Whatever the methods to clean bad data or handle external exceptions are, data cleaning algorithms must be shown to operate on both live-time and historical data. Data cleaning algorithms can add latency to real-time systems. Algorithms that cannot be performed in real time prior to trade selection should not be used on historical data, or else the cleaned, historical data will skew backtesting results.

Cleaning of historical data corrects errors and updates the dirty data source with clean data, or more preferably creates a new data source to hold the corrections set. Maintaining the original, dirty data source in its original form allows the team to go back if a mistake was made in the cleaning algorithms that consequently further corrupted the data. This is true also when reformatting data.

Depending on the time interval desired, the format of the data may not match up with those increments, or bars. (Bars being fixed units of time with a date/time, open, a high, a low, and a close and maybe even a volume and/or open interest.) Given tick data, for example, and a trading strategy using bars, the team may want to analyze bars of different durations—a minute in length, five minutes, a day, a week, or a month. In order to convert the data, reformatting may have to take place, which can, if not controlled properly, introduce new problems.

Since many forecasting models, like GARCH, are extremely sensitive to even a few bad data points, we recommend the team look carefully at means, medians, standard deviations, histograms, and minimum and maximum values of time series data. A good way to do this is to sort or graph the data to highlight values outside an expected range, which may be good (but outlying) or bad data. For other types of bad data, we recommend running scans to detect suspicious, missing, extraneous, or illogical data points. Here are a few methods used to scan data.

TABLE 15-2

Scanning for bad data

Intraperiod high tick less than closing price

Intraperiod low tick greater than opening price

Volume less than zero

Bars with wide high/low ranges relative to some previous time period

Closing deviance. Divide the absolute value of the difference between each closing price and the previous closing price by the average of the preceding 20 absolute values

Data falling on weekends or holidays

Data with out-of-order dates or duplicate bars

Price or volume greater than four standard deviations from rolling mean

15.1.2. Winsorizing Outliers

Outliers are extreme values, that is, data points far out on the tails of the distribution, that will disproportionately affect statistical analysis. Outliers (that are not errors) contain important information, but their presence should not obscure, or even obliterate, all other data and information. To reduce the distortion, data cleaning can either delete outliers from the sample, or, more likely, winsorize them using a compressing algorithm. Winsorizing pulls outliers in toward the mean by replacing them with a value at a specified limit, say three standard deviations. For example, for 90% winsorization, the lowest and highest 5% of observations are set equal to the value corresponding to the 5th and 95th percentile. A winsorized mean will be a more robust estimator because it is less sensitive to outliers. A problem with winsorizing all the data is that volatility may shift over the time series, so we recommend winsorizing on a rolling basis.

15.1.3. The Point-in-Time Data Problem

Dirty data is of course problematic, but cleaned data also has problems. Consider the following scenario: stock price data for a day is cleaned after the close of business and an adjustment file is sent out the next day, reflecting the corrected price data. This occurs regularly due to block trades, paper trades being entered late, and crossing trades, all of which become part of the end-of-day pricing set.

With the new price data, many calculations for derivatives, which were based on the incorrect data, are now wrong. Implied volatility calculations will be wrong. All OTC derivative contracts that are based on the stock's implied volatility will be wrong. End-of-day rebalancing algorithms could also be wrong due to dirty data.

The cleaned data arrives several hours, even up to a day, later. The cleaned data may or may not be the actual value that would have been seen in the market in real time. The cleaned data, now in a historical database, could be used to make a trade during backtesting. But, again, this data was not available when the trade would have taken place.

A cleaning algorithm for end-of-day prices is very important, but not as easy as it sounds. At the close, block orders affect prices, traders sometimes push bids and asks around, and small orders can move the market in the absence of late liquidity. All these things blur the definition of closing price. (Closing price data for futures is generally clean since contracts trade usually only on one exchange, but for stocks and bonds, the calculation is more difficult. With commodity futures, however, closing price data can pose a problem on days where prices are lock-limit down or up. One may not be able to ascertain which price is the closing price. Even where one can make such a determination, OTC contracts which continued to trade may differ. Likewise, the market for a stock can be closed for news or other anomalies. In such cases, the exchange may or may not set a closing price.)

- **End-of-day stock prices.** To calculate a clean closing price, we recommend getting a nonofficial closing price five minutes (the closer to close you get the data, the higher the probability you will have an error) prior to close across selected exchanges. Throw out all locked or crossed bids and asks and then determine the midprice. Finally, weight those prices by order book quantity. We recommend you ask your data vendor how they calculate end-of-day NBBO values. How do they calculate VWAP for the day? For the whole market or just for certain exchanges? And can I select exchanges? Do they do average weighted bid based upon real size 100 lot or 1000 lot.

- **End-of-day option prices.** We recommend first getting the option contract bid and ask prices five minutes before the close. Second, get the borrow and stock loan rebate rate for the day as well as the risk-free rate. Third, choose the appropriate option pricing model, preferably one that includes jumps for key events, and obtain (for stock options) the next earnings date and projected dividend dates and amounts. Fourth, calculate the implied volatility on a strike-by-strike basis and on a surface basis, based on clean inputs. Fifth, calculate a clean delta, and delta weight the implied volatility by strike for calls and puts. Sixth, deal with zero bid or ask prices, that is, calculate the wings. Seventh and last, calculate a clean option price, which should be between the market bid and ask to confirm accuracy.

  We recommend (unlike stocks where we recommend blending multiple prices) using the exchange with the highest volume for that contract as the official market for that contract, and ignoring volume on other exchanges. If there are two that are close in volume for a particular contract, calculate an implied volatility for the bid and ask in each market and then blend the implied volatilities together.

  In summary, if you are unable to take market bid and ask data, run it through a cleaning/smoothing algorithm, get an implied volatility, and recalculate a fair price that is not between the market bid and ask, then you probably do not have a good closing price cleaning algorithm.

The point-in-time issue also applies to fundamental data, which also may be cleaned by the vendor or revised according to accounting rules. In a backtest, the team may select fundamental data, for example, quarterly free cash flow data, that was revised sometime after the quarterly release date. This revised data taints the backtest; it is different data than was available on the release date. Based upon the new data, a stock that was originally bought may have been immediately sold since the original calculation was now in retrospect incorrect. The data adjustment may affect the entire sector as well, since the adjusted numbers may alter the sector mean and standard deviation, resulting in a complete reranking of the outputs of the trading/investment algorithm. To solve this point-in-time problem, many firms require a one to two month lag of data for backtesting. A lag is an artificial time interval introduced into the data to account for this point-in-time problem.

15.1.4. Demeaning and Standardization

Factor demeaning, where the average value is subtracted from the observed value, removes bias from the factor. For example, to demean book-to-price by industry, you subtract the average book-to-price for the industry from each company's book-to-price figure. This reduces the industry bias, and makes companies from different industries or sectors more comparable in analysis. This is quite an important step in model construction, since book-to-price for a high tech firm will differ significantly from that of an electric utility, for example.

When combining factors into a model, it is useful to measure the factors in the same terms, or on the same scale. Standardization, or detrending, accomplishes this by rescaling the data distribution so that it has a specific mean and standard deviation (usually 0 and 1, respectively). Once a sample has been standardized, it is easy to determine a number's relative position in that sample. To standardize a factor, the mean of the sample is subtracted from an observation, and the resulting difference is divided by the standard deviation.

15.1.5. Scaling and Ranking

The strongest and most direct way that scaling influences most nonlinear models is through the implied relative importance of the variables. When more than one variable is supplied, most nonlinear models implicitly or explicitly assume that variables having large variation are more important than variables having small variation. This occurs for both input and output. Most training algorithms minimize an error criterion involving the mean or sum of squared errors across all outputs. Thoughtless use of such criterion will cause the training algorithm to devote inordinate effort to minimizing the prediction error of the $100, while ignoring the $1, stock. The fact that 100 times as many shares of the $1 stock may be purchased is not taken into account. The scaling of each variable must be consistent with its relative importance.

We also recommend ranking fundamental data. For example, earnings should be reflected in percentile by sector, as should implied volatility. A biotech company will always have a higher implied volatility than a consumer products company. Therefore, call away returns for a biotech would always be higher since implied volatility is higher. We also recommend ranking the call away return to ensure against selling covered calls on all biotechs.

15.1.6.   Synchronizing Data

Databases of the different types of data have different updating periods. Take splits, for example. Price data vendors update daily. Balance sheet vendors update weekly. As a result, a given ratio, such as sales-to-price, may contain an unsplit sales figure and split price. Fixing this problem is called synchronizing the data, accomplished by either buying synchronized data or performing the task in-house. (Because divide-by-zero errors can cause problems, we recommend adding a filters flag to very small divisors. Any calculation that has division as part of the calculation needs to have clean data to avoid problems.)

The real key to synchronizing data, or blending data, is a Rosetta Stone. A Rosetta Stone is the set of unique identifiers used to link data and instruments across vendors. A proper Rosetta Stone is highly valuable since it will allow the trading/investment system to trade many instruments—stock, options, bonds, CDs, and OTC products—on a single underlying. Furthermore, unique identifiers across underlyings and across vendors enable the blending of proprietary data with purchased data. We believe the ability to trade multiple instruments of a company using both vendor-supplied and proprietary data is a key to building a system that will beat its index or peer group benchmark.

15.2.   STEP 2, LOOP 2: Clean and Adjust for Known Issues

The purpose of this step is to take the manually built cleaning algorithms (probably done in Excel) and convert them into tools that can be used by junior people, with well-defined GUIs and outputs along with algorithms that can be manually run against the entire database. The cleaning algorithms at this point should be viewed as prototypes. Also, the tools built for this step should be placed in a library for future use for all other projects that use the data set.

15.3.   STEP 2, LOOP 3: Document Cleaning Algorithms

Over the last loop, the product team should produce and document the algorithms that will be run everyday to clean data. We recommend the team write the documentation as use-cases or sample code from Loop 2. The use-cases should illustrate what the inputs are; what the outputs are; plus, a written description. The team needs detailed descriptions of the algorithms with sample code and test cases, so that in Stage 3 they can implement the algorithms as part of the software development process.

The team must also produce a schedule of cleaning activities and a time line, that is, what happens when and how long it will take. For example, historical price data for the day may come in at 3 p.m., and fundamental data at 8 p.m. The team must schedule jobs accordingly. The document should also outline what manual GUI tools need to be built, for example, charts, with user manuals.

If the pricing data is missing, or is late, everything else must stop until it shows up. The interactive tools let someone overwrite the data with clean data, for that we again suggest separate tables. (If you clean the data, why tell your vendor?) Overwrite the vendor's data. There is no need to tell the vendor about their dirty data. All the corrections should be in a separate table of changes. This is the loop where the database programmers get involved in how much time, how much money, and how complex it will be to build the data cleaning algorithms and produce a plan on the time, cost, and structure to accomplish it.

15.3.1.   Trade Cost Analysis

Backtesting results depend on execution assumptions. For a working system, in Stage 4, poor execution may cause nonconformance with performance metrics experienced during the backtest. In this step, we also recommend that the product team document best execution policies, trade cost analysis, benchmarks, and algorithms. In a working system, we further recommend that the product team automate posttrade reporting and analysis. Execution performance should be monitored to ensure that it is delivering competitive advantage and reviewed on a periodic basis.

Developing and documenting a formal policy will make communication with top management and investors a straightforward exercise. Investors now demand that money managers both achieve and prove best execution, where best execution is generally benchmarked against implementation shortfall, arrival price, or volume-weighted average price.

15.4.   Summary

For many systems, the size of the databases used to store data is in the half-terabyte plus range. So, you should expect with this amount of data to have errors, omissions, and issues. In a world where the difference between the 25th percentile and 75th percentile of returns is measured in basis points, not understanding and cleaning your own data relegates you to average performance at best. Therefore, we suggest that your most senior financial engineer along with your most senior programmer commit a large amount of time to cleaning data so that you have a competitive advantage over those who do not clean data.

15.4.1.   Best Practices

- Design data cleaning algorithms to operate on live-time as well as historical data.
- Initially analyze distributions graphically with scatterplots and histograms. Build tools to allow junior-level people to quickly determine the quality of data.
- Winsorize, scale, rank, demean, and standardize data and define methods for dealing with point-in-time data problems. Also, create a Rosetta Stone to link data.
- Benchmark and document all cleaning algorithms.
- Standardize methods for calculating national best bid and offer closing prices.

CHAPTER • 16

Perform In-Sample/Out-of-Sample Tests

A backtest is a simulation of a trading/investment strategy's response to historical data. Essentially it is an elaborate quality assurance test to check the model parameters and assumptions, and verify the system's ability to meet required performance specifications in a prototype production environment.[1] Performing proper in-sample and out-of-sample tests is perhaps the most critical step in the trading/investment system development process.

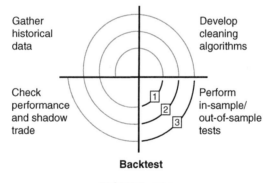

FIGURE 16-1

In backtesting, financial engineers are keenly aware of the extent to which in-sample results may differ from out-of-sample results and trading algorithms must be examined against both before progressing to the implementation stage. A well-developed system will perform similarly out of sample as it does in sample, so it is important to save some of the historical data for out-of-sample testing. A backtest will result in one of three outcomes for a trading/investment system:

1. Profitable both in sample and out of sample.
2. Profitable in sample, but not out of sample.
3. Unprofitable both in sample and out of sample.

If the system is profitable both in sample and out of sample, it will very likely receive capital to begin implementation and trading as soon as possible. If a system is profitable

157

only in sample, it may be allocated additional resources for continued research and/or sent back to Stage 1. If, however, the system proves to be unprofitable both in sample as well as out of sample, management will likely scrap the project altogether mainly due to the nonscalability of the trading idea.

The purpose of backtesting is not simply to identify returns, standard deviations, and drawdowns, but also to identify the common cause and any special cause variations in the trading/investment system. Key components of performance measurement will be the expected fees charged by brokers, exchanges, regulators, custodians, and auditors as well as taxes. Backtesting should always be performed in light of these fees.

Modern computer modeling techniques have allowed very complex models with many parameters to be estimated and fitted. Beyond this, the creation of new models itself has been automated. The result is that model selection and validation has become more difficult. The concept of "model error" while once mostly an ignored issue must frequently be directly addressed.

16.1.   STEP 3, LOOP 1: Define Testing Methodology

In the original testing conducted in Stage 1, the product team used a small set of clean data to prove the calculations and trading algorithms. The focus now is on tests of the performance of the entire trading/investment system using historical data. To perform this task, the team should lay out a testing methodology. The question is the following: how do we take the black box test from K|V 1.4 and roll it into a multiyear, multi-instrument test?

The first step is to build a reliable set of instruments to test the algorithm against. We will call this set the investable universe, and it will be used for the entire backtesting process. (The trading system will only buy and sell instruments within this universe. In Stage 4, risk managers will monitor the trading/investment system's positions to ensure compliance.) The selection of the instruments should be based on the following items, that is, investable instruments:

- Must have data with both a beginning price and an ending price over the appropriate time interval. Which is to say, we will select only those instruments that have sufficient price/valuation data to calculate returns.

- Must pass a liquidity screen. A screen may filter out low priced stocks, bonds with limited issuance, or contracts with low outstanding notional value. For instruments that are inherently illiquid, additional slippage must be added to execution prices. A liquidity screen should make sure that as the pool of investment capital grows, the system will scale properly. As a general rule, the trading/investment system, in its maturity stage, should not purchase more than 2% of the outstanding shares or open interest (except for market making systems).

- Must have the data necessary to calculate the factors or signals that comprise the trade selection algorithms.

The team can either build this data set themselves, or they may be able to purchase vendor software to run these screens. Instruments that pass these filters become the investable universe, a locked-down data set which the team will use for all backtesting and regression testing from this step forward.

The next step is for the instruments in the investable universe to calculate the return, volatility, and drawdowns for each instrument for each time period, adding in dividends. All this must be done before backtesting begins. For stocks, this is trivial. For derivative products that include hedging these calculations can be very complex.

The goal here is to lock down and control the universe of instruments and data used for testing. The team then has to determine if the universe is large enough to allow testing. If only 50 stocks make the universe, then your universe creation rules probably have a problem. The next item to address is the appropriate time lag for the testing scenario. A time lag is required to handle the point-in-time data issue. If you have perfect data, then your lag will be zero. Otherwise you need to determine the appropriate lag.

16.1.1. Data Proportions

In classical statistics a subset of data is selected for building and optimizing algorithms. This subset may be selected by using the data furthest back in time, a randomly chosen data, or a manual process to ensure that a good distribution of economic cycles is represented. The normal rule is to use one-third to one-half of the data for the initial algorithm testing and optimization.

The next one-half to two-thirds of the data can then be used to confirm the algorithm with out-of-sample data. The purpose of using this data is to prove that the algorithm works properly with data that was not used to make the algorithm. Since researchers normally like to reoptimize an algorithm if it does not work, we recommend that one-third of the data be used for in-sample testing, one-third for out of sample, and one-third for a final test set. The last third is only used after all optimizations and adjustments are done; this is a double safety to ensure that the researcher does not overfit the data. If the trading/investment machine fails the final one-third then the project should be considered for cancellation; researchers may have data mined the first two-thirds of the data so all the research results should be viewed with suspicion.

For more specific situations, we recommend the following allocations:

- **High frequency systems.** For each of the three test sets, allocate one-third of the data. Tune on the first third. In-sample test on the first two-thirds, and out of sample on the last third. Assign a random number, 1, 2, or 3, to each day. Use the 1 day for tuning, 1s and 2s for in sample, and 3s for out of sample.

- **Equity portfolio systems.** By random, select three portfolios of stocks. These portfolios should mirror the sector weights and credit score weights of the benchmark. Use portfolio 1 for tuning, portfolios 1 and 2 for in-sample testing, and portfolio 3 for out-of-sample testing. An alternative is, given say 15 years of data, to tune on the first five years, in-sample test on the first ten years, and out-of-sample test on the last five years.

We also recommend the use of a data set that contains fundamental equity factors pre- and post-Sarbanes-Oxley. Specifically, let us consider a system that uses insider trading as a predictor of earnings surprises. Such an indicator would clearly perform differently before Sarbanes-Oxley than after it. As a result, hold back from the in-sample test the years of data since the legislation was passed, as this data represents the real-world today.

What are we trying to accomplish? If we are trying to create a system that performs well in market downturns, overweight the selection of data for in-sample with downturn years. Then, test out of sample on a blend of years using both down and up. Likewise, if we intend to create an algorithm for any type of market, weight the in-sample data set uniformly, but subsequently perform the out-of-sample test on, say, only the down years, and then retune it and run it again on, say, only the up years. This will give you an understanding of how your algorithm performs in both up and down economic cycles. Sometimes, all that is needed to become successful is to match the benchmark in average and good years, but substantially outperform the benchmark in down cycles.

- **Fixed income portfolio systems.** For fixed income data, indicators are created from macro indicators such as economic data and Fed actions along with underlying corporate data for bonds, CDOs, convertibles, and other structured products. Fixed income data is normally very clean for month ends due to the requirements of marking a bond portfolio using dealer prices. Since most corporate bond investors hold their positions for several months, we recommend performing a backtest that only uses month end prices and calculations.

We also recommend producing a return for each security for each period using the same rules. This will then be used in the backtesting step for the returns. We realize this is not an industry standard practice. However, our method produces a stable return stream that does not vary with the backtest. Our method forces, very early in the testing cycle, the discussion of how to consistently measure returns.

With respect to database structure, we recommend separating the raw data from the returns and from the indicators. This will enable reusability of returns and signals. Of course, the ability to reuse returns assumes a fixed holding period. For a nonfixed holding period, new returns would have to be generated.

16.1.2.   Return windows

During a backtest, returns over different holding periods should be consistent. For example, if you are optimizing an algorithm over three-month holding periods, returns for one-month, two-month and six-month periods should be consistent with three-month periods. You should not accept results where, say, one-, two- and six-month returns were negative, while three-month returns were positive. We recommend backtesting over different holding horizons. If an algorithm does not work or is inconsistent for multiple horizons, you should reject it. This should also be true for high frequency trading systems.

We also recommend applying this cross-holding period testing strategy to sectors, countries, market capitalizations, etc. We have found that the best quality control tool to identify these effects is the fishbone diagram and that the analysis and the structuring of these tests are done very efficiently using design of experiments.

We recommend that the product team decide up front what results will be gathered from the backtest: maximum drawdowns, number of winners versus losers, portfolio turnover ratio, average monthly return, standard deviation of returns, average return per trade, Sharpe ratio, Sortino ratio, and how to produce a time series of returns. Again, we suggest that this be done using a fishbone diagram that will link common causes of variations in these calculations such as economic cycle and investment cycle. At the end of this loop, the team will be able to perform cause and effect analysis for the variations in the returns.

16.2.   STEP 3, LOOP 2: Perform In-Sample Test for Large Sample

In-sample testing is very time intensive, because the team manually checks the calculations and results. During the in-sample test, algorithms may calculate the averages and standard deviations for trades on, say, three instruments. Is the math right? Is the trading logic right? If it does not work properly, the team will still be able to make modifications to the data or to change the logic steps.

In-sample testing is a time-consuming and very complex task (which deserves its own book). This is the step where the team converts all the prototype examples into prototype production-level code. From the manufacturing analogy, this is where the team builds the prototype production facility. To summarize the standard steps for this loop, we recommend that you:

- First calculate the returns and store them in separate table.
- Then, calculate all the factors or signals.

In-sample testing will expose irregularities in the data (e.g., fiscal year changes), so that they can make modifications. If the modifications require new quantitative methods, however, the project will need to revert back to Stage 1, and be reresearched and reprototyped before moving again to the backtesting stage. For this step, we expect the appropriate exception handling to take place, such as catching changes in reporting cycles. These types of quality control issues are similar to manufacturing issues encountered when going from a test beaker of chemicals to a 50,000 gallon batch.

After calculating the returns and factors, graph compounded performance by factor or signal. For trigger trading systems, graph the linked trigger P&L versus the P&L of the investable universe and graph the excess return versus investable universe. For filter systems, graph the performance of the selected basket versus both the basket of unchosen instruments and the investable universe. For multifactor systems, graph each quantile versus the investable universe. We recommend keeping it ordinal; the bottom quantile should be decreasing, the top quantile should be increasing, to form a fan shape. If the graph is not ordinal, then there is a problem with the indicator.

The team should perform this graphical statistical analysis for each indicator by itself and with all indicators combined together. The team can use a design of experiments (DoE) approach or fishbone diagram for individual (i.e., unblended) factors to investigate the interaction between the predictive capability of a given factor with other factors, such as economic cycle, that have not been modeled in the system due to the lack of this data in real time. Given a fishbone diagram, the team can decide which combinations of factors to look at together. Also, because the trading/investment algorithms are locked after Gate 1, stick with algorithms defined in K|V 1.2. At this point the team is optimizing the signals. The factor weightings may change, but not the underlying signal algorithm.

The team should decompose the returns, producing return charts and tables, to allow the team to engage in introductory risk control discussions, such as is the algorithm overweighting technology stocks? To facilitate this, these returns should be calculated per sector or per bond class, etc. The team should look not at the end returns, but rather how these returns were created. Ideally, returns are generated by picking better securities versus over- or underweighting classifications.

The team is trying to figure if the algorithm has a bias. For example, in the basket, what percentage is large cap, or small cap? In a basket of securities, what are the credit ratings of the companies purchased—A, BBB, C? Is it effectively going long large caps and short small caps? Is the algorithm effectively going long companies with junk credit ratings and short companies with A or better credit? We recommend getting the positions taken in statistical format and analyzing the outputs. There may be some unexpected, hidden factor model. Given the returns of the algorithms, there may be some principal component analysis that explains most of the returns outside of the chosen factors or signals.

Ideally, graph the returns by as many classification factors as possible. This means probably producing 30 to 40 graphs in order to determine how stable the trading algorithm is, given different slices of the universe. From a database view, given a selected basket, take from the table of everything you bought, SELECT WHERE Sector = 'Oil'. SELECT WHERE Cap <= 1000000.

This loop is very much a "field of NASCAR" loop. Statistics and mathematics are your tools to modify and build trading/investment systems. However, there is a large amount of trial and error. Nothing replaces seasoned researchers, traders, and programmers that have proven they have the ability to tune an algorithm since they have done it before successfully. Use stats and mathematics to make it work properly. Compounded performances (when stated) were calculated by taking a hypothetical starting equity amount and calculating the total return for the period. Each subsequent period then uses the resulting equity balance as its start to calculate that period's total return.

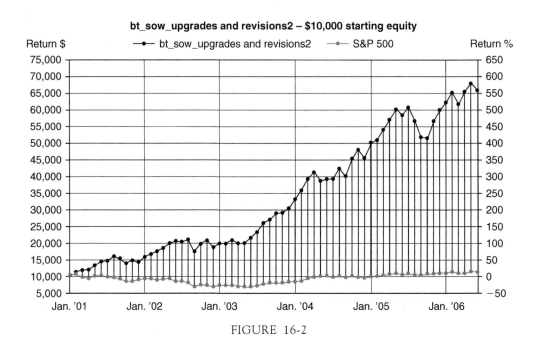

FIGURE 16-2

16.3. STEP 3, LOOP 3: Perform Out-of-Sample Test

Out-of-sample testing is done to ensure everything is working properly, with no adjustments, with almost real-world data and samples. During the out-of-sample testing, no more modifications can be made. Out-of-sample testing is backward looking (whereas shadow trading is forward looking).

Trading algorithms and quantitative models must be examined against both in-sample and out-of-sample data before progressing to the implementation stage. It is of utmost importance to save some of the historical data for out-of-sample testing.

Often a trading idea at inception belongs in group three, but arrogance leads us to believe that our idea falls in group one. And so it can at times be tempting to manipulate historical data and find periods of time where a particular system shows profitability. Manipulation of this sort will lead to incorrect conclusions and furthermore will certainly generate inconsistent if not disastrous results. Bad ideas are not all bad. Knowing what does not work can sometimes be a giant step forward. A complete failure may be the exact catalyst toward finding a profitable solution.

16.4. Summary

This step is the make or break step of the entire design process. In the step, the product team will have produced an algorithm that can beat the benchmark or they have proven that the current strategy is wrong and they need to go back to Stage 1 to change the algorithm.

16.4.1. Best Practices

- Use fishbone diagrams to identify special causes of variation.
- To ease reuse, separate raw data from the returns and from the indicators.
- Screen instruments and lock down the investable universe.
- Estimate transaction costs and slippage and incorporate them into backtests.
- Plan and document the trading/investment rules and backtesting methodology before you begin.

CHAPTER • 17

Check Performance and Shadow Trade

In-sample and out-of-sample tests of a trading/investment system generate performance metrics. Performance testing will validate the ability of the process to achieve the planned results. Performance metrics should conform to those generated during prototype testing. Trading system regression testing will detect errors. Nonconformance will cause the product team to investigate its cause. Regression testing of a trading/investment system seeks to uncover discrepancies between performance metrics the system generated during a previous stage of development and those generated during backtests. These discrepancies sometimes occur as a result of a change in tool sets, but at other times may be indicative of the underlying nature of the trading system.

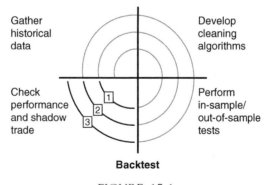

FIGURE 17-1

Experience shows that as trading/investment systems are developed and tool sets change, regression bugs are quite common. Sometimes they occur because of poor control practices during the conversion from one tool set to another (e.g., conversion of Excel prototypes into C++ algorithms, or a switch of optimization engines).

In most software development projects when a bug is located and fixed, good practice dictates that the team run and record a test to prove the fix, and regularly retest the fix after subsequent changes to the program. A test suite contains automated software tools that allow the testing environment to execute all the regression test cases automatically. Some projects set up automated systems to rerun all regression tests at specified intervals and report any nonconformance. Common strategies are to rerun the system after every successful compile, every night, or once a week. (Regression testing is an integral part of the extreme programming software development methodology. In this methodology, design documents are replaced by extensive, repeatable, and automated testing of the entire software package at every stage in the software development cycle.)

17.1. STEP 4, LOOP 1: Perform Regression Test to Validate Algorithms and Benchmark

In the first loop, the product team takes performance metrics from Stage 1, generated from a small set of sample data, and runs comparisons against performance for the investable universe. The team should also be laying out the tools of how they are going to measure performance versus the benchmark. They will look at raw returns in the IS/OS tests versus the results from Stage 1. They will look at excess returns of the Stage 1 sample against the universe and the benchmark to confirm the algorithm still outperforms its peers. The difference between the benchmark and the universe of investable instruments needs to be calculated to determine the effect of illiquid securities on the universe returns. In addition, the team should compare sample calculations of returns instrument-by-instrument against the returns of the sample universe. The team should perform all the comparisons to double check that the sample performance of Stage 1 and the performance of the investable universe are highly correlated. This is done to ensure that the data cleaning algorithm has not introduced errors into the calculations.

To clarify, let us say a small sample of data, say for 20 stocks, proved outputs of the system in Stage 1. Now, after cleaning all the data and calculating all the returns, on a stock-by-stock basis for the 20 stocks, the product should perform a white box regression test. The results should show similar performance if the cleaning algorithms are correct. Before scaling up, the product team should be sure to check all the outputs after the cleaning algorithm against the outputs from the original spiral for the original instruments.

Finally, in this step, the team should benchmark the difference between the investible universe and the benchmark itself. This can be accomplished using statistics and charts to graphically explain the difference. Also, we recommend checking the returns of the original benchmark against the universe of stocks you selected.

There are many benchmarks that contain untradable securities due to market capitalization, illiquidity, or poor credit rating. (e.g., the Crédit Suisse First Boston Convertible Bond Index has in the past contained bonds that are illiquid.) When you compare yourself against a benchmark that contains untradable securities, you may decide that your algorithm is performing poorly; however, your algorithm may be performing well against your competitors, since they have the same restrictions you have. Without this step of benchmarking the investable universe versus the benchmark, the firm may otherwise kill the project instead of fast tracking it as a peer-beating system.

Imagine this: if you could predict 100% of the future, what would be the optimal output of your model? If you knew what the top 10% returns would be (i.e., if you knew what the optimum basket would be), and you could pick everything right, what would your returns be? The outputs of this hypothetical optimum algorithm should also be used as a benchmark. This benchmark will provide a gauge of how much better you could make an algorithm. If you know what optimum is, you know how much better you can make the algorithm.

Finally, the team should decide on the tools, tables, and graphs used to mathematically validate the results of the in-/out-of-sample testing. We recommend that at a minimum the product team determine the types of graphs that will be produced as part of the check performance stage. These tools will be used in loops 2 and 3 and will form the basis of statistical control tools.

17.2.   STEP 4, LOOP 2: Perform Regression Test of In-Sample Results against Prototype

In this step, the product team performs a regression test of the in-sample results versus the investable universe and versus the benchmark in order to prove that the system performs as expected.

The quality of the trading/investment system will be appraised by a collection of regression tests that evaluate one or more of its features. A valid regression test of in-sample results will generate the verified gold standard results. Regression tests data and the gold standard results should be packaged into a regression test suite. As development progresses and more tests are added, new results from in-sample and out-of-sample tests can be compared with the gold standard results. If they differ, then a potential flaw has been found in the system.

Depending on the nature of the flaw, it may either be corrected and development allowed to continue, or development will revert back to Stage 1. This mechanism detects when new tests invalidate existing strategies and thus prevents the trading/investment system from progressing any further.

17.3.   STEP 4, LOOP 3: Perform Regression Test of OS Test Results against IS Results and SPC Outputs and Shadow Trade

In this step, the product team performs regression testing of all the performance metrics against the in-sample, gold standard test results. The performance metrics should be similar and the degree of similarity will indicate if the environment is currently favorable for this algorithm. Let us suppose, however, that you produce an algorithm that works well in sample, but that has a clear economic cycle to it. You run the out-of-sample test, and you see that the economic cycle is becoming unfavorable; the out-of-sample results show a shift in performance versus the in-sample results. This could lead to a parking of the system at the next stage gate or at least a frank discussion of risk with management. The reverse situation is that the environment is becoming more favorable for the system, which should prompt management to release resources more quickly to bring the system online.

At this stage, the team should now know the key inputs, the key factors, and performance metrics to monitor, and have graphs showing excess returns by week or by day. Now, the team can introduce SPC graphs; at a minimum a range graph showing upper and lower control limits, due to the volatility of the indicators. Included should be C_{pk} calculations between the in-sample and out-of-sample tests, and if applicable performance specification limits. The team should also consider control charts, using, for example, a moving average of performance metrics. Management should expect all of these visual performance indicators at the Gate 2 meeting to show the stability of the system and its outputs. (The concepts of control charts and C_{pk} calculations will be covered in the Stage 4 chapters. Many of the quality principles described in Stage 4 apply to Stage 2 performance evaluation.)

After this step, shadow trading may begin. The purpose of shadow trading is not to confirm the profitability of the system, but to confirm that all the pieces and all the data cleaning algorithms can be done in a timely manner to enable trading in a mock system just to put the time element into the testing algorithm.

As with K|V 1.4.4, we again acknowledge that traders may well request to trade the prototype. However, we again strongly caution that trading be delayed until after the Gate 2 meeting where top management can approve use of the system.

17.4. Summary

The product must determine what data to collect; it is then necessary to clean the data, run in-sample and out-of-sample tests, and analyze the outputs of the tests in order to validate the ability of the trade selection algorithms, position management, and risk management logic to satisfy requirements. Quality testing demands that product teams compare regression test results against gold standard results to ensure the correctness of data cleaning algorithms. These tests will also indicate whether the current environment is favorable for launch of the system. At the Gate 2 meeting, management will expect to see graphical proof of the stability of the system and its performance characteristics.

17.4.1. Best Practices

- Benchmark the benchmark. The benchmark may not consist of illiquid, untradable securities, so you need to create a new universe so you can calculate the difference between the benchmark and the investable universe.
- Measure the process capability of the system using statistical process control.
- Use regression testing to ensure that the current environment is suitable for launch.
- Create a gold standard package that includes the locked-down data and the performance results.
- Shadow trade to check the ability of the system to produce signals in a timely fashion that can be traded.

CHAPTER ◆ 18

Gate 2

In the chapter on Gate 1, we discussed many important issues regarding gates in general, and all the concepts recommended for meeting format apply to Gate 2 as well. As with Gate 1, the Gate 2 meeting provides an opportunity to refine time lines and forecasts, as the project requirements are now more detailed. Although some issues and information needed for planning Stage 3 may still be difficult to foresee, overall uncertainties should be reduced through prior experience and reassessment of processes that move the projects from inception through backtesting. Like Gate 1, Gate 2 also prevents development of the trading/investment system from moving to the next stage until the required activities, deliverables, and performance have been completed and evaluated in a quality manner.

The product team should arrive at the gate meeting with its deliverables and a recommendation supported by data. A recommendation to proceed to Stage 3 must of course be accompanied by a request for additional resources. At the meeting, management will review the recommendation and decide what course to take. We also recommend the head of the risk department for the firm attend, so that risk managers can start mapping out plans for K|V Stage 4 concurrent with Stage 3 activities. In order to pass through Gate 2, several questions must be answered.

- Do the gold standard in-sample and out-of-sample test results prove the competitive advantage of the trading/investment system?
- Is the process stable? What are the performance metrics that are stable? The stability of the system should be described using statistical process control. Included should be SPC charts and C_{pk} calculations between the in-sample and out-of-sample tests.
- Has the product team delivered the required documents?
- What are the current projections for time and budget for Stage 3? This should be compared to the original projections.
- What is the product team's plan for managing the development process and the development team?
- Are the project and the software/hardware quality attributes technologically feasible?
- Are the resources requested for implementation acceptable?
- Is the product team functioning as a team or does top management need to reform it?

- Is there a development team for Stage 3? Assignments of programmers to the development team will be done with top management to ensure lines of control and consolidated IT project plan of record.

This gate will prevent development of the trading/investment system from moving forward until the required activities and deliverables have been completed in a quality manner. At this point, the project may be put on hold until IT resources are free to proceed through Stage 3. Whatever the gate decision (i.e., go, kill, hold, return, or trade) this gate should chart the path ahead by ensuring that plans and budgets are in place.

Good traders understand the importance of good technology, and buying and developing technology takes resources. Senior traders sometimes even steal resources from other projects. We recommend the Gate 2 meeting be scheduled to coincide with a periodic IT resource meeting. This will ensure that projects that pass through Gate 2 are allocated IT resources from a firmwide perspective.

- Management should hold IT resource and gate meetings at least quarterly. At this meeting, top management must lock an IT project plan of record. This will force completion of projects before a change of focus.

- Discussion of IT resources and projects should be open to all managing directors and product team leaders. Politics in the open is better than politics in private.

- Once top management sets the IT project plan of record, it must be unchangeable. While slack may be built in for critical code fixes, these should be limited. If the IT project plan of record is allowed to change, then traders will circumvent it to steal resources. Then, money and time for IT development are up for grabs, and teams start to build competing technologies and redundant internal systems. Economy of scale is lost; good programmers will leave the firm to seek a better, more stable environment; and product teams spin off to create their own firms.

Good IT resource allocation goes beyond just IT, eventually becoming a management style keeping all employees focused on goals of the firm, not their own goals. A properly run Gate 2 meeting and the setting of an IT project plan of record cements together the firm with a singularity of purpose. A poorly run Gate 2 meeting will pull the firm apart into competing groups that believe in star traders and individual rewards.

Beware the fast-track project. "Fast tracking" is a commonly used rationale to get around or disregard an IT project plan of record. If the current project is a "fast-track" project (and speed, by the way, is a great way to introduce errors), the firm still needs to review the firmwide resource allocation. To ensure an orderly queue of work for IT development teams, reallocating resources for fast-track systems should preferably not be done; if traders or top managers learn of back doors to resources, every system will soon be on a fast track. In such a case, development of new systems under a project management framework would immediately cease. We strongly recommend that all personnel and resource allocations follow the gate-defined schedules.

Gate 2 now is the point at which the specification of the system should be considered ready for full-scale production, and a freeze applied to the strategy, execution, data cleaning, and optimization algorithms; the look and feel of GUIs and reports may still evolve through user testing. After this, specifications may be changed only through a change control process, requiring a return to a previous stage for review, testing, and verification, including an evaluation of the change's effect on other parts of the trading/investment system.

System verification at Gate 2 ensures that output documents from the backtest stage meet the input requirements of the implement stage, K|V Stage 3. The results of this verification must be documented and delivered to all interested parties prior to the Gate 2 meeting.

We believe that at this point, model risk should have effectively been removed. The backtest stage, K|V Stage 2, outputs must:

- Meet the design and development input requirements of the implement stage.
- Either contain or make reference to trading/investment system acceptance criteria for Gate 3.
- Specify trading/investment system characteristics necessary for proper implementation.
- Be in a form that allows verification against the Money Document.
- Provide information necessary for purchasing third-party components.

Also, as part of the portfolio review process at the gate meeting, new trading/investment systems will again be evaluated and prioritized, working trading/investment systems reviewed, enhanced, or aborted, and resources reallocated to higher priority projects. Gate meetings are a good time to review the market and the economic environment. The portfolio review process will again be affected by changing market and economic conditions, new trading/investment opportunities, hedging considerations, and functional interdependence among new and working trading/investment systems. Top management should consider the current investment cycle and its projected effect on the profitability of the portfolio of systems, as well as look forward to what the investment cycle might be when the trading/investment system is launched after Gate 3.

18.1. Portfolio Review

Gates serve as a checkpoint to ensure that individual projects remain on schedule, on budget, and financially and technically viable. But, no project exists in a vacuum; each project competes against all others for resources and gate meetings are natural opportunities for portfolio review.

Portfolio management for new trading/investment systems is a dynamic process where the list of active and new trading/investment systems is constantly under review and subject to revision. In this process new projects are evaluated, selected, and prioritized. Existing projects may be accelerated, killed, or reprioritized with resources reallocated to more promising projects. Portfolio decisions are often fraught with risks and confused by new information, including:

- Changing market opportunities.
- Multiple and disparate corporate goals and strategic considerations.
- Multiple decision-makers and even their geographic locations.

Portfolio review is further complicated by projects in the portfolio that are at different stages of completion, by limitations on people, time and money, and by interconnectedness among different development projects. Portfolio management processes must consider all these things.

For projects that pass through any gate, management must also consider how the project should be prioritized within the overall portfolio of trading/investment systems. For fast-paced companies like proprietary trading firms and hedge funds, the portfolio is especially dynamic; at the most successful firms, management makes a strong commitment to the decision and prioritization process. Successful firms build their product strategy into the portfolio from the ground up using both top-down and bottom-up approaches, considering both market opportunities and core competencies.

The combination of top-down and bottom-up works because it overcomes deficiencies of each approach. From the top, the best firms proceed with strategy development, a product road map, and strategic buckets of money. Concurrently, from the bottom, these firms also proceed with a review of their most promising innovations. To reconcile conclusions based on the two perspectives, we recommend using a Modified Delphi-style process with a scoring or ranking model; a ranking approach will force relative priority. The top-down/bottom-up approach:

- Analyzes the markets for different kinds of risk and the competition in those markets.
- Assesses the company's strengths and weaknesses, and innovations.
- Reconciles the two (possibly at a gate meeting) to set new product goals.

After ranking, top management must check for alignment of the tentative portfolio with strategic initiatives. If the set of projects is overweighted in one market, instrument, time horizon, strategy, or geographic region, management may need to rearrange projects and priorities. This can be an iterative process of reranking and rearranging until the right balance is found. A well-run process is messy. Everyone has a key project they will fight to build. If the process is open and fair, most will agree with the final resource allocations and the IT project plan of record. Also, all top managers must be able discuss the firm's focus and the direction with their employees. Top management must focus resources on completing projects.

18.2.   Inputs/Deliverables

- Full description of the database and real-time data feeds, including comparison of alternative data sources.
- Full investment policy outlining the investable universe.
- Complete definition of the data cleaning rules and optimization methodologies. This may be included in an updated version of a business rules catalog.
- A data dictionary, data and data flow maps, and a database design document.
- Gold standard run package with in-sample and out-of-sample results and performance metrics. This package should include mocked-up reports, SPC charts, and user interfaces.
- Complete prototype of the trading system containing calculations and interfaces. This should include a discussion of software quality attributes.
- Shadow trading data, including results of regression tests versus prototypes delivered at the completion of Stage 1.

18.3.   Summary

Gate 2 is the make or break point for a new trading/investment system. At the gate meeting, top management will decide whether to commit the resources necessary for full implementation. As with all gates, the product team should distribute the gate deliverables a week before the meeting, and arrive at the meeting with a recommendation as to how to proceed, backed by hard facts. Should the project be allowed to proceed, the product team should also have an overview plan for Stage 3, including forecasts and resource needs.

Gates are also a convenient time for portfolio review, for top management to consider resource allocations among the portfolio of new and working trading/investment systems. As with all gates, the Gate 2 meeting is an opportune time to engage in a review of the portfolio of new and working trading/investment systems as well as the current market and economic cycles.

STAGE · III

Implement

CHAPTER • 19

STAGE 3: Overview

The spiral stage structure of K|V begs two perspectives—one, that of the loops; and two, that of the steps. One can look at the four steps that comprise a single loop, or the three loops that comprise each step. We will do both. This chapter will present an overview of the three loops. The following four chapters will examine each of the four steps and each pass over each step. The number of loops is not by any means fixed. (We decided that three iterations were sufficient to cover the commonly encountered substeps.)

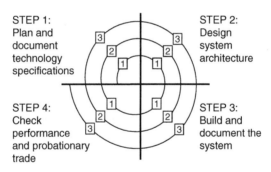

STEP 1:
Plan and document technology specifications

STEP 2:
Design system architecture

STEP 4:
Check performance and probationary trade

STEP 3:
Build and document the system

FIGURE 19-1

Stage 3 accomplishes the transformation task, turning the specifications of the trading/investment system into software and hardware. The design of the trading system from previous stages now becomes the specification requirements for the software design. By the time a product team reaches this stage, most if not all the groundwork for success has already been laid. The requirements have been gathered and tested in previous stages, and after Gate 2 are fixed. Any design errors discovered or changes made to the trading/investment strategy from this point on require a return to Stage 1 for rework and then retesting.

At this point also, our methodology assumes that the task of building software and hardware components of the trading/investment system will include a development team in addition to the product team. The lead programmer/IT member of the product team manages this somewhat agile development team, which will engage in test-driven development. In this capacity, the development team leader becomes the lead software designer. This way the development team lead understands the critical tasks, priorities and resources necessary to complete the transformation, and represents the product team's (i.e., the customers') interests to the developers. This should ensure that knowledge is properly transferred. The financial engineers from the product team over the course of Stage 3 manage software quality assurance of business tier software. The traders from the product team perform and/or oversee quality assurance over GUI, integration, and reporting mechanisms, as well as run user-acceptance tests. The marketing person from the product team can write or oversee the writing of the user documentation for the software. Essentially, the product team is the customer of the development team.

The breakdown of these roles is critical to ensuring the project moves forward quickly. Often we find the financial engineers and traders believe they should be in charge of production programming. We recommend this be avoided for the following reasons:

- Standard coding is a poor use of financial engineers' time. Programmers should program. A better use of a financial engineer's time is to work with risk managers to design risk controls and perform quality assurance testing.

- The skills that make a brilliant financial engineer do not necessarily make a brilliant programmer. Financial engineers often (and should) spend their programming time on algorithm development and prototyping, ignoring pure technology issues such as error handling, GUI design, and data interfaces. (Financial engineers sometimes consider these tasks to be grunt work.)

- Traders, on the other hand, think only about money and, since bonuses are on the line, often push for software release at the expense of its stability. Proper error handling takes time, but is not apparent to end users. Error handling can sometimes become a "future feature" when traders oversee software development. This type of fast tracking works well until fatal errors arise. Then, the traders blame the programmers, and the programmers blame the quality assurance testers. Traders should be responsible for user acceptance testing, and 100% accountable for errors. The finger pointing will then be at them. Any monetary loss due to poor user acceptance testing should be billed directly against the team's bonus. (This is the norm in standard engineering.)

We also recommend that the product team now add a risk manager, who will learn the specifics of the trading/investment system and be able to recommend how best to build out the risk management functions and reporting requirements. Risk managers must understand the trading/investment system along with helping structure what risk controls and reports will be required for Stage 4. The addition of the risk manager is critical for speed of implementation since the product team may finish a system without well-defined risk parameters. In such a case, the risk management department may not set trading or limits until they fully understand the trading/investment system.

19.1.   Development Team

Stage 3 is where the development team's senior software engineers take control of the project to design and build clean, optimized, robust, and fast software. Of course, software development processes have been researched in depth over the last 40 years, and in this step we will not rewrite the research, but rather link our K|V methodology to agile processes and the Software Engineering Institute's (SEI) models for designing and building tight software. We do, however, believe in test-driven development where the development team iteratively writes test cases first, then writes only the code needed to pass each test.

The technology development team is responsible for the design, coding, testing, and implementation of the software and network components of a trading/investment system. We recommend this team follow more agile development principles, embracing change, communication, and feedback. According to the Agile Manifesto (www.agilealliance.com), an agile team:

- Focuses on customer satisfaction.
- Self-organizes.
- Communicates face to face, often in daily meetings.
- Focuses on iterative and evolutionary development.
- Strives for technical excellence and simplicity.

A development team typically consists of a lead software designer (again, the product team's lead programmer/IT professional), software engineers, network engineers, and test engineers, who perform unit test-driven coding, hardware, and software integration testing, and refactoring in an iterative, incremental, timeboxed manner.

The typical responsibilities of the software engineers are to understand and evaluate the requirements specifications and alternative architectures, build and unit test the system, and create design documentation. Where possible the software engineers reuse software components from the firm's library of proprietary components. Furthermore, they will purchase, configure, and extend COTS components where appropriate. Management should not be allowed to select the programming language. This should be set at the firm level and followed by all teams. (While the firm may enact changes on the recommendation of programmers, nevertheless development must take place within management-approved technologies.) To ensure maintainability, management should also lock the framework for coding firmwide.

A development team develops software iteratively. As always, we believe in client-driven and risk-driven iterative technology development, where the elements with the highest business priority and risk are chosen first. Each iteration in Stage 3 covers design, programming, testing, integration, and delivery of a useful piece of software. We prefer shorter iterations where timeboxes are no longer than two weeks. This process is very similar to a prototype in K|V Stage 1 except that an iteration in this stage produces a working portion of the final trading/investment system.

Iterative development dramatically increases feedback versus sequential development, providing closer communication between the product team and the development team. Small portions, or batches, beget short feedback loops that enhance control. Shorter iterations, furthermore, force an option-based approach to development, allowing the technology to respond to proven and tested facts rather than estimates and forecasts. An option-based approach reduces risk by keeping options open rather than freezing the technology design. Unit testing and integration test engineers should be involved from the first iteration so that design problems will be exposed early on. Iterative development and testing forces points of communication, better use of time and resources, and, in the end, better quality.

The development team should consider the documents and prototypes from Stages 1 and 2 to be the base code used for testing. Programmers sometimes ignore specifications and designs, preferring to just start coding. This leads to design errors, including nonscalability, and produces poor design documentation. Instead of being encouraged that the software is finally being built, the product team will become discouraged. Without firm design documents in line with the initial requirements specifications, a completed system should not pass a due diligence process, be funded by investors, or allow the sale of the system and its fund.

Developers must follow plans. A construction team building a bridge would be fired immediately for changing designs away from the prototype structure. A development team programming flight controls would be fired immediately for not building to the prototype and simply coding on the fly. Top management must be firm on this concept or give up on our methodology. Deviation at this point will result in out-of-control development and failed projects.

19.2.   Real-Time Systems

While K|V assumes that all the functional requirements, performance requirements, and design constraints are specified prior to Stage 3, in the real world, with real-time, high frequency systems, where technological speed is the competitive advantage, more system planning and design will be needed.

Planning and design for such systems typically follow an evolutionary process. In such systems, computation times have to be short, typically measured in milliseconds or faster, and execution deadlines are critical. Late execution would defeat the whole purpose of the trade selection algorithms. Larger systems of this type may also contain a complex man/machine interface (e.g., an execution strategy control system, where fast operator response is required but millisecond deadlines are not critical). In such a case, user interfaces may need additional prototyping.

For systems that make use of high frequency data and arbitrage or market making algorithms, critical response times are accomplished in one of two ways. One model runs algorithms at regular intervals. An example is a closed-loop index-arbitrage system, having a fixed, preset sampling rate for the index's constituent instruments. This loop is a synchronous or periodic event with a real-time clock, where response times can be easily determined. The second model is where the software responds to external events that occur at random, asynchronous, or aperiodic intervals. In this case, each market event must be serviced, that is, received, understood, and responded to, within a specified maximum time. When the trading system has to cope with multiple aperiodic market events, estimates of execution time are more difficult to determine. (Trouble often arises where systems need to handle both time-incremented and random events. Development teams are encouraged to plan and design iteratively and carefully in such cases.) Through iterative planning and design, the development team can evaluate alternative implementations. In the end, the team can set estimates of best and worst performance and test the trading system through shadow or probationary trading.

19.3.   LOOP 1: Program and Test Trading/ Investment Algorithms

STEP 1:   Document Software Requirements
STEP 2:   Design Business Rules Packages
STEP 3:   Program Business Rules Packages
STEP 4:   Test System Outputs against Black Box Tests from Previous Stages and Probationary Trade

Loop 1 takes the quantified logic, that is, the business rules of the trading/investment system, and turns it into production, executable code. These activities come first because the product team may have already converted some of the trading/investment strategy algorithms, prototyped in Stage 1, into C++, Java, or .NET code objects in Stage 2. This code can be used in the production system. Where this has occurred, the development team need not spend extra time and resources reprogramming those features; regression testing in Stage 2 should have already ensured its correctness and the product team should have fully documented the architecture of these components for review by the development team and inclusion in the Stage 2 deliverable documents.

Where the development team converts prototypes from one implementation, like Excel, Resolver, or MATLAB, to code over this stage, the product team should perform regression testing to ensure that errors are detected and fixed. Our methodology assumes that regression testing is built from the successful white, gray, and black box test cases used during testing of prototypes (K|V 1.4).

While we have devoted only one loop to this section, we fully expect and advocate that the tasks be broken down into several iterations using an agile framework. In the end, the goal is to create a stable, fast running code that correctly implements the business logic. In this stage the development team performs unit tests on all software components.

19.4. LOOP 2: Build and Test Interfaces

STEP 1: Document Interface Requirements
STEP 2: Design Interface Packages
STEP 3: Program Interface Packages
STEP 4: Test Interfaces

Loop 2 integrates the trading/investment algorithms (i.e., the business logic tier) with external software components and the user interfaces. Most of these external software components have been purchased from vendors in Stage 2 and the product team is responsible for ensuring that COTS products conform to the specified requirements. External components include databases, potentially an optimization engine, and execution, risk, and accounting software. Integration into the existing technological environment should already be well understood; the data dictionary, data maps, and data flow maps created in Stage 2 should facilitate the integration process.

For integration with external components, the development team will also design, code, and test exception handling mechanisms in this step, including recovery procedures in the event of external errors. Where recovery is possible, the trading/investment system should be put into a fail-safe mode (such a mode of operation may reduce response times, but service only good elements of the system). This offers a sort of graceful shutdown, or fault tolerant operation, where full and safe performance is maintained in the presence of faults.

Trading/investment systems that use real-time data and/or automate execution must be planned and built with safety in mind, concerned with the consequences of failure. Fail-safe systems make no effort to meet normal operational requirements. Instead they aim to limit the danger or damage caused by fault.

19.5. LOOP 3: Create Network Architecture

STEP 1: Document Hardware and Network Requirements
STEP 2: Design Network Architecture
STEP 3: Buy/Build Network Infrastructure Components
STEP 4: Perform Acceptance Test

Loop 3 assembles and connects the hardware and network components that will house the trading/investment system. Now, hardware changes quickly. In fact, computer processing power doubles every 18 months, according to Moore's law. Given that trading/investment system development may take several months to complete, hardware available in Stage 1, or even in Loop 1 of this stage, may be outdated by the time development is complete. For this reason, hardware development should come last.

19.6.   Outputs/Deliverables

Building a working trading/investment system is essentially a software development project. The trading/investment logic is encompassed within proprietary software. As a result, implementation requires blueprints of the software and the connectivity between and interoperability with disparate software and hardware systems first. These blueprints will evolve, but must be firm in the end.

Software development without documentation can become a disaster. The development team, while agile, must document design alternatives and the rationale for the design decisions. The development team should write and maintain a rationale and structure document, but that document should be brief and to the point and discuss the designs and rationale at the highest level structures of the system. However, too much documentation can be worse than too little. Massive documentation takes a great deal of time and even more time to update as designs change, but if documentation is out of sync with reality it can significantly misdirect future action.

The ability of a development team to respond to change often determines the success or failure of a trading/investment system design and development project. When the development team builds plans, those plans must be flexible, ready to adapt to changes in the market and technology. In the end, the development team will deliver their documentation to the product team. The product team will deliver these documents at the Gate 3 meeting. At this meeting management will expect:

- Software requirements specification document.
- Software and hardware architecture documents.
- Proof the system meets the quality attribute requirements as per SAS 70 or ISO 9000.
- Working software and hardware with documentation.
- User documentation.
- Signed user acceptance test report.
- Full probationary trading performance report, including trade selection reports and results of regression tests versus the gold standard run package results from Stage 2.

(For best practices regarding writing stage deliverables, we refer you to K|V 1.1.)

19.7.   Summary

In Stage 3, the product team contracts with a development team to build a running, to-specification trading/investment system. The agile development team designs and programs proprietary software, integrates that software with COTS components, and implements it in a hardware and network environment in order to meet the specifications originally set forth in the Money Document. All these activities should be planned and documented as the team encounters the tasks. For high frequency systems, where technology is the competitive advantage, planning, testing, and evaluating alternative designs take on particular importance.

We recommend the use of client-driven and risk-driven iterative development, where at the completion of each iteration, the development team delivers a working component of the system. Because the business rules may have been codified and compiled in Stage 2, we recommend the initial iterations build the proprietary business logic components, follow iterations to integrate these components with external software components, and create network architecture in the final iterations.

CHAPTER • 20

Plan and Document Technology Specifications

After passing through Gate 2, the requirements of the trading/investment systems are fixed, except for the look and feel of user interfaces and reports. The product team can no longer add to or change the trading/investment strategy without returning to a prior phase of the model. This is an important milestone in the development cycle. It is more important to deliver a working system that meets specifications at this stage than to develop a perfect system. One of the main reasons that software projects run over budget and behind schedule is scope creep due to the programmers striving for perfection too early in the life cycle of software product. At this point, scope can no longer creep. The development team should build software iteratively to meet the specifications and requirements from previous stages—no more, no less. Any major enhancements should be withheld until the Kaizen stage, that is, after Stage 4, as part of the continuous improvement process.

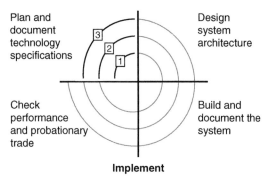

FIGURE 20-1

The product team began development with a vision and scope document—the Money Document—which they used to acquire resources for Stage 1. By Stage 3 the evolving project description should clearly lay out the inputs, data processing, functionality, and outputs, as well as special technology performance requirements and behaviors, called quality attributes. Furthermore, prototypes should provide a full decomposition of the software. Additionally, constraints with respect to resources, risks, and delivery dates should also be well documented.

Nevertheless, the product team must still communicate clearly the scope and specifications so the development team knows exactly what is expected. To this end, we recommend the product team assemble a Software Requirements Specification (SRS). An SRS for a trading/investment system consists of the combined, ordered, and linked descriptions and documents, and prototypes created in earlier stages, including data dictionary, data maps and data flow maps, GUI requirements, error handling maps, and report generation maps. An SRS will allow the development team to quickly build the system to the proper specifications. In this respect, K|V Stages 1 and 2 were essentially requirements gathering for Stage 3.

20.1.   Software Requirements Specification

A trading/investment system SRS, adapted from the IEEE Standard 830-1984, includes all of the required features and functionalities and all of the items that the development team will need to design and build the production trading/investment system (or at least the automated parts). The SRS is the parent document; all subsequent Stage 3 documents, such as design documents, software architecture documents, testing and validation plans, and documentation plans, will be derived from it. A well-written, agreed-upon SRS is the product team's assurance that the development team understands the problems to be solved and the necessary software behaviors. Furthermore, the prototypes that become part of the SRS also serve as the parent document for testing and validation strategies that will be applied to the requirements for verification. As software design and development proceed, the design elements and the actual code should be tied back to the requirement(s) that defines them using code comments. Once the team has regression tested and accepted objects, then quality assurance testers should review and approve all final code comments prior to user acceptance testing.

While prototypes already exist for most of the application, the development team will encounter and address them one by one. As with all high-level documents in engineering, we expect these to be revised in an orderly process as the team iterates through Stage 3. (This is no different than with the revision process of quality management using ISO 9000.)

20.1.1.   Elements of a Trading/Investment System's Software Requirements Specification

While an SRS may appear to be lengthy, most of it is already complete, based upon the work of previous stages. For specifications that are unclear or non-sequitur, the product team should take care to link and prioritize concepts with additional written explanation.

I. Introduction
   A. Purpose of the system
   B. Project scope
   C. Quality attribute requirements
   D. User documentation requirements
   E. References

    II. Functional requirements

        A. System features

        B. Operational risk requirements

        C. Design and implementation constraints

        D. Assumptions and dependencies

   III. Interface requirements

        A. User interfaces

        B. Network interfaces

        C. Data interfaces

   IV. Reporting requirements

        A. Trade execution/cost analysis reports

        B. Performance/risk monitoring reports

    V. Appendixes

        A. Glossary

        B. Business rules catalog (prototypes)

            1. Trading selection algorithms

            2. Position management rules

            3. Data cleaning rules

        C. Data map, data flow map, data dictionary

        D. Performance/risk monitoring rules

        E. Gold standard IS/OS test run package

From the IEEE standard, the SRS should address the following:

- **Functionality.** What is the software supposed to do?
- **External interfaces.** How does the software interact with people, the system's hardware, other hardware, and other software?
- **Performance.** What is the speed, availability, response time, recovery time of various software functions, etc.?
- **Attributes.** What are the portability, correctness, maintainability, security, etc. considerations?
- **Design constraints imposed on an implementation.** Are there any required standards in effect, implementation language, policies for database integrity, resource limits, operating environment(s) etc.?[1]

In short, the SRS should not include any design requirements. The benefits of a good SRS:

- Establish the basis for agreement between the product team and the development team.
- Reduce the development effort.
- Provide a basis for estimating costs and schedules.
- Provide a baseline for validation and verification.

- Facilitate transfer to new users or new machines.
- Serve as a basis for enhancement.

That is, an SRS can evolve, providing a foundation for continuous evaluation and improvement.[2]

20.2.   Collaborative Planning

High technology changes quickly and software development, therefore, is not completely predictable. Development teams that are agile embrace change, even while user requirements are fixed, creating first a release plan, and then a series of iteration plans as they progress.

A release plan in K|V consists of the SRS and a forecast as to when the development team believes it can complete implementation. A release planning meeting should include all members of both the product team and the development team. In this way, the release plan will communicate a shared vision for the project between the product team and the development team.

An iteration plan lays out the design-build-test scenario for each piece of the system, tackling the features with the highest business priority and risk first. Each iteration, that is, loop in K|V, of Stage 3 strives to implement a small enough feature or set of features, in fine enough granularity, so the team can confidently estimate time and effort required. If a feature cannot be completed in a single loop, the development team should break it down into smaller pieces. The team leader uses timeboxed iteration cycles to track progress of completed tasks and features as development progresses. In general, we recommend shorter iterations, at most two weeks. Shorter loops force better team communication and performance through more frequent:

- Contact regarding project risks.
- Iteration planning meetings.
- Teamwide reflection after each loop.
- Informal and formal code reviews.
- Daily scrum meetings.

The development team should also create a management plan to define the procedures for software development control processes, such as configuration management and versioning.

20.2.1.   Running a Successful Iteration Planning Meeting

At each iteration planning meeting, the development team breaks down features into tasks and assigns tasks to team members. The product team should attend this meeting to answer questions and prioritize the remaining work. During the meeting, development team members volunteer for tasks and as they finish them, sign up for more. Often, after collective brainstorming, the development team leader will list ranked tasks on a whiteboard or cards. (Subsequent daily scrum meetings are then held in view of the whiteboard or the posted cards.) When team members complete tasks, they erase them or cross them out. The same process can be used for project risks as well.

Given customer priorities, we recommend ranking tasks by risk, or uncertainty. Uncertainty can be in the form of technological complexity, amount of effort, interdepartmental politics, or user testing of the interface. The development team should also consider coverage, so that all major parts of the system are touched on in early loops. The goal is to discover and stabilize the major components and their interactions. Task ranking is necessarily based on experience and qualitative factors, and again we recommend using a scoring method, where each team member ranks the tasks. On completion, the leader can sort and discuss priorities in a Delphi framework.

As we have said, iterations should be timeboxed. Because size is the basis for a discussion of effort, the team should estimate size, that is, thousands of lines of code, using their experience, and more importantly function point estimates based on completed prototypes. (Evolutionary prototypes or code developed in Stage 2 speeds things up. Throwaway prototypes provide a basis for discussion of function points.) Also included in estimates should be time allocated to daily scrum meetings. Team members should also be able to budget, or at least eyeball, their own total work hours or uninterrupted development time for each task, say five hours a day. Between task size estimates, meeting times, and time budgets, the team should be able to arrive at a reasonable timebox estimate and/or put together a meaningful Gantt chart. With a flow of new trading/investment systems and a little experience, estimates as to effort, staffing, and cost will naturally become more precise.

During iteration meetings, the team should also make estimates for computer capacity, server and database use, and network capacity, which should all be documented as they impact departments and personnel external to the development team. The team should also be cognizant of risks to external dependencies, such as delays caused by other departments or vendors.

Lastly, the development team should also plan for intraloop code reviews, both formal and informal. During an informal code review, programmers look at and criticize each other's code. During a formal review, programmers make notes regarding design decisions and their rationale. Later, the rationale can be criticized, changes recommended and recorded, and version numbers updated. Through code reviews, development teams quickly confront design risks, overcoming them, scaling back, trying other paths, or even in extreme cases canceling the project where risks are insurmountable. A development team can provide immediate, factual feedback, not shallow assurances before they miss deadlines or the project fails. At the end of each iteration there must be a demonstration of progress to the product team, so that the finished features will be ready for quality assurance testing.

20.3. Buy versus Build

The quickest way to shorten a software development schedule is to buy components or reuse existing software. The development team makes recommendations as to which components to buy, which to reuse from internal libraries or past projects, and which to build from the ground up. Because this decision will affect the rest of the project, iteration plans should also address the process for selecting a solution to the buy versus build problem. If the team intends to base a trading/investment system on a COTS application, they will need to incorporate aspects of that software into the design of glue code or middleware that is developed in-house. Of course, reuse has dramatic implications for costs and schedules as well.

We recommend the product team establish controls over vendor-supplied components. That is, the development team should evaluate third-party components through a process, basing their selection on a vendor's ability to meet requirements. Furthermore, the development team should maintain a record of vendor and vendor component evaluation results. Such a process should consider:

- Accurate identification of needs and specifications of vendor products.
- Evaluation of the total cost, including licenses, scalability, delivery, and performance implications on trading/investment system results.

- Warranty replacement for nonconforming products.
- Existence of complete documentation.
- Vendor experience, reputation, and viability and references.
- Support and effectiveness of response to problems.
- Ability to comply with laws and regulations.

The advantage of custom-made systems is that products are optimized for the application at hand, which is particularly important for high frequency trading systems. Unfortunately, design and development of one-off hardware and software is costly and time-consuming. As prebuilt tools become more sophisticated, it will become more and more difficult to compare the performance of various components simply by reading their specifications. Tests must be developed that allow for comparison across multiple vendors. For example, the team may purchase a statistical package from a third-party vendor, but calculations may be different from their own, and assumptions may not be clearly defined. Doing the hard work of building benchmarks and a system that can be benchmarked against other people's assumptions certainly pays dividends.

Vendors who sell trading system components have a long history setting up their tests to show unrealistically high performance that may not be replicated in real usage. Vendors of course only report those tests that show their components in the best light. They also have been known to misrepresent the significance of underlying assumptions, again to show their products' best side under specific configurations.

We recommend that product teams establish benchmarks, and take claims regarding performance (particularly those provided by vendors themselves) with ample grains of salt unless the underlying assumptions are explicitly provided. According to ISO 9001:2000 clause 4.1: "Where an organization chooses to outsource any process that affects product conformity with requirements, the organization shall ensure control over such processes." Amanat Hussain adds that "the overhead of developing, supporting and enhancing an in-house system needs to be assessed against the cost, functionality, technology, flexibility, and the level of support available from third-party vendors." Trading and money management firms seeking to gain a competitive advantage understand that proprietary systems enable them to differentiate their trading/investment systems and that when buying third-party systems, platform compatibility and integration issues must be considered carefully.[3]

Technology benchmarks furthermore give developers the ability to measure performance attributes and make trade-offs in buy versus build decisions. For example, a benchmark could extract the key algorithms that contain the performance generating aspects of a system. Running the much smaller, prototyped benchmark can give clues about the vendor's assumptions and furthermore how to improve performance.

20.4. Hitting Deadlines

Development teams naturally want to discuss their elegant technology and the significant progress they are making. But, teams also need to frankly discuss development risks with both the product team and top management. Risk factors might involve cost and schedule overruns, technological feasibility issues, performance issues, or other factors that may cause the reality of the final implementation to be lower than expectations. Development team members may feel threatened by conversation that shines light on solutions that did not work or estimates they wish to reconsider. But, if both the development team and product team make project risk management a priority, discussion will be more fruitful. Teams that avoid defensiveness move forward faster and with their credibility intact.

Development projects sometimes get behind schedule. It is a fact of life in software development. But, top management and product teams expect timely delivery of technology, especially where the technology creates competitive advantage. This puts pressure on the development team. If deadlines must be met and the team is behind, the team can simplify the scope or designs or cut features.[4]

Sometimes unavoidable design decisions complicate the implementation of a feature, such as integration with legacy code or functionality, or support for multiple environments. In general, the team should always implement the simplest solution that meets requirements today. Planning too far ahead or too broadly can induce delays. Some development teams get bogged down designing robust architectures, portions of which may be irrelevant to the success of the trading system. Overdesigning and overbuilding are signs that the development team is unable to focus and prioritize features.

Sometimes, a specific feature may by implemented through a simple, alternative method that still solves the business purpose. For example, if a trader wants real-time, straight-through processing of trades, he may actually accept hourly batch processing. While the alternative solution may be suboptimal, the quicker implementation may speed up development and permit trading to start on schedule.

As a last resort, the development team may need to eliminate low priority features to satisfy a timebox deadline. This is why business priorities must be understood before each iteration. The development team may spend weeks working out a technically difficult problem that is relatively unimportant. They may spend even more time explaining why several simpler features with higher priorities are not done.

A development team spent several months building redundant and backup systems for real-time, market data feeds. A year behind schedule, they still had not yet programmed the algorithms for performance metrics. The customer's priority was working software and performing systems. Backup data feeds were a luxury that could wait till later versions. The firm missed a tremendous business opportunity.

The development team must communicate with the product team and top management about simplifications and proposed cuts as soon as possible. This will allow all interested parties to renegotiate priorities. In the end, the customer, that is, the product team, decides which features to defer. When its people involve others in tough decisions early, an organization can build mutual trust, respect, and confidence, rather than blame and adversial relationships.

20.5. LOOP 1: Document Software Requirements

The product team creates the SRS, the starting point for the development team. The SRS defines the functional and software quality attribute requirements needed by the product team. (Software quality attributes are defined in Chapter 2.)

Together the two teams agree upon a release plan. From then on, the agile development team plans, designs, builds, and tests the technological implementation of the trading/investment system. Before each loop, the development team should meet to plan features and tasks and schedules for the ensuing iteration. The first loop will design, build, and test the business tier. While we have devoted only one loop to this section, we fully expect and advocate that the tasks be broken down into many, smaller iterations.

20.6.   LOOP 2: Document Interface Requirements

Trading/investment systems bring together several disparate technologies that must work together, including:

- Relational databases.
- Real-time data feeds and FIX engines.
- Third-party APIs for execution, quant libraries, optimization, charting, and report generation.
- Internal connections to risk management and accounting software.
- Client-based graphical user interfaces and reports.

These disparate technologies, either proprietary or off-the-shelf, must be able to work together. Glue code makes interoperability happen.

20.7.   LOOP 3: Document Hardware and Network Requirements

The development team will base estimates of hardware and network capacity requirements for the trading/investment system on experience. Network facilities and support tools include:

- Front-end clients, database servers, network gateway servers, and peripherals.
- Network infrastructure, including cables, T1/T3 lines, hubs, routers, etc.
- TCP/IP, UDP, Tibco, etc.

As with software development, the development team assigns responsibilities to develop these facilities.

20.8.   Summary

The SRS is the foundation on which the architecture, design, and implementation of a trading/investment system are built. While prototypes have been created for most features, the team will encounter and address them one by one in an iterative fashion. An iterative approach to planning and development reduces uncertainties. In this case, the sources for the SRS are the completed documents and prototypes from previous stages: business rules, quantitative methods, data cleaning algorithms, performance requirements, system requirements, data maps, etc.

The push toward component-based software architectures means that many elements of the trading/investment system architecture may be purchased as commercial off-the-shelf (COTS) technology. Buy versus build decisions, and their trade-offs with functionality, should be viewed within the context of the trading/investment system's competitive advantage, development time, and expense. Furthermore, the product team should have in place processes for evaluating and benchmarking third-party components.

20.8.1. Best Practices

- Use agile methods to plan iterations, identifying project priorities and risks up front. Plan, design, code, and test collaboratively.

- Write, or rather assemble, a Software Requirements Specification to ensure proper communication between a product team and a development team.

- Establish controls over vendor components ahead of time.

- Build the hardware and network infrastructure last.

- Communicate progress of and risks to technology development to the product team and top management regularly.

CHAPTER • 21

Design System Architecture

Software and hardware design are the activity of transforming requirements into the technologically feasible solutions and selecting optimal architectures. Design is a search for the best technologies, the ones with attributes that will generate superior trading/investment performance. Design must be documented either with team-specific notations, or more formally with the Unified Modeling Language (UML) to view use cases, object models, and other components.

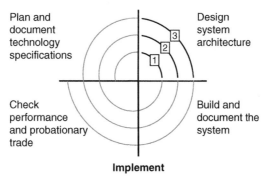

FIGURE 21-1

Unlike most software projects, in K|V the key business elements are already prototyped via Stages 1 and 2, and the key users have been involved in requirements gathering since the fuzzy front end. In Stage 3, the software engineers are free to focus their attention solely on technology design and not on requirements gathering. In this step, the development team translates requirements into feasible, high-level design alternatives. Good design practices will reduce development time, software errors, and bugs, as well as minimize the need for additional resources for refactoring and fixes later on; ample research proves that finding and fixing a software problem after delivery costs 100 times more than finding and fixing the problem during design. Good design up front is important because decisions may fix constraints for the life of the software, for example, the choice of programming language.

Traditional, sequential development methods force all design decisions to be made as early as possible, which causes the cost of changes to rise exponentially as development moves forward. The iterative development process we support allows the development team to delay crucial, constraint fixing decisions to as late as possible in the process, that is, an iterative process and benchmarked designs reduce project and operational risks.

21.1. Software Tiers

Most fully functioning trading/investment systems make use of a multitier architecture. Multitier designs promote modular software development with well-defined interfaces. The main advantage to multitier design is that it allows developers to replace or refactor any individual tier as needed without affecting the other tiers. A fully automated trading/investment system incorporates several separate tiers, or layers, in its architecture. We generalize these into three tiers.

- **Presentation tier.** This tier covers the user interfaces that contain presentations of real-time data, positions, performance metrics and controls for any dynamic inputs, and trading system on/off/shutdown states on a client computer. This tier also includes reporting mechanisms.

  A user interface enables traders to manage the working system intraday. For example, sector deltas may be on the user screen continuously so a trader can hedge manually in real time. Charts containing price data, time series of earnings, or dividends, may also be fed through the user interface. Some firms update the user interface with one minute VaR calculations.

  In the presentation tier, we also include mechanisms for printed or Web-based reports, including, for example, intraday and end-of-day batch reports. In these reports, junior-level analysts may scan data for errors, while traders or portfolio managers may review performance metrics or new information after hours or on the train the next morning when things are quiet and they can think more clearly.

- **Business tier.** This middle tier covers the business logic, that is, the trading/investment strategy, housed on an application server.

- **Data access tier(s).** This tier includes database interactions on a database server for historical data as well as connections to accounting and risk databases. This tier also includes real-time data feeds and trade execution processes on a gateway server(s).

Tiers provide a way of grouping different parts of the software architecture. For maintainability, it is generally advisable to store the business logic of the trading/investment system in separate objects and modules in the middle tier. Business logic that is unencumbered by type conversions, API connections, and database rules keeps the tier divisions clean. For reusability, it is important to segregate data access modules into distinct components.

A good design is easily adaptable to changes in the business logic or technology. Since no design can be infinitely flexible, a good design groups things that are likely to change together and hides them from the rest of the system. Changes then will only have a local impact. A good development process helps the team get the basics right, and then lets the details and new discoveries evolve. Successful teams nevertheless plan on regular refactoring to keep the architecture up to date.

Multitier architectures facilitate software design since each tier is built, tested, and run on its own separate platform. This allows the development team to program different tiers in different languages—the graphical user interface language for the top tier; C/C++, for the middle tier; and SQL for much of the database tier. Two widely recognized best practices for multitier implementations are that:

- Tiers should be agnostic of consumers. That is, the data tier should not know about or depend on the business logic tier that is using its services. Neither should the business tier depend on the presentation layer.

- Tiers should be independently testable, maintainable, and versioned. Preferably, each tier should be able to be tested independently, by simulating the behavior of the other tiers.

Finally, though the presentation layer may seem to be the least important layer (at least to the performance of the trading/investment strategy), particular attention should be paid to it. The product team's perception of the quality and integrity of the system as a whole will be greatly influenced by their perception of the user interface design.

21.2. Design Process

Software development is most naturally done through learning loops, identifying problems, and discovering best practice solutions through short iterations, including test design, software design, coding, unit testing, refactoring, and then improving the design as the system develops. This is the most effective way to rapidly acquire and apply new knowledge.

Design starts with domain analysis. During domain analysis the development team studies as completely as possible the features and users of the trading/investment system. The team leader is responsible for defining the vocabulary of the system and ensuring that programmers understand the application domain. Misunderstandings create problems. Domain-level analysis models the interactions of a trader, real-time and historical data, and the system software in use cases. (A use case is a scenario that illustrates how the system should interact with the users and real-time markets.) This necessarily involves communication between the development team and the product team, including iterative reviews and evaluations.

The development team later will add lower-level designs, but all business-related features will be validated against domain-level models. Modeling of both domain-level features and lower-level constructs should ensure that a design will solve the right problem and at the same time be effectively implementable in software.

Once the domain is understood, the iterative design process can be broken down into parts:

- **Decomposition.** Decompose problems into modules and relationships.
- **Test design.** Create test cases first, then design architecture.
- **Conceptual design.** Produce designs of modules. A team may create many alternative designs over several iterations.
- **Evaluation/Benchmarking.** Evaluate alternative architectures, called candidate designs, to arrive at a benchmark design. (The next step, K|V 3.3, will transform the design into software. The final software will implement the best practice design.)

As part of design processes, all engineering disciplines apply abstraction to reduce complexity. Within each level of abstraction, the team can perceive two views—dynamic and static. A dynamic view shows the interactions between modules or objects, and a static view shows the structure. Apart from structuring design, abstraction can also form the backbone of documentation of the system. User documentation can address domain-level requirements, whereas the software architecture document addresses conceptual designs.

21.2.1.   Decomposition

In decomposition, the team reduces complexity by constructing a set of independent abstractions to describe the system, separating functionalities into components that have defined interfaces. This way the development team first views the system as a single component within some physical environment and then works from the top down into the individual tiers. Modules form the highest-level decomposition view of a tier's static structure. The high-level architecture can be shown as a set of interconnected modules or components. At this phase, the internal mechanisms and objects that comprise modules and components are irrelevant.

During decomposition, the dynamic views depict the behavior of the system; for example, how the historical and real-time data feeds in, how the system processes the data, and how the data flows out of the system. Whereas domain analysis modeled the real-world abstractions, this phase models the abstractions as they are to be represented inside the system.

With respect to performance, as a development team decomposes a design, the team often gives each component a budget for execution time and memory space. Changes that improve performance may make the program harder to work with and can slow development. We recommend the team write tunable software first, then tune it for speed. That is, we recommend the team ignore performance until a later optimization loop. Nevertheless, well-factored code will give a development team more time to spend on performance tuning.

21.2.2.   Test Design

Test-driven development requires that the team design unit tests prior to coding. Fortunately, the product team has already created test cases for the trading/investment strategy, execution, and data cleaning algorithms over the course of Stages 1 and 2, so the development team should not need to design new tests before coding. For user interfaces and data integration modules, the development should design unit test cases prior to coding.

We believe in test-driven development and tests require plans. While quality assurance testing will occur in Step 4 of this stage, we assume in this step that programmers are employing code reviews and test-driven development, where:

- **Unit tests** verify the correctness of every single method of every single object and module.
- **Integration tests** verify unit tested software modules as a group.
- **System tests** verify that the complete system complies with the specified requirements.

Tests should be designed and written first, and this forces a new perspective. The programmer develops each object from the perspective of a consumer of that object's services, making the object's interface as important as its function. By writing test cases first, the team forces the software to be testable. Writing test cases depends on a good design document, a good requirements document, and a good development team leader, who budgets sufficient time (likely 30–40% of coding time) for proper testing.

Testing should consist of a cohesive collection that attempts to cause failure under controlled conditions. Ideally, testing will commence with the same toolsets that will be used live and for this reason many exchanges and third-party vendors offer a simulated trading environment. However, the order matching (i.e., fill characteristics) will likely be significantly different from those experienced during live trading.

Writing tests is a form of documentation. Test cases used to test prototypes in K|V 1.4 should be used to test corresponding implementations in this step. Regression tests against the results of tests in K|V 1.4 will verify correctness of the coded implementations.

21.2.3. Conceptual Design

During conceptual design, the development team analyzes decomposed problems, experiments with possible solutions, and creates a set of candidate architectures, which they can further analyze and evaluate. The design step focuses on refining the description and selecting from among alternative designs, potentially using a UML package and class diagrams with dependency associations. An architectural design becomes a blueprint, that is, a technical description of a system that can be looked at and criticized. The development team categorizes these perspectives on designs into views:

- **Logical view.** Defines the software tiers and major abstractions that perform the system functionalities.
- **Object view.** A view of the classes and their composition into components and modules.
- **Data view.** Defines the design structure of the persistent data.
- **Data flow view.** A way of looking at the relationships between components.
- **Concurrency view.** A view of processes and threads and how they communicate with each other and interact on shared resources.
- **Physical, or deployment, view.** A description of the system's hardware resources and network topology.

During conceptual design, some coding of prototypes or stubs may take place. Often, a team will build a skeleton of the system as a proof of concept. This skeleton may serve as the basis for further development during the following step.

21.2.4. Evaluation

The goal of Stage 3, Step 2 is to arrive at best-of-breed technologies, the hardware and software that best satisfy the prioritized quality attribute requirements. Design evaluation is where the development team analyzes candidate technologies and designs as soon as they are stable, but before the team makes any real commitment to development.

Evaluation allows the development team to argue benefits and problems with designs while they are cheap and easy to address. A design evaluation should answer two questions: is the proposed design suitable and which of the competing designs is the best?

The Software Engineering Institute has developed methods for evaluating software architectures. Most appropriate for the purposes of trading/investment system development is the Architecture Tradeoff Analysis Method (ATAM). The ATAM for architecture evaluation should reveal the ability of a particular architecture to meet quality attribute requirements. A full-blown ATAM meeting consists of nine steps:

1. **Present the ATAM.** The leader describes the ATAM steps.
2. **Present the business drivers.** A reiteration and discussion of the business goals defined in the Money Document and software quality attributes. We believe that everyone should come to the ATAM meeting having read the Money Document and the Stage 2/Gate 2 documents.
3. **Present the architecture.** A review of any business logic and data objects that were created for Stage 2. These objects may or may not be used in the final architecture. If the objects are unusable or unscalable, the development team will create new objects.
4. **Identify the architectural approaches.**
5. **Generate the quality attribute utility tree.** Using high priority scenarios, or use cases, the software quality attributes are ranked.
6. **Analyze the architectural approaches.** During this step, risks and trade-offs are discussed.
7. **Brainstorm and prioritize scenarios.** Create a large set of use cases and prioritize them in a Delphi framework.
8. **Analyze architectural approaches.** Retest to confirm results from Step 7.
9. **Present the results.**[1]

Now, regular, full scale evaluations of this type can be burdensome. For speed, we recommend "quicker and dirtier" evaluations of architectural decisions made during the most recent iteration. Once a fixed architecture is proposed, a full-blown ATAM meeting should take place. Once the architecture is complete, the team must document it and be sure to update the documentation as designs evolve. The product team should check the progress of documentation at iteration meetings. Developers must have all documentation updated before providing demonstrations at the completion of each iteration.

21.2.4.1.   Benchmarking COTS

One key component of the architecture is the identification of which components will be purchased commercially, which will be reused from internal sources, and which will be created from scratch. The project's approach to reuse affects the rest of the software's design, and so it should be defined at architecture time. If the development team prefers to base an application on a COTS package, for example, the rest of the software will need to be designed around that framework. Reuse of existing, benchmarked components saves time and money. Buying components saves time, but platform compatibility and integration issues may be significant.[2] Run-off tests will verify that a vendor's software package can produce the appropriate data or calculations within tolerances. One problem, though, is that a vendor may change some assumptions or models without our knowledge in later versions or updates.

The overhead of developing, supporting, and enhancing an in-house system needs to be assessed against the cost, functionality, technology, flexibility, and the level of support available from third-party vendors. An important consideration as trading and money management firms seek to gain a competitive advantage through technological innovation is that in-house systems are proprietary and the firm will be able to differentiate its strategies and technologies from competitors. Where a firm chooses to outsource any process that affects conformity with specification requirements, the development team must demonstrate control over such processes.

The development team should not limit its reuse considerations to source code; they should also consider how to reuse data, detailed designs, test cases, plans, documentation, and even design processes.

21.3. Software Architecture Document

The SAD is the project blueprint. A SAD contains all of the items that a software engineer will need to design and build a product. The main benefit of producing a SAD is that it forces the prototype and the software engineer to formally address key items such as calculations, GUI, and reports prior to starting the development and implementation of the trading system software. Since many of the key items of a project get revised regularly as the details get flushed out with prototypes, it is important that the research and backtesting done in earlier stages be fully documented in light of the SAD to come.

SADs can get large and unwieldy. Because of their potentially large size and complexity, SADs are best decomposed into smaller and simpler documents, subvolumes documenting the architecture at different tiers. Every architecture decision should be documented with an associated rationale. The contents of a SAD should be:

    I. Introduction
       A. Purpose
       B. Scope
       C. Definitions, acronyms, and abbreviations
       D. References
       E. Overview
   II. Architectural representation
  III. Architectural goals and constraints
  IV. Use-case view
       A. Use-case realizations
    V. Logical view
       A. Architecturally significant design packages
  VI. Process view
 VII. Deployment view
VIII. Implementation, or tier views
  IX. Data view
   X. Size and performance
  XI. Quality attribute requirements

The team should also document unit tests and objects early in the software design process so that junior-level programmers can start building the GUIs, databases, and reports. Unfortunately, many programmers believe that documentation of objects should come after the software is complete, and furthermore that someone else should do it. Programmers enhance job security by avoiding documentation. If a system becomes profitable, the programmers that built it, but avoided documenting it, will want raises. After all, they are the only ones who understand how it works. At such a point, the firm has two choices: either make the programmers partners, or hire even pricier programmers to reverse engineer the system.

We recommend the product team call weekly documentation review meetings until the initial object documents are complete. Developers have less leverage early in the process. Programmers who avoid documenting tasks should be removed from the development team. The financial engineers should audit documentation to ensure that it is properly done.

21.4. High Frequency Trading Systems

High frequency trading systems are event-driven software applications (EDAs) that require message-oriented middleware. Unlike traditional applications, which follow their own program flow, event-driven programs react to external events, in our case, to events that occur on electronic exchanges—changes in bid and ask prices and ladder volumes and trades. EDAs rely on event loops, to look repeatedly for new data. When new data arrives, the kernel calls back the program which executes an event handler function. Programming the business tier of a high frequency trading system is a matter of writing the event handlers that gather the new information and make trading decisions. Real-time trading systems must deliver the right answers in the right order and at the right time. To meet these objectives the software must have deterministic behavior. It must perform correctly and on time.

As a quality attribute, performance represents the responsiveness of the system measured by either the time required to respond to an event or by the number of events that can be processed in a fixed time. Typically a performance requirement is expressed as a number of transactions per unit of time or the length of time required to complete a single transaction. Some aspects of performance are architectural and many performance problems stem from the architectural design decisions. A performance bottleneck that can be traced to a single, isolated code routine can be easily fixed.

Performance is the driving factor in architectural designs for high frequency systems and is partially a function of how much communication and interaction occurs among system components. Performance can be modeled at the architectural level in terms of arrival rates and distributions of service requests, processing times, queue sizes, and latency. With the price/performance ratio of hardware dropping and the cost of software development rising, longer-term, less arbitrage-oriented strategies are moving to the forefront.

21.5. LOOP 1: Design Business Rules Packages

The product team may have already converted some of the business logic prototyped in Stage 1 into C++, Java, or .NET code objects in Stage 2. This code can be used in the production system. Where this has occurred, the development team need not spend extra time and resources redesigning and reprogramming those features. This code may comprise most or all of the business layer. Regression testing in Stage 2 should have already ensured its correctness and the product team should have fully documented the architecture of these components for review by the development team and inclusion in the Stage 2 deliverable documents.

The development team should append the data dictionary started in Stage 2, creating an entry for each class, including attributes, methods, and scope. We recommend creating object models quickly and analyzing the life cycle of each class. Further, programmers should consider which use cases lead to an instance of each class and which cause changes or destruction. The programmers should also update the data flow maps to include flow of message between objects and methods calls using collaboration diagrams.

21.6. LOOP 2: Design Interface Packages

In a multitier architecture, the business tier is generally a middleware application, communicating with data and presentation tiers running on other machines across a network of (potentially disparate) platforms. (Typical developers create middleware as a publish/subscribe system, where sources publish data to the entire network and consumers of the data subscribe to messages.) Fortunately, a database design document, data maps, and data flow maps have to a large extent been documented in Stage 2, which will speed the design of the code that connects the business logic, that is, the trading engine, to other packages.

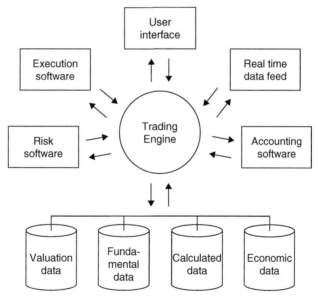

FIGURE 21-2

Message-oriented middleware is a client/server architecture that increases the interoperability, portability, and flexibility of an application by allowing the application to be distributed over multiple platforms. It reduces the complexity of developing applications that span multiple operating systems and network protocols by insulating the developer from the details of the various operating system and network interfaces and APIs. Message-oriented middleware typically supports asynchronous calls between the client and server applications, enabling applications to communicate without having to understand the technology of the other application within the network.

21.7.   LOOP 3: Design Network Architecture

A trading/investment system is implemented as a network of nodes, each node config-
ured with hardware and software. The three software layers in the logical view (presentation, business, and data) are coded and deployed onto these nodes. Software designers,
however, need to understand the physical layer, too, in order to decrease latency, improve
speed, and avoid network bottlenecks.

Computer speed has usually been defined in terms of MHz or GHz (cycles per second), though a computer with higher MHz rating may not necessarily have faster speed.
Manufacturers now measure speed in terms of MHz and processor cache. More speed and
more cache make for faster processing. Memory, bus speeds, and the quality of the written
code will also influence processing speed.

Latency is how long it takes to complete a process. Throughput is the amount of work
done per unit of time. Interrupt latency is the guaranteed maximum response time of the system to an event. There are trade-offs among different design choices: adding cache usually
increases latency (which is bad) but makes throughput better. As you can imagine, computers
that run automated trading/investment systems need low interrupt latencies—a real-time trading strategy may lose money if market data is not analyzed within a specified amount of time.

Benchmarking hardware and network technology should take all these factors into
account by measuring the time a computer takes to run through a series of test programs.
As we have seen with other vendor-supplied technology, some vendors optimize their
products to execute specific tests quickly to meet a benchmark. The same system may not
perform as well in a different environment.

Nevertheless, a new system will likely involve new hardware. This means software
designers will need to develop programs to interface with the physical level. A system cannot
be fully tested until the hardware is benchmarked and ready, but concurrent development of
hardware and software is usually a recipe for long development cycles. We recommend that
designing a network architecture should be performed using an ATAM process, including:

- Review specifications and quality attributes requirements of the network.
- Predictions of network traffic.
- Location and types of terminals, servers, and their required protocols.
- Technical specifications and pricing of vendors' products.
- Documentation of the network design.

21.8.   Summary

Technology design transforms requirements into the technologically feasible solutions
and selects optimal architectures. It is a search for the technologies that will generate
superior trading/investment performance. We recommend test-driven development, where
tests are designed first, prior to design and development of a three-tier (or n-tier) architecture—business tier, data access tier, presentation tier.

An iterative process of decomposition, test design, conceptual design, and evaluation/
benchmarking should enable a development team to build the technology to specification
and meet the technology quality attribute requirements efficiently. Given the short life
cycles of hardware and network components, we recommend network design come last.
Lastly, we recommend the use of the ATAM method for evaluation when possible, and
creation of a software architecture document as a primary deliverable for Gate 3.

21.8.1. Best Practices

- Ensure that all developers understand the domain and its vocabulary before designing software.
- Use decomposition processes to break down the high-level requirement into workable modules.
- Establish a standardized methodology for evaluation of alternative architectures and benchmark internal and external technologies.
- Design test cases prior to coding.
- Create a Software Architecture Document.

CHAPTER ◆ 22

Build and Document the System

Finally, construction and testing of the automated portions of the trading/investment system are ready to begin. While some trading systems are fully automated, many consist of varying components—tools and reporting processes—that are automated. Whatever the case, Step 3 consists of construction of the software components as well as the hardware and network infrastructure, transforming the designs laid out in the system architecture documents into real technology. The objective is to produce high quality components that implement the system's competitive advantage as well as its quality attributes.

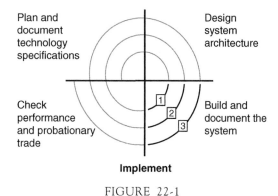

FIGURE 22-1

By the time the project reaches this step, the groundwork for success has already been laid. From here, all that is required is proper execution, that is, sticking to the fundamentals. The idea of construction is to build something every day, even if it is only a very small piece. At the end of each day, a compile can take place followed by automated unit tests. If the software compiles and the tests pass, the developers have been synchronized. This is an ambitious schedule, but the logic is that more frequent compiling provides better, more immediate feedback. Steve McConnell in his book *Rapid Development* lists the following construction fundamentals:

- Coding practices, such as variable and function naming, and documenting code.
- Data-related concepts, such as scope, persistence, and binding time.
- Guidelines for using specific types of data, such as integers, enums, and pointers.
- Control-related concepts, such as using conditionals and loops, and controlling complexity.
- Assertions and other code-centered error-detection practices.
- Rules for packaging code into routines, modules, classes, and files.
- Unit-testing and debugging practices.
- Integration strategies.
- Code-tuning strategies and practices.
- The ins and outs of the programming language.
- Use of construction tools, such as development environments, source-code control, and code libraries.[1]

Good fundamentals mandate code documentation. Further, the development team must produce a user manual. These are best produced along the way rather than at the end. Together, these documents will allow a junior trader to operate the system and a junior programmer to maintain it. (Of course, since trading/investment systems are proprietary, complete user and code documentation should not include sensitive information.)

The team also needs to update other documents started in previous stages. The data maps continue to grow to clearly show the calculation of each data field and where it came from and where it is used. As development progresses, the product team may request additional user interfaces or reporting features. GUI documentation will grow to include a screen shot of each form, the data item displayed in each field, and a data map that maps the data back to a calculation, data table, or data feed. The development team should also document error handling mechanisms, including a discussion of all known issues that have been addressed.

In the end, following good construction and documentation fundamentals is good operational risk management as well as a time-saving practice. Good coding and good documentation improve predictability and control over implementing trading/investment systems and increase the odds of delivering on time and under budget.[2]

22.1. Programming Considerations

Generally, we recommend business logic objects and modules be broken down in an instrument-centric fashion, that is, starting from the tradable instruments. A futures contract is a tradable instrument, as is a stock or an option. All of these can be objects in a program. (OOP enables the developer to organize large programs logically and perform very large and complex tasks with fewer lines of code.)

A simple abstracted instrument class may look like the following:

TABLE 22-1

Nouns	Description
Symbol	The ticker symbol or CUSIP (unique identifier) of the instrument.
Bid	The highest bid price.
Ask	The lowest ask price.
Last Trade Price	The price at which the last trade was executed.
Last Trade Qty	The quantity of the last trade.
Bid Qty	The volume on the bid price in the exchange order book.
Ask Qty	The volume on the ask price in the exchange order book.
Expiration	The date of the expiration of the instrument, if any.

Verbs	Description
Enter Order	Sends an order to the exchange.
Cancel Order(s)	Sends a request to the exchange to cancel an order or orders.

Developers can create instances of instruments and collections of instruments or, more appropriately, portfolios of instruments, to build the business logic layer in a manner that is logically and structurally equivalent to reality. An instrument class will allow developers to connect to electronic exchanges via APIs. (In the class definitions, a singleton may in fact perform the asynchronous connection to a gateway server.)

Asynchronous messages are sent and received to and from a computer's queue in separate processes. An application using asynchronous communication can send a message to a queue and immediately go on to other tasks without waiting for a reply. In synchronous communication, on the other hand, the sender of a message must wait an indeterminate amount of time for a response from the receiver before continuing. Sockets manage both synchronous and asynchronous communications of messages. As you can imagine, synchronous sockets, which make use of multithreading, are generally not preferable in trading applications, which use networks heavily for price updates and order routing. Rather, asynchronous sockets that do not suspend processing while waiting for network operations are a better choice.

While message queues can provide temporary storage of data when the destination program is busy or disconnected, real-time trading systems generally have little or no use for old data and so message expirations are essential. Because message-oriented middleware (and business logic tiers are often message-oriented middleware) is stateless, in many cases if a server is not connected, the middleware will be unaware unless there is some process that monitors the state of the connection periodically.

Multithreading allows a program to perform multiple blocks of code concurrently, or in parallel, and developers can use them to, for example, communicate asynchronously over a network or with a database, perform time-consuming calculations, or to distinguish between operations with different priorities. High priority threads can be used to manage real-time data feeds and calculations while low priority ones can be used to perform less critical tasks. In general, however, while multithreading is advantageous, fewer threads are still better than more. Managing multiple threads can eat up a large amount of processor time and create new problems. Namely, multithreading can create conflicts between threads that are trying to use the same resource. In order to make our multithreaded programs safe, we may have to control access to different resources or blocks of code or objects, a process called synchronization. Incorrect synchronization of resources can create deadlocks or race conditions. (A deadlock happens when two threads stop responding because each is waiting for the other to finish. A race condition happens when abnormal events or results are generated due to an unknown dependence between events in different threads.)

22.2. Database Connections

SQL statements that trading/investment systems are most often concerned with are those that retrieve data, although at times they also need to write, change, or delete data in a database. SQL statements are simply groups of those words logically arranged to pull specific data from the data source or manipulate the data in the data source. Computer programs can send SQL messages to a database in their code, but things called stored procedures are preferable.

Precompiled stored procedures are a faster way (executionwise) to construct logic that would otherwise be coded in the business tier, because they are actually stored in the database. Applications can call the stored procedures directly rather than sending multiple SQL messages one at a time and waiting for the results.

22.3. Refactoring

Well-written, or "well-factored," code is simple, easy to maintain, suitable, and has no extraneous features. Nevertheless, later improvements will often be necessary, especially in complex, performance-driven systems where not all the facts are well understood at design time. Suboptimal choices are an intrinsic part of the process of engineering complex designs in the real world. Refactoring may also be needed where new user interface or reporting features are requested by the product team. Sometimes it takes five or six tries to get a module right. Great designs evolve. Even great software and great trading/investment systems must be continuously improved over time.

Refactoring means changing code and object organization. When changes are made, regression tests must be used to ensure that the new code works the same way as the old. And regression testing is performed, in part, using unit tests. Generally, software engineers start with something that works and improve the low-level design. Once the riskiest objects are built, the rest of the programming will just be a step-by-step grind through the Software Architecture Document. Where refactoring is necessary, the development team can augment the SAD as new and better knowledge and features are added.

To optimize code, a software engineer should follow approved policies and procedures. Generally, a programmer starts by running the program under a profiler that monitors execution and indicates where algorithms and objects are consuming time and memory space, called hot spots. Then the programmer focuses on those hot spots and applies optimization techniques. After each step, the software engineer will compile, retest, and rerun the profiler. If performance has not improved, he can back out the change or make new changes. This process of finding and removing hot spots can continue until performance satisfies the requirement for the performance quality attribute.[3]

22.3.1. Code Reviews

During code reviews, development team members systematically review coded units. (Some firms choose to use pair programming as an alternative to individual coding with reviews.) There are even tools to automate parts of the review process. Some development teams, though, skimp on code reviews and walkthroughs. Just like in K|V 1.4, a decision to ignore review techniques that are proven to find defects is tantamount to a conscious decision to postpone corrections until later, when they will be more expensive and time-consuming to fix. While formal code reviews can be time-consuming, more informal review processes, such as pair programming, still yield excellent results. Whatever the case, preventing or detecting and removing defects early in this step yields significant schedule benefits. We recommend developing a lightweight code review process and integrating it into development. Formal software reviews should be conducted at the completion of each software layer to identify problems.

22.4. LOOP 1: Program Business Rules Packages

In Loop 1, the development team programs the business layer according to the designs of the previous step. As we have said, the product team may have already converted some of the trading/investment algorithms prototyped in Stage 1 into code over the course of Stage 2. This code can be used in the production system. Where this has occurred, the development team should not need to spend extra time reprogramming and retesting these features; regression testing should have already ensured correctness. Furthermore, the product team should have fully documented the architecture of these components.

Where the development team does need to convert a prototype from one implementation, say in Excel, to code over this stage, the development team must perform regression testing against Stage 1 results to ensure that errors are detected and fixed. Conversion often creates problems. Hopefully, experienced product team members will have designed prototypes in such a way so as to ease the conversion process. In the worst case, conversion becomes a reverse engineering project by programmers who may or may not understand the underlying finance theory or trading/investment strategy. A common programming error at this point is changing data cleaning algorithms. A programmer may try to enhance these algorithms, failing to understand that a revision of input data requires a new backtest, a reversion to Stage 2. A complete regression test of the Stage 2 cleaning algorithms against the real-time implementations is critical. The development team should also discuss shutdown criteria due to bad, or too much, data with the product team to ensure that these algorithms do not affect the performance characteristics from the backtest.

White box, gray box, and black box unit testing, also performed by software engineers, will validate the smallest testable parts of their code. (In object-oriented programming, the smallest unit is the class.) For correct unit testing, each test case must be independent from other cases. Traditionally, a unit test should never go beyond a class. But, unit testing on classes alone is not sufficient. Just because the objects and methods are working correctly, does not necessarily mean that they work together to correctly form working modules. For our purposes, the term unit testing consists of testing each class, as well as related objects that comprise modules. (This approach will evolve into what is called bottom-up integration testing in Loop 2.) Unit tests may be either performed manually or in an automated fashion. Manual unit testing should follow approved unit testing policies and procedures. The team should keep records and results of the tests.

As one might imagine, version control is essential. If a new version fails a test that a previous version passed, version control software should be able to provide a list of changes in the new version. Automated testing tools will run tests and document results. In either case, good unit testing should force discipline and motivate the development team to stick to good fundamentals. A common approach to speeding up automated unit testing is to only simulate time-consuming operations.

Unit tests will not find every problem, however. Unit testing will not uncover higher-level integration errors, such as data flow problems. Say, for example, that when a trade confirmation is received, unit tests may not guarantee that it will be entered into the accounting database or the risk engine. Such data flow will require more sophisticated integration tests.

22.4.1.   Exception Handling

All trading/investment systems must be designed to handle unforeseen problems, that is, exception handling. If COTS packages are brought in, their quality must be assessed. Claims are regularly made concerning the benefits of using one operating system over another. Yet users of such systems often experience unpredictable behavior, including system hang-ups. Could this really be trusted for a real-time trading system that drives the firm's bottom line?

Where no recovery action is possible, a trading/investment system can be put into a fail-safe mode or condition. Or, the system could keep working, but with reduced service. This may reduce response times or permit servicing only of good elements of the system. This offers a sort of graceful shutdown—or, fault tolerant operation—where full and safe performance is maintained in the presence of faults.

Trading/investment systems that use real-time data and/or automate execution must be designed with safety in mind, and be concerned with the consequences of failure. Fail-safe systems make no effort to meet normal operational requirements. Instead they aim to limit the danger or damage caused by fault. For high frequency systems, software may need to discard any commands not complete within a certain timeframe.

22.5.   LOOP 2: Program Interface Packages

In Loop 2, the development team programs the presentation and data interface layers according to the designs of the previous step. Interfaces to the business layer include: the graphical use interface; database interfaces for price, valuation, calculated, fundamental, and economic data; real-time data interfaces for price updates and order execution; and interfaces to external systems for accounting and risk management. Glue code is computer programming code that is written to interface between disparate proprietary modules and commercial off-the-shelf applications. Objects and modules comprising these layers must also be subjected to unit testing, but integration of the business tier with these other tiers will require black box integration testing.

Integration testing takes unit tested objects and modules and applies tests defined in an integration test plan. Integration testing should verify that the software's quality attributes meet requirements, including functional, performance, and reliability requirements. Test cases, both successes and error cases, will likely be simulated, where use of shared data areas and interprocess communication is tested and individual subsystems are exercised through their interfaces. Test cases are constructed to test that all components interact correctly. Integration testing will include:

- COTS integration tests of two or more COTS components to determine if they contain any interface defects. For example, order management software and FIX engine.
- Database integration tests to determine if the software components interface properly with the database(s).

Any conditions not stated in specified integration tests, outside of the confirmation of the execution of design items, will generally not be tested. Integration testing concludes with multiple tests of the completed software, preferably in market and data scenarios that mimic those the system will encounter in real trading.

22.6. LOOP 3: Buy/Build Network Infrastructure Components

In Loop 3, the development team buys and/or builds the hardware and network infrastructure components, the physical layer of the system, according to the designs of Step 2. Now, hardware changes quickly. So, given that trading/investment system development may take several months to complete, hardware available in K|V Stage 1, or even in Loop 1 of this stage, may be outdated by the time development is complete. For this reason, we recommend hardware and network development come last.

Using a three tier, or three layer, architecture—presentation, business, data access—is an effective, distributed client/server design that provides performance, flexibility, maintainability, reusability, and scalability. The business tier server accomplishes this by centralizing process logic. Centralized process logic makes administration and change management easier by localizing system functionality so that changes must only be written once and placed on the middle tier server to be available throughout the systems. In addition, the middle process management tier controls transactions and asynchronous queueing to ensure reliable completion of transactions. Connectivity between tiers can be updated for changes requested by the product team or necessary to comply with new quality attribute requirements.

After the physical layer is complete, the development team can conduct integration and black box system tests on the complete system to evaluate the system's compliance with the Software Requirements Specification and the quality attribute requirements. Before full system tests are run, additional integration tests should be performed, including:

- Hardware integration tests of two or more hardware components on a single platform to induce failures in interfaces.
- System integration testing of two or more components distributed across multiple platforms.
- Performance tests of hardware and software against its performance requirements under normal operating circumstances to identify inefficiencies and bottlenecks.
- Stress tests to cause failures under extreme but valid conditions (e.g., heavy volume (i.e., fast markets), slow fills, extreme price movements).

System testing takes into account all of the integrated and tested software components as well the software itself integrated in a hardware and network environment, and seeks to detect defects within the system as a whole. (System testing makes sure the software and hardware are working right, not whether the trading system makes money.)

During system testing, the development team should throw everything possible at the system, up to and beyond the bounds defined in the requirements specification. In the end, system testing is important, but its limits must be recognized. Design flaws can often be picked up early on by running the program in an emulated environment. Most testing is done by simulation of the environment, but it is difficult to provide realistic test exercises (can we simulate all possible price changes in markets? Including extreme cases and gaps?). Furthermore, it is difficult to predict and simulate all failure modes of the system; and hardware failures can complicate things. System testing is the final test undertaken by the development team before the product team engages in user acceptance testing.

22.7. Summary

Any trading/investment system will consist of proprietary and off-the-shelf components. New software should be unit tested; components that work together should be integration tested; and the completed software and hardware implementation should be system tested. Code reviews are critical for finding and fixing bugs.

Every software module has three functions: its intended functionality, its ability to change, and its communication to the consumer of its services. Test-driven development should ensure both interfaces and functionalities are emphasized. Since all trading systems and all code will likely change over the lifetime, sound coding and documentation practices are critical. It is the responsibility of programmers to make sure that such changes are as simple as possible to make. Developers unfamiliar with the module should be able to read and understand code documentation without undue mental gymnastics.

22.7.1. Best Practices

- Plan and conduct unit, integration, and system tests.
- Use instrument-centric OOP and stored procedures where possible.
- Refactor, refactor, refactor.
- Document code thoroughly while coding, not at the end.
- Stick to the fundamentals.

CHAPTER • 23

Check Performance and Probationary Trade

The product team must be confident that the development team has built the hardware and software in a quality manner. The product team can accomplish this through independent verification and validation; the term quality assurance (QA) generally refers to these activities. Systematic auditing of both the development process and the developed products will ensure that development has been done properly and that the software and hardware components meet specifications and quality attribute requirements. QA processes naturally escalate development issues to the product team level, forcing a constructive dialog with the development team, a critical determinant of success. That is, QA does not create quality, but it does measure it.

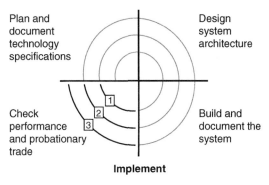

FIGURE 23-1

QA does not prescribe a set of procedures, only that they be created and followed. The product team, who after all is accountable for the performance of the working trading/investment system, must be confident that the development team:

- Designed components and evaluated alternative implementations.
- Benchmarked various technologies.
- Properly conducted buy versus build comparisons.

213

- Documented the rationale for design decisions.
- Planned and conducted unit, integration, and system tests.
- Documented test results and followed issue resolution procedures.

The product team members now expand their roles to oversee their respective areas of expertise. Each product team member is now in charge of testing the trading/investment system, that is, they are the domain experts/managers for quality assurance in their own area. The financial engineers manage quality assurance of business tier software. The traders from the product team perform quality assurance of the GUI, integration control and reports, as well as run user-acceptance tests. The marketing person from the product team can write and/or review the user documentation for the system. At the completion of Stage 3, however, the whole product team is nevertheless accountable for the success of the entire system.

23.1. Quality Assurance

Quality assurance (QA) by the product team should prove that development processes are being performed properly, and that the software and hardware products will satisfy specifications and quality attribute requirements. To this end, the product team should monitor the development team's processes for conformance to plans and product for conformance to specifications. The main objective of QA after each loop is to ensure that the product is ready to proceed with the next phase of development.

Periodic audits, that is, at the end of each iteration, are a key technique used to operationalize QA. The product team should plan these audits in advance to be systematic. The first products audited should be the development team's iteration plans and documentation, and a comparison of the actual steps carried out with those in the documented plans. One purpose of an audit is to verify that the development team's status reports accurately reflect the status of development. QA reviews plans and provides a mechanism for follow-up on nonconformities.

QA assures that the development team performs formal software testing, such as unit, integration, and system testing, in accordance with plans and procedures. The documentation review includes test plans, test specifications, test procedures, and test reports. Furthermore, good QA monitors code reviews, inspections, and walkthroughs. In this role, the product team oversees, participates in as needed, and verifies that the development team conducts and documents code reviews properly. In summary, QA encompasses any and all audits and tests necessary to provide adequate confidence that the trading/investment system will perform satisfactorily in service, including auditing design development and testing processes. The ultimate goal of QA is to ensure a trading/investment system will pass an SAS 70 audit.

This includes auditing activities of the development team from planning to design, to building software and hardware, including documentation of:

- Release plans.
- Iteration plans and timebox schedules.
- Buy versus build decisions.
- Processes for benchmarking designs and evaluations.
- Status of all deliverable items.

All approved designs and software should be placed under configuration management, which is accurate with respect to the numbering or naming protocols of executable programs, software modules, software units, and associated documents. Software development libraries must provide for proper handling of code and documentation from their initial approval until they have been incorporated into the final version.

QA should also include auditing of the test results of individual units, modules, and components, and integration of modules and the system as a whole. QA assures that:

- Test procedures truly follow test plans and that these procedures are verifiable.
- Tests are conducted on the correct version of software.
- Changes to code are made properly, and that no unauthorized changes are made.
- Nonconformities discovered during testing are recorded and that procedures to address nonconformities are followed.
- Regression testing is conducted to assure nonconformities have been corrected. (This is to say that resolution of all nonconformities must take place prior to Step 4. QA is not debugging.)
- Test reports are correct and complete.

Lastly, QA will include regression testing of the outputs of the trading/investment system against gold standard, black box results experienced in Stage 2.

Tools exist to assist the QA process and the product team should evaluate its need for proprietary tools versus those available off the shelf. Useful tools include QA audit and inspection checklists as well as automated code screens, reports, and calculation testers.

23.2. LOOP 1: Test against Black Box Results from Stage 2

Over the course of Loop 1, the development team has built and tested the business layer of the trading/investment system. To ensure that this layer correctly implements the quantitative methods and business logic designed over the course of Stage 1 and 2, the financial engineers perform regression testing using static data. Validation of the business layer will demonstrate the ability of the system to achieve the planned results, that is, to do what it is supposed to do.

QA regression tests take known data (i.e., data used during K|V 2.4) and known model inputs for calculations. The financial engineer leads QA regression testing and makes sure the tests are done to specification, mapping inputs to outputs. For example, the financial engineers may run 100 products and five years of data through the production software to verify that all inputs lead to all the correct outputs. If the outputs are not identical, the team will have to hunt down the differences. A normal source of difference is in rounding algorithms. Rounding algorithms in C++ of COTS components may not match the rounding algorithms in Excel or MATLAB. All differences in rounding algorithms, interpolation algorithms, and precision tolerances in optimization should be investigated with a documented conclusion. The financial engineers should keep a list of known differences and their causes for future discussion with the product team or top management. Depending on those causes, they may or may not need to run additional regression tests, say for 1002170 instruments and ten years.

A QA test of the business layer should regress the mean returns, standard deviations of returns, Sharpe ratios, etc., and range of the time series of outputs using SPC. Using historical data, the SPC charts from Stage 2 and Stage 3 should be nearly identical. The stability of the system using prototypes must be very, very similar to that using the production software if the system is to pass Gate 3.

23.3.   LOOP 2: Test Data and Graphical User Interfaces

In Loop 2, the development team has built and tested the presentation and data interface layers. Now the traders and financial engineers, along with a risk manager, will perform QA for validation and verification of the GUIs, integration, and reports. The traders should run live data examples between prototypes and the coded implementation using regression. To accomplish this task, the traders will need, say, 1000 snapshots of real data in the correct format. The traders can run this data through the system to make sure GUIs and graphs and reports are running properly.

Auditing the presentation and data interface layers and the development team's integration testing will uncover data mapping issues, error handling issues, data cleaning issues, and anything unexpected using real-time data. Using inputs and outputs, the traders test:

- GUIs by changing user-defined data, or putting in error/boundary conditions. Does the system catch it and respond correctly?
- Reports through interactive testing using scenarios. Are reports coming out correctly? Are the graphs and colors right? Does printing work right?
- Data integration to search for truncation errors. What happens if a bond has a name longer than 20 characters. Does it get truncated? What happens if the portfolio grows from $100 million to $10 billion? Does the data or do fields get truncated?

GUIs and reports will change after implementation. Over the following year, GUIs and reports will evolve to help the traders better manage the system. QA testing must also test for supportability and the modifiability of GUIs and reports over time.

23.4.   LOOP 3: Perform Final Audit and Probationary Trade

In Loop 3, the development team has built the hardware and network infrastructure to house the trading/investment system and performed system tests. The product team, led by the traders, must verify that the operation, functionality, and quality attribute requirements are met. Acceptance testing refers to the functional testing of a working trading/investment system by the product team prior to implementation. As the customer, the product team runs black box scenarios to test different components and behaviors of the system and whether those components have been correctly implemented. A component or behavior can have one or more user acceptance tests, whatever it takes to ensure that it works to specification. Each acceptance test must have a predefined, expected result. The product team is responsible for verifying the correctness of these tests and reviewing test results to decide which tests failed and which ones succeeded. As always, acceptance tests should include regression tests of the outputs of the system against Stage 2 results.

The product team's user acceptance tests confirm through trial and review that the system in its entirety meets the specification requirements and quality attribute requirements.

Users of the system, generally the traders, perform these tests. Test designers draw up formal tests and devise a range of severity levels. User acceptance testing acts as a final verification of the proper functioning of the system, emulating real-world market and trading conditions on behalf of the product team. If the system works as intended and without issues, the product team can reasonably infer the same level of stability in production. These tests are not usually focused on identifying simple problems, which the team should have previously identified and had fixed. The results of these tests give confidence to the product team as to how the system will perform in production.

User acceptance testing is a critical level of testing because it is the final opportunity to identify any problems before the trading/investment system is put into production. In addition, this testing concludes with signed-off acceptance of the working system by the product team as a whole. User acceptance testing must be conducted thoroughly and accurately to give the final assurance of quality and checking that the system meets the user and business requirements. Only when testers can no longer find errors can the product team be confident that the system will run correctly and as expected.

Before commencing user acceptance testing, be sure that the acceptance criteria have been defined. Whatever the case, any changes or fixes performed at this step must be proved with a new and complete round of unit, integration, system, and user acceptance tests. This means that new acceptance tests must be created for each iteration. Rounds of testing continue until the acceptance criteria are met and the product team signs off that the system is ready for implementation.

In user acceptance testing the users execute the user acceptance test cases according to the testing strategy. The user acceptance testing process needs to be managed and controlled to ensure that:

- Tests are executed in the correct order.
- Test results are recorded.
- Testing progress is monitored and reported.
- Test incidents are reported and actioned.
- Complete retesting is performed following any code changes and the results reported.
- All required test cases are executed, acceptance criteria are reached, and the acceptance testing is signed off.

A user acceptance test is an interactive process between the trader, the product team, and the development team. The risk department may also perform user acceptance testing. During user acceptance testing it is important to monitor the progress of the execution of test cases and the resolution of incidents reported as a result of testing. Regular progress meetings should be held to report on progress with the testing. Where multiple acceptance test teams are used, such as for different business areas and/or large projects, each team leader should provide a separate report. A consolidated report should also be prepared.

Loop 3 in this step is the final audit. Are regression tests done and documented? Everyone must agree. The product team signs off that the audits and tests are complete. All must feel comfortable that, if the senior trader is unable to run the system, the rest of the team can do so. (Investors may even require this before providing capital.) All test results will be submitted to management for review at the Gate 3 meeting.

23.5.   User Documentation

The product team includes a marketing person and we recommend the marketing person, along with the trader, read and write the user documentation and training manuals. These documents must be well written, describing how the system works, what it is supposed to accomplish, and how a user can operate the system in step-by-step fashion. By having a marketing person lead the user documentation process, the team can be confident the manuals will be written from the perspective of a lay user.

This way, if the trader is unable to run the system, for whatever reason, another member of the product team can read the user documentation and training manuals and operate the system properly without any additional assistance or expertise. Of course, this does not require documentation of proprietary algorithms, which will be kept secret. The other members of the product team should also review the documentation and manuals for clarity, correctness, and maintainability. Once the system is in production, product team members will be too busy running the system or working on other systems to deal with new additions to the current documentation.

These documents should make the trading/investment system SAS 70 and/or ISO 9000 auditable, since many large firms are starting to invest only in firms that have an auditable investment method due to the large number of funds that fail for operational reasons.

23.6.   Probationary Trading

Once the product team has signed off on all tests, probationary trading can begin. Probationary trading will find any remaining design flaws in the trading/investment algorithm or the software prior to trading the full investment sum, which will officially begin the track record period. The second purpose of probationary trading is to allow the traders time to use the GUI and reporting tools and determine what additional tools they will need to properly manage the trading/investment system.

This time, when the product team checks performance, they will have real-time, live trade data to measure. This is the final step in the testing stage of the trading system life cycle. Following probationary trading is Gate 3, where top management must still approve trading of investor assets. Placing simulated trades against real-time market data will give us a true and final test of the potential of a trading system. At this point, the returns of the system will be similar to those of the final product.

23.7.   Summary

The product team must be confident that the development team has built the hardware and software in a quality manner. Quality assurance audits will verify that processes have been followed and that the software and hardware are built to specification and satisfy quality attribute requirements. Because the product team is ultimately responsible for the trading/investment system, the team must conduct planned user acceptance tests before implementation. The goal of QA is to ensure a trading/investment system will pass an SAS 70 audit.

Once user acceptance tests are completed and signed, all operational risk should essentially have been removed. For Loop 4, the team can focus on market risks.

23.7.1. Best Practices

- Prove that processes are followed and software meets requirements through QA audits.
- Write user documentation so the team can run the system in the absence of the lead trader.
- All changes to code must be proved with a new and complete round of unit, integration, system, and user acceptance tests.
- Use probationary trading to uncover any remaining flaws.
- Regress performance metrics against past results. Differences must be researched and their causes documented for discussion at the Gate 3 meeting.

CHAPTER • 24

Gate 3

In the chapters on Gates 1 and 2, we discussed many important issues regarding gates in general, and all of the concepts recommended for meeting format and portfolio review apply to Gate 3 as well. Gate meetings also are a good time to review the market and economic environment.

The product team should arrive at the Gate 3 meeting with its deliverables and a recommendation supported by data. A recommendation to go to launch and Stage 4 must of course be accompanied by a request for investment capital. To convince top management that the hardware and software implementation work properly, the product team can deliver user acceptance tests reports, which should ensure that working system meets the Stage 4 input requirements. These results should be documented and delivered to all interested parties prior to the Gate 3 meeting. These documents must be in a form that allows verification against the original Money Document.

By Gate 3, the trading/investment system is fully validated. Quantitative methods and business rules have been tested and proven. All technological uncertainties have been resolved. All the support infrastructure should be in place. All concept, model, and operational risks are gone. The team and top management should be confident that the system will achieve its competitive advantage. In Stage 4, the product team will focus on controlling market risks. Nevertheless, top management must still make a go, kill, hold, or return decision. In order to pass through Gate 3, several questions must be answered:

- Does the market opportunity still exist? Does the competitive advantage still exist?
- Is there investment capital available to start trading immediately?
- Does the probationary trading prove successful implementation? Is the process stable? What are the metrics that are stable?
- Have the required documents been delivered?
- Is the product on time and on budget?
- Are the systems for the report generation for the system in place?
- Are the resources requested for ongoing management of the system acceptable?
- Is there a plan for moving continuously through Stage 4?

Gate 3 will prevent implementation of the trading/investment system until the required activities and deliverables have been completed in a quality manner. Furthermore, this gate will chart the path ahead by ensuring that plans and budgets have been made for Stage 4. A go to launch decision will mean the product team will receive investment capital to start trading immediately.

While a system may be ready to go, management will consider external factors before giving a final go ahead. The portfolio review process will again be affected by changing market and economic conditions, new trading/investment opportunities, hedging considerations, and functional interdependence among new and working trading/investment systems. Top management should consider the current investment cycle and its projected effect on the profitability of the portfolio of systems, as well as look forward to what the investment cycle might be when the trading/investment system is launched. External factors may also include commitments by investment capital providers.

Given the late stage of development, shutting down a project at this gate will undoubtedly result in a full-blown political battle. Of course, it is better to win a battle to close down or park a project versus losing tens of millions of dollars in a trading/investment system that has poor information coefficient ratios.

24.1. Process Improvement and Benchmarking

Gate meetings are also convenient times to review:

- The design and development processes that produced the trading/investment system up to this point.
- The performance of the product team.
- The documentation protocols and how they may be improved.

After each stage (or even after each loop, especially the first loop of a new stage), we recommend holding a poststage (or postloop) review meeting. Reflecting on experiences of the previous loop or stage is a critical factor to improving design and development processes, that is, to evolving a successful methodology. Incremental improvement in processes, then, mirrors incremental development. Done regularly, process review meetings should become part of the rhythm of the design and development process.

Successful teams develop the ability to communicate and criticize each other honestly and openly. The first condition for good teamwork is that each team member understands that he alone is responsible for the whole. A team must be able to look at itself and learn from its successes and failures. Some key questions might be

- What did the team learn?
- What can the team do better/faster next time?
- What factors are really making the team perform well or poorly?
- Are we communicating effectively?
- Could interteam relationships be improved?
- Are the team's goals of output and quality being achieved?
- Did the team have the right resources to achieve success?

The responses to these questions will cross every boundary of the project, from management interaction to documentation, to interpersonal communications, seating arrangements, and the makeup of the team itself. Just like poor teams, even the best teams make mistakes and must be open to criticism; the best teams learn more quickly from their mistakes than do poor teams. The best teams avoid repeating mistakes again and again.

Process improvements can make future design and development projects better, easier, and faster, eliminating errors, and fostering consistency, increased velocity, and cost reduction. Real costs can be reduced through the avoidance of waste and defective development processes, though simply finding out of control points in the process and removing them is only putting the process back where it was in the first place. It should be noted that putting out fires is not improvement. Similarly, finding an out-of-control step in the process, finding the special cause, and removing it is also only putting the process back where it was in the first place. It is not improvement of the process.

Process improvement serves not only to correct past mistakes, but also to incorporate new strategies or technologies that can make things better. New technologies especially are always coming on the market. Effective process improvement strives toward efficient technology transfer from outside the organization to processes within it. Product teams should compare, that is, benchmark, themselves to performance goals, other teams within the firm, and, if possible, other teams at other firms. Effective teams are constantly looking for new ideas that can help the next time around, wherever they can be found.

As you might imagine, team members can pick up more ideas during their work, rather than at the end of the stage. Weeks after the fact, people tend to forget valuable observations and insights. We recommend team members keep a process improvement notebook, where they can each write down ideas or concerns as they arise. Further, each team member should summarize their perspectives in a lessons-learned page after each loop, for review at the stage-end reflection meeting. This midstream reflection will lead to successful process improvement meetings.

Prior to the meeting, the team leader can collect each member's notebook and prepare a list of discussion items. By the end of the meeting, after reviewing all ideas and concerns, the team should arrive at a consensus on which new ideas for improvement can be tried out. After developing several systems using the same framework of abstraction, development teams can organize and catalog repeating patterns and best practices. A catalog of best practices can form the basis for process improvement.

The team leader's role in reflection is critical. The leader must focus the team's attention on honest and open criticism of processes and other members. A good team leader will make each member contribute constructive ideas on how to improve problems. Successful leaders are people who say it like it really is. Leadership and teamwork is about communicating what each team member is doing and then pushing toward a common goal. Honest and open communication and feedback ensures this will happen.

Open communication must not be personal; every communication must be understood to be for the benefit of the team, not to insult one team member. Open and honest communication means that each team member knows what each other member thinks. Communication cannot be effective if team members are lying to each other, even if the lies are told to protect someone's feelings.

Honest, open reflection and criticism will speed process benchmarking. Robert Camp has defined a formal, four phase benchmarking process:

- **Phase 1: Planning.** Identify which processes and which people to benchmark, and gather data on alternative practices.
- **Phase 2: Analysis.** Examine the gap between true performance and best practices.

- **Phase 3: Integration.** Communicate the findings and create new performance goals.
- **Phase 4: Action.** Make plans, take action, and monitor progress toward performance goals.[1]

The first step of process benchmarking is to specify a process or a series of interconnected processes to be studied. Next, a benchmarking standard or team with superior performance in that process being examined is identified. The high performance process of the team is then studied. In this way a performance gap is established and the elements, which have led to the superior performance, can be understood. The final step is to formulate an improvement plan and implement the actions necessary to close the performance gap.

The key to reusability is not just to reuse code, but more importantly to reuse the analysis and design processes. Establishing firmwide standards and best practices for evaluation of trading/investment systems and software design is critical. These standards will provide a framework within which best-of-breed trading/investment system and technology can emerge and evolve. All steps in our methodology are examples of processes for which a firm can benchmark and standardize development processes. Benchmarks and standards may also include:

- Documentation standards that specify the form and content for, for example, Money Documents, investment policies, iteration and release plans, code and user documentation, and testing documentation, and provide consistency throughout a project.
- Design standards that provide rules and methods for translating the prototypes and software requirements into the software design and for representing it in the design documentation.
- Code standards that provide methods and rationale for translating the software designs into code. These may define language, style conventions, rules for data structures and interfaces, and internal code documentation.

Best practice evolves quickly. Honest team self-criticism forms the foundation of the drive toward better practices and toward best-in-class performance. Because financial markets change so rapidly, staying up to date, with new and improved processes, is itself a never-ending process.

24.2. Deliverables/Inputs

At this gate meeting, top management will expect several deliverables, including:

- Software requirements specification document.
- Software and hardware architecture documents, including proof the system meets the quality attribute requirements.
- Working software and hardware with documentation.
- User documentation.
- User acceptance test report signed by the product team.
- Full probationary trading performance report, including trade selection reports and results of regression tests versus the gold standard run package results from Stage 2.

24.3. Summary

By the time of the Gate 3 meeting, all operational risk should be removed. Nevertheless, management should consider risks external to the product and the product team before giving the final go ahead to implement the system. A go decision will allow the team to start trading investment capital immediately. For the coming stage, Stage 4, the product team and risk management will be free to focus on market risks.

Often overlooked are opportunities to improve the processes that produce the trading/investment system. Process improvements make future products better and easier to design and develop, eliminating risks of errors, enhancing consistency, and reducing costs.

Gates are a convenient time for reflection, for the team to look back on their own performance and the processes used over the course of the previous stage. The pressure for instant solutions leads to short-term thinking. Short-term thinking often addresses symptoms, not causes of problems. Quality management requires that teams find root causes to real problems so that processes can truly be improved. Perpetual process benchmarking will mean that processes are under constant review and change.

STAGE • IV

Manage Portfolio and Risk

CHAPTER • 25

STAGE 4: Overview

The spiral stage structure of K|V begs two perspectives—one, that of the loops; and two, that of the steps. One can look at the four steps that comprise a single loop, or the three loops that comprise each step. We will do both. This chapter will present an overview of the three loops. The following four chapters will examine each of the four steps and each pass over each step. The number of loops is not by any means fixed. (We decided that three iterations were sufficient to cover the commonly encountered substeps.)

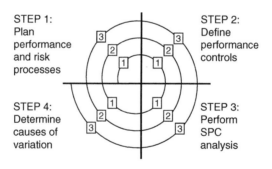

STEP 1:
Plan
performance
and risk
processes

STEP 2:
Define
performance
controls

STEP 4:
Determine
causes of
variation

STEP 3:
Perform
SPC
analysis

FIGURE 25-1

Stage 4 is different. Stages 1, 2, and 3 addressed trading/investment system design and development issues. By Stage 4, the product team has delivered a fully functioning trading/investment system, a system turned on after Gate 3, assuming financial risks and churning out performance metrics—metrics that can be measured and risks that can be forecasted. The product team is no longer involved. From this point forward, risk managers and a kaizen (i.e., continuous improvement) team will assume control of the system. Risk managers will monitor the system's outputs and the kaizen team will make and/or implement containments, which are short-term solutions, not fixes or corrective actions, investigate root causes, and make recommendations for long-term fixes of the root cause, that is, maybe month-long projects. (The long-term projects will be picked up by a newly formulated product team, which should go back to an earlier stage of K|V and work through the problem and the fix according to the methodology, adding new knowledge at each stage. This is consistent with a rapid or agile method because the new team will use all of the old test cases, as well as new ones to enhance the improved trading/investment system.)

Portfolios of securities and derivatives require constant monitoring and so successful implementation of a trading system necessitates that periodic reports be generated to determine if the system is performing to specifications. These reports will present the portfolio performance statistics, risk calculations, attribution analysis, and Value at Risk (VaR). Furthermore, quality control should determine if the system is in or out of control. If the process is out of control, a determination of the cause of the variation from the expected results and the risk managers should create an action plan to deal with those causes. The three risk methodologies represent three different sets of tools for monitoring the system.

Processes in a stochastic world change regularly. They drift within a range of values that are normally considered the upper and lower control limits. Sometimes these stochastic processes change due to a real shift in the real world. For example, the reformulating of a plastic's chemistry due to an EPA ruling would change all parts made with the plastic. In the same manner, changes in securities laws may cause real shifts, the way Sarbanes-Oxley shifted volatility around earnings. The real question in systematic trading and investment is "Is the variation normal and expected? Or, is the process out of control due to a fundamental shift in the world?" More simply, "Is this the same process the product team backtested?"

Some risk managers may not catch credit. Interest sensitive stocks, bonds, and many derivatives all contain a credit forecast embedded in their values. As a result, these instruments may become highly correlated during a credit shock. Algorithmic trading/investment requires careful real-time performance monitoring as well as pre- and posttrade analysis to ensure the algorithms are properly applied.[1]

Risk has always been at the heart of trading/investment systems. There is a difference between calculating market risks for capital reserves and using risk to control or improve a process. In the K|V methodology we propose that we use outputs of the risk calculations to improve the process instead of setting capital reserves only. Our methodology differs from the classical use of risk calculation that are used to protect the trading firm from rogue traders since in systematic trading/investment, the machine controls the process, not human traders. We believe that a firm needs both views to be successful in the competitive world of trading due to the continual drive to benchmark funds.

25.1. History of Risk and Return

Traditionally, a risk department calculates risks and returns separately from a trading group to ensure a trading group stays within its limits. The risk department defines limits through stochastic mathematics with the goal of ensuring that the firm is optimizing its risk/return ratio. We group the measures of risk into three basic categories:

- **Single performance.** These classical measures of risk and return compare a portfolio relative to itself. Examples of single performance calculations include: returns, drawdowns, Sharpe ratio, Sortino ratio. These calculations do not forecast, only document the current model outputs. We believe these outputs can be viewed as stochastic, contrary to popular beliefs. We base this view on the low ability of current systems to explain variation.

- **Performance attribution.** In the not so recent past, attribution has been introduced into the world of risk and has now become a standard for most pension funds. Attribution allows a fund manager to determine how he is performing relative to a benchmark—are the individual security bets adding value? Or is it the over-/underweighting of sectors?

Very interesting is that some of the best funded pension plans in the world do not believe that a firm can significantly outperform its benchmark without the addition of hidden risk, while individual investors believe a firm can shoot for the moon to generate 50% returns a year with no additional risk. Our view is closer to the pension fund world than the individual investor's world. All successful trading/investment ideas become known to smart investors quickly. Smart investors enter the area of excessive returns quickly due to their superior ability to gather information. Very quickly an informal benchmark is created by the smart money to measure which firm to place capital with. Once a benchmark has been formed and outside capital is put to use, the focus shifts from absolute returns to asset gathering to generating fees. The best way to gather assets is to beat the benchmark with lower risk.

- **Value at Risk (VaR).** Value at Risk can be viewed as a forecast of the future return of a system. Risk managers choose a distribution since they must believe a substantial amount of the process variation remains in the system. The purpose of the forecast is to determine what the worst case is given a predefined distribution and threshold. If the trader hits this predefined threshold then the risk department forces the trading desk or group to post additional margin or to close down the desk. This is done in the third spiral since we will use this to determine if the underlying process variation is stable or shifting. A process standard deviation should be stable as measured in the VaR calculations. If a process's standard deviation shifts from a low volatility regime to a high volatility regime, risk managers and kaizen teams will need to quickly determine its effect on the output of the algorithm or even better switch to a high volatility algorithm.

The real problem with all three levels of risk management is that many traders and money managers view the risk department only as a necessary evil. They do not want to help the risk department since this could lead to lower bonuses due to risk-based haircuts. Some traders believe a major part of trading is hiding profits and risks from the risk department, done by shifting inputs in theoretical models. The goal is to have money for rainy days where the market goes against you so you can smooth out your returns. This cat and mouse game has been played for years by the traders and risk managers. In fact the risk managers unofficially encourage this game since they are the ones that have to discuss with senior management any unexpected losses. By smoothing out the returns everyone wins, according to many traders.

The problem with the smoothing out of the returns and managing expectations is we live in a stochastic world. We should be using the stochastic outputs to improve the process by identifying shifts in the investment environment early so we can do something about it before everyone in the peer group loses money. Sometimes the way to win is not the best but may avoid periods where everyone loses money by closing down or scaling back a trading algorithm (during a period when it is no longer predictive) or switching investment styles.

Academics have a static view of risk, one that claims to explain the majority of the variation of returns. In such a view, risk is a snapshot of a stochastic process that is assumed to be stable and well defined. In the nonsystematic trading/investment world, risk managers assign abnormal, or assignable, variation to a person. Large downside deviations, that is, drawdowns, are pinned on people—a trader or a portfolio manager. The normal reaction is to reduce trading limits until the person recovers his emotions. (Think red bead experiment. In a red bead experiment, several players (employees) select ten beads from a box containing 10% red and 90% white beads. A manager then yells at the employee who draws the most red beads in the hope of improving his or her performance on a subsequent trial. Deming used the red bead experiment to illustrate typical management response to common variation in a process.) In systematic trading/investment, however, there are no emotions in periods of drawdowns and no people to blame for outliers.

Furthermore, systems are not scaled up or down in backtests; they assume a steady state. The snapshot view of risk does not distinguish between what is a normal, or common cause, variation and what is a special, or assignable cause, variation. The snapshot view of risk ignores tolerancing and, furthermore, lacks a stochastic view of risk outputs arising from stochastic inputs from the real world.

25.2.   A Brief History of Quality Control

In industrial engineering, engineers learned a long time ago that a stochastic process can be controlled using very basic statistical tools. The tools do not fix a broken process but tell engineers when a process is no longer working as designed. In the K|V methodology we apply this quality process control to manage the automated trading/investment systems. The key point of SPC is to use statistics to quickly identify when a process mean, standard deviation, or range has shifted due to special causes. In manufacturing we are able to measure most of the inputs and outputs of the process. In trading/investment, we are not able to measure many of the inputs into the system since we do not know for sure that we are in a recession until we are nine months into a recession.

It is well understood in quality that an engineer should not adjust a machine after every part, which leads to overcompensating. In SPC as long as parts are within tolerance, that is, within control limits, no adjustments are made, a process which produces higher quality parts. The analogy to finance is traders lowering risk capital during periods of drawdowns, which leads to being undercapitalized when the market bounces back. When it does bounce back, they often overcompensate before a big downturn.

One can perceive dollar cost averaging as a quality view of the market. During a down market, dollar cost averaging does not consider the machine broken. The market is not broken, so keep adding money to the market machine. No changes are made to investment policy in either up or down markets. The CBOE S&P 500 BuyWrite Index (BXM) is also a quality control view. (A buy/write strategy is one where the investor buys a stock (or a stock index) and writes call options (i.e., the options are "covered") on the stock (or stock index).) Option premium is highly correlated with market uncertainty. When investors are uneasy, they demand more premium. When they are sure, they demand less. Effectively, the market widens its tolerance level in uncertain times. When the market goes down, an investor gets paid for the increased uneasiness by selling higher premiums. The BXM is like trading an SPC mechanism. When control limits are hit, it naturally changes the trading structure by selling volatility.

25.3.   Combining Performance and Quality Control

The combination of classical risk calculations and the application of quality control for automated trading system are based on our beliefs that a trading algorithm works in a stochastic environment. The algorithm does not remove a significant portion of the stochastic nature of the environment and thus the output of these algorithms is stochastic. The standard control of the stochastic process embedded in the output is to build a large portfolio. The large portfolio is used to create a stable mean, based on the law of large numbers. The stable mean concept is identical to statistical quality control where we take a sample and measure the mean, standard deviation, range, etc. The distribution of these sample means is normal due to the central limit theorem. The distribution of the sample means is then used to control the process through SPC charts.

The actual risk measurements can be displayed using quality control. We use these risk calculations and SPC to determine whether the input process(es) to the trading/investment algorithm has shifted. If the input process has changed, then we need to investigate the causes of the change in the risk values. The cause could be a shift in the underlying stochastic process caused by, say, economic or political issues, or a change in the regulatory environment.

Therefore, this spiral has been designed in an interleafed fashion. The first spiral is the measurement of the algorithm against itself. This is classical risk management. The second spiral is the measurement of the algorithm against a benchmark. The last spiral is the measurement of the algorithm against the universe through simulation of the future.

The three categories of risk measurements are essentially snapshots at a point in time. SPC links all these through time to find out what is normal, and to find changes in inputs and processes early, not late. By addressing these items early, a trading/investment system should be able to outperform its competitors who adjust after losses have taken place, when everyone understands the risks in hindsight.

25.4. LOOP 1: Assess Single Performance

STEP 1:   Specify Single Performance Controls
STEP 2:   Benchmark Single Performance Calculations
STEP 3:   Perform SPC Analysis
STEP 4:   Determine Causes of Variation in Single Performance

In this step, risk managers assess the performance of a trading/investment system versus itself, that is, versus the performance observed during the backtest. The first round of risk control measures the system's performance versus the out-of-sample test results from Stage 2 to see if the machine is producing the expected performance metrics.

25.5. LOOP 2: Measure Performance Attribution

STEP 1:   Define Benchmarks and Attribution Controls
STEP 2:   Benchmark Attribution Calculations
STEP 3:   Perform SPC on Attribution Metrics
STEP 4:   Determine Causes of Variation in Attribution

Performance attribution will analyze performance of a trading/investment system relative to its benchmark. We believe that risk managers should perform SPC on excess returns using attribution analysis along with the over- and underweighting versus key factors. The SPC will indicate if the machine is working according to the initial design constraints.

A stock-selection machine was severely overweighting in tech stocks in 1998 and 1999. This was justified by excess returns. However, in 20 years of historical data, the algorithm never overweighted a sector to this extent, nor were the excess returns ever to this level. Therefore, the machine was deemed to be out of control. The owners had two choices: shut down the machine, or monitor the machine for early signs of further breakdown and possible reversion to the mean. When the sector's excess returns turned negative, a human overrode the machine and brought the tech sector weight to below the benchmark weight. This allowed the fund to outperform all other peer funds that remained overweighted in technology till 2001.

25.6.   LOOP 3: Assess Value at Risk

STEP 1:   Choose VaR Methodology
STEP 2:   Benchmark VaR Calculations and Software
STEP 3:   Perform SPC on VaR Metrics
STEP 4:   Determine Causes of Variation in VaR

Single performance and attribution analysis quantifies only what has happened in the past. Risk is the potential for loss in the future, so a risk manager needs a forward look-ing methodology. Value at Risk is just that; it helps predict how a portfolio will behave in potential shocks. However, without attribution a manager's ability to control risk is limited since there can be little definition of which risks to hedge (credit risk for equities, sector risk for bonds, etc.). A key point here is that a firm may or may not hedge an item that is underweighted relative to the benchmark weight since underweighting is itself a form of hedging. With VaR, simulations can be done to determine where the stress points in a portfolio are so they can either modify the portfolio or hedge the risk. Also, risk managers use VaR to determine risk-based margins (which is why traders are generally hesitant to help the risk managers build better systems).

25.7.   Deliverables

- Periodic SPC charts and analysis reports.
- Return attribution and risk attribution report.
- Root cause analysis reports.
- Identification of future risk distributions.

25.8.   Summary

The primary difference between the classical view of risk and our view of risk in the systematic trading/investment world is that the former attempts to manage a person (i.e., a trader or portfolio manager), the latter a machine. A machine does not change its behav-ior after a stern conversation with a risk manager. A machine does not fear losses, nor does it celebrate winning. A machine can effectively work forever if the inputs and the economic environment were to stay constant. A machine simply changes raw data into a working product.

In our view of risk, the machine has predetermined performance and predetermined risk/reward ratios, which are stochastic outputs that should be monitored using SPC. The purpose of SPC is to notify risk managers of a problem in the machine, to make them aware of special, unassigned but assignable, variation in the system. The task of the risk managers and the product team, then, is to determine the root cause of the special varia-tion in the performance of the machine.

Our process is more complex than the traditional risk overview process due to the complexities of continuously monitoring a process. In manufacturing, variation in proc-esses is usually quite small, sometimes measured in thousandths of an inch. In trading, variation is most often quite large. The demands on a risk manager should naturally be more complex, since they should be part of a continuous improvement team. Management tasks such a team with fixing trading/investment machines. The risk manager must understand all forms of traditional risk, statistical process control, and process improvement methods such as design of experiments and kaizen. In the following chapters we will not focus on the calculations of risk (these are well covered in the many excellent papers and books on the subject), but rather on the structure of blending classical risk and traditional quality together to control trading/investment systems.

CHAPTER • 26

Plan Performance and Risk Processes

The inputs into a trading/investment system, that is, into the trade selection, execution and position, and risk management algorithms, are data—price data, valuation data, fundamental data, calculated data, and economic data. In basic statistical terms, all the trading algorithms are trying to forecast future performance using stochastic, independent variables. In manufacturing, effective coefficient of determination (r^2) is very high, in excess of .95. In finance, they are much lower, normally less than .60. The goal is to use both risk management and Six Sigma techniques to increase the effective r^2. The unexplained variation is the cause of uncontrollable risk. This risk can and has been catastrophic to trading/money management firms. The variation a model does not explain is itself stochastic—what we call common cause variation in the outputs of the system, or the unpredictable part of the profit.

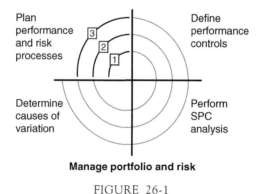

Manage portfolio and risk

FIGURE 26-1

A risk manager attempts to understand how and why a trading/investment system is making and losing money and what the potential for loss is. He or she currently does this using three tool sets:

- Single performance measurements.
- Performance attribution.
- Value at Risk.

237

All these tool sets, however, generate estimates and forecasts that are only snapshots in time of what might be a poorly explained stochastic system (as determined by the r^2 of the model). If an output of a trading/investment system has changed, the risk manager must understand whether that change is within a normal range or due to special, or assignable, changes in the inputs. If inputs have changed, this may have caused the distribution of the outputs to change. To make this determination, the risk manager looks not only at returns and standard deviations, but also at many process outputs—sector weights, credit score weights, average drawdowns, number of winning trades—and asks a simple question: have the output distributions changed?

If the trading/investment system is not producing the same outputs again and again and again, then the product team must figure out what is broken and how to fix it. A trading/investment system may exhibit nonconformance, that is, be broken, if an input distribution has changed, because, for example:

- Other trading/investment systems have come online and are now competing.
- Competing systems have evolved to explain more variation. For example, competitors may have changed from static to Bayesian statistics.
- Laws have changed. For example, Sarbanes-Oxley completely changed the meaning of earnings estimate revisions.
- Exchange matching algorithms have changed and/or execution processes no longer outperform their benchmark.
- Technology has changed from single to multiprocessor.

Successful firms automate the process of monitoring and reporting portfolio statistics, trade limits, and risk factors. Essentially, these reports will help risk managers understand whether or not the system is working within specifications relative to the backtest, the index benchmark, and risk forecasts. These records prove conformance with expectations and document nonconformance, including the types and nature of nonconformities, and actions taken to repair or preclude its further use. There are three ways of dealing with nonconformity:

- Finding and correcting the nonconformity (this requires at least a reversion to Stage 2).
- Authorizing its use, release, or acceptance if concession is obtained from a relevant authority.
- Shutting down the system.

A defect causing a nonconformity may cause the firm to rework or repair the trading/investment system. The product team will have to demonstrate conformity of a previously nonconforming trading/investment system that has been corrected. This must be done by reverification through the same gates and acceptance criteria in previous stages.

Most trading system developers view that performance outputs of the system are for the risk department and the sales department after the system is running; they believe the machine is optimal and contains very little variation. The product team has built a complete database on the performance of the trading/investment system and now must continuously measure the ongoing performance of the machine versus the backtest data. This continuous checking, this automated feedback mechanism, enables the people running the system to quickly identify problems, begin analysis, and take corrective actions. This action may include a trader overriding the system. Risk and performance metrics are not only for the risk department in well-run firms, but also by the traders that operate the systems. These calculations are similar to sensors on a machine, used in real time to focus the Six Sigma quality improvement process.

We will discuss the most basic concepts of risk only, due to the enormous body of knowledge on market risk and risk calculations, discuss how to use SPC to show when the system has changed, and then DoE to find the root cause of the changes.

26.1. LOOP 1: Specify Single Performance Controls

To effectively evaluate the performance of a trading/investment system relative to itself, that is, to normalcy arrived at during backtesting, the team will have to specify time intervals—by minute, hour, day, month, year—and time spans, consisting of series of time intervals, to create a time series of performance metrics. (The product team will have defined these metrics in Stage 1, captured them during Stage 2, and now must plan to monitor these metrics periodically.)

The performance over a number of time intervals can be calculated arithmetically, geometrically, or continuously. Key components in performance measurements are the fees charged by brokers, exchanges, regulators, custodians, and auditors as well as taxes. Performance should always be calculated net of these fees.[1]

26.2. LOOP 2: Define Benchmarks and Attribution Controls

Traders sometimes argue that they should be measured solely on absolute returns, that the uniqueness of their strategy renders their performance incomparable. Of course, the trader has an incentive to convince management of his true genius: if something good happens, he must be right! While some strategies are in fact unique (especially macro strategies), most are not.

Traders prefer to have few, or better still no, quantifiable methods of determining the value they add. In the world of systematic trading and investment and automated execution, the trader adds no value in times of normal operation. The purpose of a trader is to simply monitor and oversee the trading/investment machine. Only if the machine breaks down, that is, the algorithm stops working, and SPC charts show nonconformance, may the trader step in to "land the plane safely" by unwinding positions. This role is critical.

According to market lore, Leland, O'Brien, Rubenstein Associates (LOR) began selling portfolio insurance in 1983, without any backtesting, only probationary trading in personal accounts. In 1987, LOR's clients and licensees executed the programmed sales, contributing to selling that swamped the market. Their programs underestimated volatility and overestimated liquidity. Proper backtesting would have uncovered algorithm failures under extreme market conditions. Several firms went bankrupt. At Wells Fargo, however, a trader ditched the algorithm and traded on his own to manage positions. He may have saved Wells Fargo itself. Wells Fargo lost money, but remained in business. A good trader adds value through crash management when a system is out of control. SPC will signal an out-of-control state.

When it comes to performance and risk, the real question to be asked is the following: which algorithm(s) is/are adding value? Most systems have effectively two algorithms. One algorithm for position selection, and another algorithm for optimal weighting of positions in a portfolio. The goal is not to overweight sectors, market caps, credit risk, etc. versus the benchmark, but to generate pure alphas without accepting unforeseen risk. Using portfolio attribution we can understand the performance of a trading/investment system relative to an index benchmark.

Performance attribution is a technique used to analyze the sources of excess returns of a trading/investment system relative to a benchmark. Attribution will assess the ability of a trading/investment system and identify where and how it is adding value. Performance attribution is the process of decomposition of returns and risk into the position selection algorithms to measure the value added by the active investment management and to communicate the risk components of the trading/investment strategy.

So, to make sure that a trading system consistently outperforms its benchmark we need to perform attribution analysis on portfolio versus a benchmark. This is done to understand the sources of active returns in an investment portfolio. Product teams mostly use the most common method of attribution, the Brinson method, which uses three factors to explain the active performance of a portfolio:

- Sector allocation
- Stock selection
- Interaction.

The next question is how to select an index benchmark, or construct a benchmark for strategies that do not have a well-defined index.

26.2.1.   Index Benchmark

In most cases, the product team chooses a market index as the benchmark for a trading/investment system. Generally, the instruments traded will be largely drawn or derived from the constituents of the index. Because indexes track returns on a buy-and-hold basis and make no attempt to determine which instruments are the most attractive, they track passive investment and can provide a good standard against which to compare the performance of a trading/investment system that is actively, though systematically, managed. Using an index, it is possible to see how much value a trading/investment strategy adds and from where or through what positions that value comes.

Selecting a specific benchmark is an individual decision, but there are some minimum standards that any benchmark under consideration should meet. According to Carl Bacon, in his book *Practical Portfolio Performance Measurement and Attribution*, to be effective, a benchmark should meet most, if not all, of the following criteria:

- **Unambiguous and transparent.** The names and weights of securities comprising a benchmark should be clearly defined.
- **Investable.** The benchmark should contain securities that an investor can purchase in the market or easily replicate.
- **Priced regularly.** The benchmark's return should be calculated daily, weekly, or monthly.
- **Availability of historical data.** Past returns of the benchmark should be available in order to gauge historical returns.
- **Low turnover.** Ideally, there should not be high turnover in the securities in the index because it can be difficult to perform monthly portfolio allocation on an index

whose makeup is constantly changing. However, this does not apply to high frequency trading or systems with high turnover by design.

- **Specified in advance.** The benchmark should be constructed prior to the start of evaluation.
- **Published risk characteristics.** The benchmark provider should regularly publish detailed risk metrics of the benchmark so that the investment manager can compare the actively managed portfolio risks to the passive benchmark risks.[1]

Choosing the right benchmark for a portfolio is important because the benchmark establishes the risk and return parameters for managing the portfolio. There are many benchmarks to choose from in the market, and making a choice depends on many factors that are individual to each money manager. Choosing the right benchmark depends on identifying those that meet certain minimum requirements and then selecting the index that best matches the investor's goals for the portfolio and the level of risk the investor is willing to assume in order to meet those goals.

Benchmarks should be appropriate, investable, accessible, independent, and unambiguous. We recommend attribution be performed under the Brinson–Fachler method. Returns are attributed to asset allocation and stock selection effects and presented according to the industry sector, region credit rating of the company, security type, model rank, etc.

26.2.2. Alternative Benchmark Construction

For many strategies, an appropriate index benchmark may not exist. Nevertheless, a good, clean investable universe will. (The investable universe will have been defined in Stage 2.) The team can create a randomly selected portfolio from the investable universe for use as a benchmark that conforms to agreed upon portfolio constraints. This is called the Monte Carlo portfolio.

A Monte Carlo portfolio simulates multiple portfolios from the investable universe. These randomly generated portfolios produce a distribution of performances—returns, standard deviations, drawdowns, etc.—using simple portfolio construction constraints.

The median, mode, upper/lower quartile, upper/lower decile, etc. portfolios can be used as the benchmarks for risk/reward comparisons, attribution analysis, and SPC difference monitoring. An alternative way to construct a benchmark is to simply build a random basket of securities and consider this to be the benchmark. The issue with this method is that you could have picked the black swan winner and thrown a very good strategy. (According to Nassim Teleb, a black swan is an event rare beyond the ability of normal expectations to predict.) The reverse of this is you could pick the black swan loser and keep a poor strategy. Therefore, we recommend many simulations and using the median simulated benchmark.

This technique could also be used in qualitative funds to create a benchmark, even if the manager objects. We recommend all trading/investment system developers and managers embrace the Monte Carlo benchmark as a starting point for kaizen, the continuous process of measuring performance and implementing solutions that boost performance of trading/investment strategies.

Money managers must stay focused on beating the competition. By constantly measuring performance versus a Monte Carlo benchmark and quickly adjusting for root causes of special variation, trading/investment systems can consistently beat competitors that do not benchmark performance or engage in continuous improvements to strategies.

However, management should not reward product teams solely on beating a Monte Carlo benchmark. Top management should view beating a benchmark, for bonus purposes, largely as a red bead experiment, because of the large amount of unexplained variation in the process. Consistent with Deming and Ishikawa, management should measure the product team on project management and improvement of the system based on the reduction of variation in the system's performance outputs versus the Monte Carlo benchmark.

We also do not embrace the concept of sending out these Monte Carlo benchmarks to customers due to the confusion of what it actually represents and the fact these benchmarks contain proprietary portfolio construction information.

Finally, to get the named fund manager to accept this, all fear must be driven out of the firm by top management. If a person fears this information will be used to lower a bonus or to terminate them, then they will fight the Monte Carlo benchmark approach. They will be motivated to find reasons why it does not work and why they will not accept it. Only after everyone understands the only purpose of the simulated benchmark is to better the results of the trading/investment system can the process improvement system be implemented.

26.3.   LOOP 3: Choose VaR Methodology

Risk is generally considered to be the potential for loss in the future. Financial risks are those risks assumed by taking positions in the financial markets. The distribution or dispersion, that is, the standard deviation or volatility, of outcomes in financial markets creates both positive and negative risk. As Phillippe Jorion points out, "Extraordinary performance, both good and bad, should raise red flags." In systematic trading and investment, we use performance measurement to test conformance with backtest and benchmark results. Extremely good performance may portend extremely bad performance. Past performance can be measured, but risk must be predicted. Stage 4 focuses on measuring performance to understand what is normal performance, the common variation of the system. We use SPC to uncover out-of-control performance, which may portend high risk. Financial risk arises from randomness in markets, which are traditionally arranged into the following categories:

- **Market risk.** Arising from fluctuations in the market prices of tradable instruments.
- **Interest rate risk.** Arising from fluctuations in yields across the different maturities.
- **Currency risk.** Arising from the fluctuations in values of currencies.
- **Basis risk.** Arising from fluctuations in the correlations between instruments.
- **Credit risk.** Arising from fluctuations in the abilities of counterparties to meet financial obligations.
- **Liquidity risk.** Arising from fluctuations due to lack of market activity.

Risk management is the process by which various risk exposures are identified, measured either on an absolute or relative basis, and controlled. Financial risks must be rigorously defined. The product team cannot control the volatilities of markets; however, they can know the exposure of a trading/investment system to those volatilities. This exposure is the common variation of the system.

Value at Risk attempts to forecast the distribution of P&L over some time horizon and within a given confidence level. The objective is to aggregate all risks and boil them down into a single number that expresses the probability and size of loss in the future. There are six steps to forecasting risk:

- Decompose each instrument into its fundamental categories of risk.
- Aggregate the exposures of all instruments in the portfolio into these categories.
- Combine exposures to risk factors and the joint characteristics of these risk factors.
- Understand what is normal or common variation within the system.
- Determine causes of special variation in a system.
- Forecast the movements in risk factors and special variation.

The Value at Risk of a portfolio is a sum of the risks of the constituent instruments, where the sum takes into account not only the risks of the individual instruments, but also the cross-instrument interactions.

- Delta normal Value at Risk, where risk is a linear combination of exposures.
- Historical simulation, which better allows for nonlinearities and nonnormality.
- Monte Carlo simulation and stress testing, which incorporates a range of risk types and extreme scenarios.

Most trading/investment systems, especially those that make use of leverage, are subject to some form of VaR for trading limits. The real value of VaR is not in its calculation of current risk, but in its calculation of what-if scenario risks, and therefore we recommend Monte Carlo simulation, because (among other reasons) scenarios can be used to perform kaizen improvement of the system. A new security or ETF or option can be added to a VaR representation of a portfolio to generate a theoretical result. Of course, over the long term the logic behind a systematic hedging strategy must be backtested.

26.4. Summary

Portfolios of securities and derivatives require constant monitoring. No system, no matter how well planned or well built should be left unattended. Calculations to monitor a trading/investment system will be unique to the system itself, although systems of different types—trigger, filter, signal strength—will have metrics in common. In any case, we prefer graphical representation of complex calculations; interpreting graphs is easier than interpreting data, especially time series data.

- Is this system in conformance with the backtest?
- What performance calculations do I want to monitor?
- Is my system placing bets that I do not understand?
- If any of these three are out of control, how do I control and adjust my system?

All the way back in K|V 1.2 the product team should have determined the monitoring metrics and measurement components needed to provide evidence of conformity of product to requirements. Risk managers will use performance and risk metrics to identify and control nonconforming trading/investment systems to prevent losses.

26.4.1. Best Practices

- Plan to integrate evaluation of performance relative to the backtest and to a benchmark and Value at Risk.
- Use an index benchmark, peer group benchmark, or Monte Carlo benchmark for every trading/investment system.
- Automate the process of retaining all data and calculating all metrics. These should have been prototyped in Stage 1.
- Plan and document risk management processes up front, not after the fact.
- Plan for out-of-control systems during extreme market movements, assigning responsibilities to human traders to "safely land the plane."

CHAPTER ◆ 27

Define Performance Controls

Monitoring performance and risk metrics requires keeping track of individual trades and their respective payoffs. With the choice of so many methods to calculate performance metrics and the potential for errors and abuse, top management must establish internal controls and policies with respect to calculations, performance presentation standards, and independent verification in accordance with CFAI/GIPS/NAPF guidelines, including:

- Consistency of calculation methods.
- The treatment of fees and transaction costs.
- Currency translations.
- Handling of intraperiod cash flows.
- Accuracy of pricing data and algorithms.
- Accuracy of input data for theoretical values of illiquid securities.

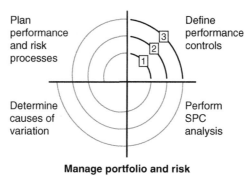

Manage portfolio and risk

FIGURE 27-1

While the calculations of these metrics may appear simple, small differences or nuances, such as average capital invested, can have significant impacts on return calculations.[1]

245

27.1.   LOOP 1: Benchmark Single Performance Calculations

Determining which metrics to calculate depends on the nature of the system. For single performance calculations, many or all of the following are important:

- Mean/median P&L.
- Average returns.
- Standard deviation of returns.
- Sharpe ratio.
- Sortino ratio.
- Percentage of winning days.
- Number of winning trades and losing trades, winning days and losing days.
- Drawdowns.
- Average holding period.
- T-statistics for trigger and filter trades for comparison of universe to selected trades.
- Information coefficient/Spearman correlation.
- Hurst index.

For SPC charting purposes, the mean value for these metrics will be that experienced in the backtest. However, these values may be smoothed using group averages, rolling means, and/or exponential moving averages due to the need for normality in classical SPC. Trading/investment systems normally have substantially more output variation compared to traditional SPC controlled processes in the manufacturing world.

Many of these metrics will vary wildly. The average of the sum of a large number of independent, identically distributed random variables converges in distribution to a normally distributed random variable. So, use a cumulative sum over five or more samples.

When quality principles are applied to trading/investment system performance metrics, data-related problems often occur. Non-normally distributed data is a typical issue. We often use time series data of cumulative averages to estimate process efficiency in a trading/investment system.

The mean and standard deviation of the metric is combined with the upper and lower control limits (UCL, LCL) from the backtest with the result reported graphically. The data usually results from the cumulative average of errors of random variation and follows a normal distribution. The areas falling outside of the control limits represent a defect within the process.

27.2.   LOOP 2: Benchmark Attribution Calculations

Some systems have a well-defined benchmark such as the large cap, relative-value (filter-style) system and long/short Nasdaq 100 (signal-strength style) system. Many hedge fund managers claim they are out only for absolute return. But, every system should be compared against a benchmark alternative; to beat the benchmark a trader has to place bets that have a higher chance of winning than the bets in the benchmark.

Here is an example. It would be easy to make a lot of money on a volatility dispersion trade, if for some good fortune you were short volatility on companies with high credit and long volatility on companies with poor credit during a credit crunch. The credit market default spreads would open up for poor credit companies as people bought credit default spreads, and credit default traders would purchase leaps in the puts to hedge their positions. Implied volatility of poor credit companies would spike, stock price of poor credit companies would gap down, and you would look like a genius.

However, using a portfolio attribution system you would clearly identify that the excess profit of above the benchmark for the volatility was provided by a credit bet. In the bet explained above the trader won; however, the reverse could also be true. Therefore, to make sure that a trading system built consistently outperforms its benchmark you need to perform attribution analysis on the portfolio and the benchmark.

For attribution analysis, a risk manager must understand where the risk and return is versus the benchmark. Metrics will include first standard statistical outputs, plus additional deliverables such as, for example, a linked chart showing the growth of $10,000 for fund versus the benchmark, and calculations for:

- Alpha and beta.
- Excess returns/Sharpe ratio of excess returns.
- Average credit ratings.
- Average market cap.
- International exposure.
- Number of weeks top ranked stocks out-/underperform lowest ranked.
- Brinson–Fachler attribution metrics.

All of these calculations are useful for comparing how your trading/investment system is performing relative to the benchmark. For charting purposes, the mean value of these metrics will be that experienced during backtesting relative to the benchmark. However, these types of calculations do not answer a fundamental question: are you making money by over- or underweighting factors or are you making money by picking better trades, or by combining the two together. In an ideal world, a system should make money from both the over- or underweighting of factors and by picking better trades. We recommend that where possible all systems are analyzed using the Brinson–Fachler method to clearly understand returns.

27.2.1. The Brinson–Fachler Method

The best known approach to performance attribution is the Brinson–Fachler method, which uses weighted sums, compounding, and value added for performance analysis. Performance analysts use weighted sums to combine returns for a group of assets. Consider the following table:[2]

TABLE 27-1

	Portfolio sector returns	Benchmark sector returns
Portfolio sector weights	Q4 Portfolio $$\sum w_i^P r_j^P$$	Q2 Active asset allocation fund $$\sum w_i^P r_j^B$$
Benchmark sector weights	Q3 Active stock selection fund $$\sum w_i^B r_j^P$$	Q1 Benchmark $$\sum w_i^B r_j^B$$

where:

- Q1 is the benchmark return, the weighted sum of the benchmark sector weights and benchmark sector returns.
- Q2 is the weighted sum of portfolio weights and benchmark returns.
- Q3 is the benchmark sector weights times the portfolio sector returns. Q3 shows the return that would have been realized if the asset allocation stuck to the benchmark weights, but stock selection was active.
- Q4 is the portfolio return.

In terms of quadrant returns, the interaction term provides the missing piece that makes the attributes sum exactly to the active return:[3]

Asset allocation	= Q2 − Q1
Security selection	= Q3 − Q1
Interaction	= Q4 − Q3 − Q2 + Q1
Total value-added	= Q4 − Q1

Since the attributes sum to the value added, the Brinson model is additive.

The Brinson–Fachler model decouples the sector returns relative to or in relationship with the overall return. If a sector had positive return, but a return nevertheless below the overall return, then the asset allocation difference will be negative and the sector selection effect negative. In such a case, the portfolio manager would be penalized for investing too much money in a bad sector, a sector that lowered the index benchmark return. If, however, the sector outperformed the overall benchmark, then the sector effect would be positive. The Brinson–Fachler model looks at how the sector did in comparison with the benchmark and reports the results.[4]

27.3.   LOOP 3: Benchmark VaR Calculations and Software

Monte Carlo simulation approximates the behavior of instrument prices by using computer-generated random numbers to build hypothetical price paths through time. The VaR can be read directly from the distribution of simulated portfolio values. A main advantage of the Monte Carlo method is that it is able to cover a wide range of possible values in financial variables and fully account for correlations. Essentially, the method has five steps:

- Specify a stochastic process for each financial variable as well as process parameters. Parameters, such as standard deviation and correlations, may be based upon historical data or implied volatilities. A commonly used stochastic process model for random price movement is geometric Brownian motion, where the change in the asset price, S, is a function of the mean return, π, the standard deviation of returns, σ, the change in time, t, and a standard normal random number, ε, where:

$$\Delta S_t = S_{t-1}(\mu \Delta t + \sigma \varepsilon \sqrt{\Delta t})$$

The Cox, Ingersoll, and Ross model is a commonly used stochastic, mean-reverting process of interest rates where:

$$dr_t = \kappa(\theta - r_t)dt + \sigma \sqrt{r_t}\,dz$$

where $\kappa < 1$ is the speed of mean reversion toward the long-run value θ, and the variance is proportional to the level of the interest rate, r.

- Generate a path for each stochastic variable.
- Value the portfolio given the random variables as inputs, that is, mark-to-market.
- Repeat the generation of random paths and portfolio valuation, say 10,000 times.
- Compile a distribution of portfolio values, from which a 2 standard deviation VaR (95% confidence bands) can be measured.

As we discussed in K|V 4.1, portfolios generally contain more than one source of financial risk. The Monte Carlo methodology can be easily extended to a general multivariate case, to account for any number of risk sources. Some random variables may be correlated, others uncorrelated. In the case of correlation, a correlation coefficient must be added. This is often done using Cholesky factorization.

Monte Carlo simulation is by far the most powerful method to calculate Value at Risk. First and foremost, it can consider any number of financial risks: nonlinear price risk, volatility risk, model risk, credit risk, time varying volatility, nonnormal distributions and fat tails, implied parameters, and extreme or user-defined scenarios. The only drawback is the computation cost. Monte Carlo is expensive in terms of time and money. When portfolios contain complex derivative instruments, full portfolio valuation can take a long time and a lot of technological and intellectual horsepower to calculate. We recommend that these calculations be done using standard, internal, existing systems or third-party stand-alone systems COTS. The reason for this recommendation is twofold:

1. The calculations in these systems should be industry standard, not proprietary.
2. The time to build these complex systems can be measured in years. To get a trading system up and running quickly, a firm should not spend six months to a year to get an attribution system and/or VaR system built. (As with all vendor components, the organization must confirm COTS package's ability to satisfy the intended application when used in the monitoring and measuring processes. This confirmation must be accomplished prior to initial use and reconfirmed as necessary.)

We do recommend that you program a custom database that stores all the inputs and outputs of these systems, so that all the output data can be graphed and monitored using SPC, and data mined during the kaizen process. The proper storage of these results and analysis should allow a system to beat any competition that does not store and statistically analyze the performance output data for continuous improvement.

We recommend that you adopt a VaR framework, not only to view risk, but also to have a tool that accurately measures "what-if" scenarios. This what-if analysis becomes a key tool of the kaizen process. The kaizen team can make changes to the portfolio construction and run the Value at Risk. The results will either confirm or disprove the root cause of the system and allow a kaizen team to move forward with scenario analysis.

27.4. Summary

While many, mostly small, trading groups ignore risk metrics or perform the minimum calculations, we recommend all firms embrace real-time performance and risk metrics. Firms should view risk and performance as a continuum from single point estimates to beating a benchmark to what-if scenarios.

Think again of the world of NASCAR. In the old days, only one thing mattered: track time. In the competitive world of racing today, hundreds of performance outputs are measured and optimally adjusted to conditions in real time. After a race, the outputs and the team results are mined to understand the performance of the car under differing conditions and environments. The racing team gains knowledge through research and implements that knowledge in the next race and in next year's race at the same track. To beat the competition, the skill of the driver is important, but the continuous improvement of the car is critical.

Management of working trading/investment systems is no different.

27.4.1.   Best Practices

- Benchmark unique performance metrics for every system.
- Use the Brinson–Fachler model for attribution.
- Follow CFAI/GIPS/NAPF guidelines.
- Store all system outputs for SPC analysis and data mining.
- Use Monte Carlo simulations to analyze what-if scenarios; part of the continuous improvement processes.

CHAPTER • 28

Perform SPC Analysis

Because of the uncontrollable variations of the inputs from the real world, a trading/investment system can never achieve a stable output process. This is why we use SPC. The instability of inputs leads to variation in the output factors of the system. (This is similar to variability in a manufacturing process, such as the diameters and lengths of parts.) We apply the processes used to control machinery in manufacturing to control trading/investment systems. Statistical process controls around input data (CPI, PPI, VIX, trading volumes, etc. as defined in K|V Stage 2) and outputs (percent winners, Sharpe ratio, sector weights, etc. as defined in K|V 4.2) can tell risk managers when the system is experiencing common variation and when the system is out of control.

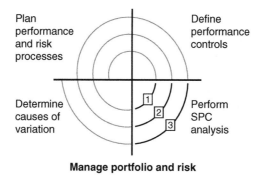

Manage portfolio and risk

FIGURE 28-1

Just like in manufacturing, when monitoring of a process uncovers excessive variation in a trading/investment system, a manager can either shut down the machine, or have it monitored more closely until investigation uncovers the root cause of the excessive variation. (Shutting down a system means only closing trades. A good trader, like a good pilot, can essentially land the plane safely after the autopilot is switched off. A human trader adds value during disasters and abnormal environments.) The main difference between manufacturing and systematic trading is that in manufacturing the monitoring is done by sampling finished pieces (i.e., a random sample is used as the basis for accepting or rejecting an entire lot), whereas in systematic trading/investment managers can perform a

100% inspection of inputs and outputs since there are essentially no additional costs versus sampling. Nevertheless, sampling will remove noise from the data.

Applying statistical process control is contrary to the view of most financial mathematicians, who are constantly looking for closed-form equations that accurately describe process variation and predict the future. We use SPC to monitor the process and to determine when a statistical process has changed. SPC does not try to forecast, rather, it monitors. Flags raised by SPC spur investigation into the root cause of the change using statistics and common sense.

The determination of the root cause of the change in the process in quality is normally a blend between applied statistics and fundamental knowledge of the process. Perhaps it is the separation between the scientists who believe they can forecast the future and the practitioner who tries to explain using simple facts that has led to SPC not being adopted in finance. What we are trying to accomplish with SPC in finance is to use SPC to identify when the underlying process, either inputs or outputs, have switched distributions. We, like most people in finance, believe in mixtures of normals with jumps, which are difficult (if not impossible) to forecast. The biggest objection to this form of mathematics in finance is that it is not predictive, but simply descriptive of the past. This is a large step forward from simpler risk limits. Now a trader or risk manager and top management can make informed decisions about when to rely on the machine and when not to rely on the machine. When the machine is broken, the firm will need a good quality engineer, who combines statistics, common sense, and a deep understanding of the underlying processes, to oversee a kaizen team tasked with finding the root cause and proposing solutions that might lead to a reformation of a product team.

28.1.   A Brief History of SPC

The history of statistical process control goes back to the 1920s and Western Electric, part of Bell Labs, where Walter Shewhart perceived that real-world processes, such as manufacturing, rarely generate normally distributed data. He concluded that these real-world processes display variation that is inherent in the process (i.e., common variation) and extra variation (i.e., special variation). The absence or presence of special variation determines whether a process is in or out of control. Shewhart's book *The Economic Control of Quality of Manufactured Product* demonstrated that industrial processes could yield data, which through statistical methods could signal the state of control of the process.[1] Deming applied Shewhart's methods during World War II to improve the quality of weapons. After the war he took SPC to Japan and transformed Japanese industry.

The underlying assumption in SPC is that any production process will produce products whose properties vary slightly from their designed values, even when the production line is running normally, and these variances can be analyzed statistically to control the process. For example, a machine may turn out parts 2 inches long, but some parts will be slightly longer than 2 inches, and some will be slightly shorter, producing a distribution of lengths. If the production process itself changes (say, e.g., the machine breaks), this distribution can shift or spread out. If this change is allowed to continue, the parts produced may fall outside the tolerances of the customer, causing product to be rejected.

Quality Money Management should ensure that all the activities necessary to design, develop, and implement a trading/investment system are effective and efficient with respect to the system and its performance. Quality practitioners solve basic problems with seven basic tools:

- Fishbone diagram
- Pareto chart
- Check sheet
- SPC charts
- Flowchart
- Histogram
- Scatter diagram.

Chance causes are those that are continuously active in the process and are built in. Assignable causes are those that can be detected because they are not always active in the process. If the variations in the product (caused by materials, machines, etc.) are due to chance causes alone, the product will vary in a normal, predictable manner. The process is said to be stable. We want to know how the product varies under normal, stable conditions. If any unusual change occurs, we can see this change in our normal distribution curve. We can say that it is the result of an assignable cause and not due to chance causes alone. When assignable causes are present, the curve has shifted.

If you make no effort to measure or monitor the variation normally expected, you could find yourself in a lot of trouble. All processes that are not monitored go downhill. So, it is necessary to measure the output of any process to know when an input process has changed. The source of variation in a process can be found in one or more of five inputs: price data, valuation data, fundamental data, calculated data, and economic data. We recommend using a fishbone diagram, which can be useful for searching out root causes of trouble in a process. The variation when measuring outputs will result from chance (or system) causes and assignable (or special) causes.

By using statistical tools, the operator of a production line can discover that a significant change has occurred in the production line and investigate the root cause of the change. He may even stop production before parts go outside specifications.

28.2. Process View

A trading/investment system is a machine and we apply SPC to each and every one of the outputs of the machine. Now, most trading/investments machines at best explain 40–70% of the variation of the process, hence, we recommend using the early quality control tools, those developed when manufacturing produced large amounts of variation. The best man-made algorithms have an $r^2 \leq .7$. Therefore, we believe that SPC, which is meant to control stochastic processes, is the proper tool to measure, watch, and control the trading machines that run on stochastic processes.

If you are running a quantitative hedge fund with a long–short or other multifactor system, under-/overweighting is normally a direct result of either portfolio optimization, which can be controlled through construction of appropriate constraint functions, or the portfolio selection algorithm. Because both of these are machines, you would expect the outputs of these machines to be stable and measurable using SPC. When the machine drastically over-/underweights a sector, or your take out ratio changes or excess returns drastically change, you should see that in control charts, which means the environment and inputs have changed. Therefore, you must investigate the root cause to determine the special cause. In current methods of risk analysis, there are two outcomes: one, the system performs perfectly, or two, it performs imperfectly. The impulse is to react to imperfect behavior with modifications to the system without determining if the variation is normal or abnormal.

With quality, action is only taken when the trading/investment system is out of control. If control limits are hit, or patterns inside the limits are experienced, then and only then is action taken. What we are proposing is the use of statistical process control, which triggers no changes as long as a trading/investment system is in control. If there are exceptional returns, good or bad, then the system is out of control. For example, if the top ranked stocks underperform the bottom ranked stocks more than usual, the system is out of control. Does this mean that the system must be down? Maybe. Does this mean switching to manual trading from automatic trading? Probably. Does this mean start looking for assignable, root causes? Absolutely. SPC charts:

- Figure out a special model to get you through the shift, all along still using the original model.
- Figure out the root cause.
- Remove the special model and return to the original once stability comes back.

Risk calculations and reports give management a snapshot of the returns and potential losses and drawdowns both on an absolute basis and relative to the benchmark over a given time horizon. Essentially, these reports will help us to understand how the system is performing relative to the market and the rest of the industry.

The actual application of SPC depends on the type of trading/investment and the backtesting method. Metrics and their SPC charts will be different for every system. The standard application of SPC is to graphically monitor the trading/investment system outputs at regular intervals. Maybe every day.

28.3. SPC Control Charts

The purpose of statistical process control for trading is a new concept for most money managers. The basis of this concept is on the following facts:

- A trading algorithm's ability to produce excess returns is stochastic since the underlying process is stochastic.
- A trading algorithm's measurable output will be stochastic because the underlying process is stochastic.
- Most quants try to build trading algorithms that produce an output with zero variation. Many quants believe they have achieved this goal until their algorithm blows up and loses money as described in Teleb's book *Fooled by Randomness.*
- SPC monitoring of a trading system based on a stochastic process has two key outputs:
  - The mean of the input and/or outputs.
  - The standard deviation of the inputs and/or outputs.
- A trading system based on a stochastic process needs a tool to determine if the output is exhibiting normal variation or if the underlying process has changed.

The tool that has been developed over the last 80 years for the above facts is called SPC. The goal of this tool is not to predict the future, but to notify the operator of the machines that the process is no longer deemed to be stable and in control.

A control chart is a record of the performance outputs, a running record of the system. Control limits are boundaries on a control chart within which a trading/investment system can safely operate. These limits are based on past performance (i.e., backtest) and show what to expect from the system when nothing has changed. Each time a risk manager checks the system, he should compare the output results with the control limits. If the results are within the limits, then there is no problem. If some points on a control chart fall outside the control limits, something has happened and the trading/investment system is no longer operating normally. There are two types of control charts:

- **Variables charts,** which are used where a performance metric is a number. The Xbar and R charts are variables charts.
- **Attribute charts,** which are used where a performance metric is Boolean, either acceptable or unacceptable, like say winning or losing trades. Quality practitioners assign numerical values to the results to enable statistical analysis. A percent defective chart for winning trades versus losing trades is an example of a variables chart. These are particularly helpful for monitoring trigger trading systems.

The enactment of Sarbanes-Oxley is a perfect example to illustrate the benefits of SPC. Sarbanes-Oxley changed the validity of historical earnings data and research. When the bill became law, every firm that used earnings per share as an indicator needed to completely retune their algorithms, because the input process changed. While it is now well understood that this change shifted stock volatility around earnings, index volatility during key earnings months, it was not understood at the time. By applying SPC on outputs, a risk manager could have identified the shift. Analysis would have identified the root cause. A product team could have retooled and backtested again.

A firm may need to build parallel systems, ready to go if there is a regime switch. This is what keeps a firm at the top. The replacement technique is far superior to the "I got caught in a regime switch and lost faith in the model so now I am making side bets out of control to keep my job" technique. SPC will detect early shifts in assumptions in models, shifts in distributions, and forces risk managers to look at and understand what has changed in the market. SPC forces statistical decisions about trading strategies. The amount of money a trader can make by successfully driving around a perceived short-term shift is pennies on the dollar compared to what a system can make by understanding the long-term, fundamental nature of the shift and responding correctly.

28.3.1. Xbar and R Charts

Xbar and R charts are the most commonly used SPC charts. Together Xbar and R monitor the behavior of a process over time. Xbar shows sample means, and R sample ranges. Interpreted together they allow tracking of both the center and variation of a process, and detection of out-of-control performance. To illustrate the calculations for Xbar and R charts we will use the following table of 20 weeks' worth of daily returns for a trading system.

TABLE 28-1

M	T	W	Th	F	Xbar	R
−0.0050	−0.0270	−0.0093	−0.0122	0.0246	−0.0058	0.0516
0.0239	−0.0133	−0.0067	0.0148	0.0221	0.0082	0.0372
0.0232	0.0163	−0.0005	0.0137	−0.0278	0.0050	0.0509
−0.0230	−0.0120	−0.0208	−0.0148	−0.0058	−0.0153	0.0172
0.0181	0.0005	0.0100	−0.0193	−0.0090	0.0001	0.0374
−0.0148	0.0032	0.0144	0.0260	0.0082	0.0074	0.0407
0.0037	−0.0115	−0.0096	−0.0173	0.0009	−0.0068	0.0210
0.0100	0.0154	0.0045	0.0144	−0.0180	0.0053	0.0334
0.0013	0.0235	0.0256	0.0221	0.0022	0.0149	0.0243
−0.0079	0.0099	0.0085	−0.0078	0.0002	0.0006	0.0178
−0.0246	0.0169	−0.0037	−0.0051	0.0102	−0.0013	0.0415
0.0012	−0.0110	0.0008	0.0088	0.0115	0.0023	0.0226
−0.0417	−0.0036	−0.0181	0.0178	0.0164	−0.0058	0.0595
−0.0096	0.0075	0.0254	0.0030	−0.0063	0.0040	0.0350
0.0006	0.0218	−0.0008	0.0101	0.0140	0.0092	0.0226
−0.0045	0.0209	0.0022	0.0169	−0.0018	0.0068	0.0253
−0.0008	0.0025	0.0112	0.0181	−0.0115	0.0039	0.0296
0.0141	0.0230	−0.0096	−0.0307	−0.0112	−0.0029	0.0538
0.0266	0.0238	0.0001	−0.0128	−0.0224	0.0031	0.0490
0.0016	0.0078	0.0350	−0.0069	0.0214	0.0118	0.0418
					Xbarbar	**Rbar**
					0.0022	0.0356

In this example, both Xbar and R are observations of a random variable. Given the sample, the mean and the range of each week's returns can be computed and are shown by Xbar and R.

$$\bar{\bar{X}} = \frac{\sum \bar{X}_i}{k}$$

and

$$\bar{R} = \frac{\sum R_i}{k}$$

Xbarbar is the estimate of μ_X and Rbar is the estimate of μ_R. Thus,

$$\mu = \bar{\bar{X}}$$

and

$$\sigma_{\bar{X}} = \frac{\bar{R}}{d_2}$$

These values can be used as known values of μ and σ, and the control charts can be constructed. For the *X*bar chart, the upper and lower control limits can be written as:

$$UCL = \bar{X} + A_2\bar{R}$$
$$CL = \bar{\bar{X}}$$
$$LCL = \bar{\bar{X}} - A_2\bar{R}$$

For the *R* control chart for range, the control limits can be calculated as:

$$UCL = D_4\bar{R}$$
$$CL = \bar{R}$$
$$LCL = D_3\bar{R}$$

The factors used in construction of control charts for various values of *n* are shown here:

TABLE 28-2

Value	Basic factors		Factors for averages			Factors for ranges			
of *n*	d_2	d_3	*A*	A_1	A_2	D_1	D_2	D_3	D_4
2	1.128	0.853	2.121	3.760	1.880	0	3.686	0	3.267
3	1.693	0.888	1.732	2.394	1.023	0	4.358	0	2.575
4	2.059	0.880	1.500	1.880	0.729	0	4.698	0	2.282
5	2.326	0.864	1.342	1.596	0.557	0	4.918	0	2.115

For the sample data, where $n = 5$ and $k = 20$, the *X*bar control values are

$$UCL = .0022 + .577(.0356) = .0227$$
$$CL = .0022$$
$$LCL = .0022 - .577(.0356) = -.0183$$

For the sample data, the *R* control values are

$$UCL = 2.115(.0356) = .0753$$
$$CL = .0356$$
$$LCL = 0(.0356) = 0$$

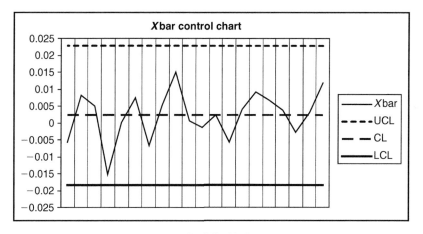

FIGURE 28-2

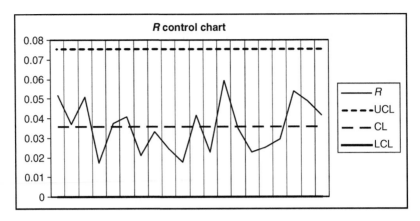

FIGURE 28-3

A common complaint about SPC is that it reacts too slowly. The real question is the following: would a risk manager stop a trading/investment system sooner? And the answer is no, for two reasons:

- A risk manager never stops a trading system when it makes too much money, even though the predictive nature of the algorithm may be flawed and no longer predictive.
- SPC does not work only on three standard deviation control limits. A "yes" answer to any of these questions may indicate that the system is out of control:
  - Are points outside the upper or lower control limits?
  - Do two out of three points land above or below the two standard deviation limits?
  - Do four of five consecutive points fall above or below a one sigma limit?
  - Do seven consecutive points fall either above or below the center line?
  - Do seven or more points trend in the same direction?
  - Do all points hug the center line, within plus or minus one standard deviation?[2]

SPC measures means, standard deviations, and ranges of many different things, any one of which may signal an out-of-control state. If anything, SPC may be too sensitive! Of course, the more tests, the greater the probability of a false alarm. This can be controlled by smoothing data through sampling. The thoroughness of SPC vastly exceeds the standard risk review process at most firms.

With both a UCL and LCL, winning big is just as bad as losing big; in either case SPC indicates that the process has changed. If the system is out of control to the upside, then we may expect mean reversion or lack of future predictability. So, maybe the risk manager should reduce the risk capital or suggest buying puts. The product team may need to retune the trade selection algorithm for a new environment. Or, maybe traders choose to accept the risk, but remain cognizant of the necessity to get out fast. Of course, any change must cause the product team to revert to Stage 1 to ensure the change's ability to add value. We also recommend that the team run shadow trading as well, as these results can be the new benchmark.

28.3.2. *d* and *p* Charts

Manufacturing industries use several types of control charts for defective parts. Two types of control charts are for the number of defective units, usually known as a *d* chart, and the control chart for fraction defective, known as a *p* chart.

Let us assume that a trading system performed 100 trades, of which 47 were profitable, 33 were unprofitable, and 20 were scratches. If d is the number of defective, or unprofitable, trades, then $p = d/n$ is called the fraction defective. If the number of unprofitable trades $d = n \cdot p$ is more than expected or traditionally acceptable, the process is out of control. The acceptable limits for d can be shown on a control chart. Like control charts for variables, a d chart can be constructed from given standards obtained from the backtest. The control limits for d are

$$UCL = \mu_d + 3\sigma_d$$
$$LCL = \mu_d - 3\sigma_d$$

Upper and lower control limits (UCL and LCL) represent bands three times the standard deviation above and below the mean of a variable. Upper and lower specification limits (USL and LSL) are bands above and below the mean which define acceptable performance of a process.

Sometimes the fraction defective, p, is controlled. The control limits for p can be easily derived:

$$UCL = p' + 3 \cdot \sqrt{\frac{p'(1 - p')}{n}}$$
$$LCL = p' - 3 \cdot \sqrt{\frac{p'(1 - p')}{n}}$$

respectively, where p' is the mean of the fraction defective for the whole population. d and p charts are both useful, but the p chart is more robust when different sample sizes are used.

28.3.3. Other Charts

There are many other statistics-based tools that organizations can employ including:

- SPC control for other known distributions.
- Pareto charts to separate the important few factors from the trivial many.
- Check sheets to display collected data in a manner that is easily interpreted.
- Histograms to chart the frequency of occurrence. Looking at the pattern of a histogram will tell you:
  - Whether the process is normally distributed.
  - Where the process is centered.
- Scatter diagrams to determine correlation between variables.
- Run charts to display process results over time.
- Control charts (SPC) to determine whether process variation is the result of the process's inherent capability or caused by some controllable external factor.
- Cause and effect diagrams.
- Stratification.
- Scatter diagrams.

Over time, other process-monitoring tools have been developed for different underlying process distributions, including:

- Pareto diagrams
- Scatter diagrams
- CUSUM chart.
- EWMA charts.

A cumulative sum control chart (CUSUM) plots the cumulative sum of deviations of successive samples from the average. An exponentially weighted moving average (EWMA) chart plots the weighted average of current and all previous values, giving greater weight to more recent data and decreasing weights for older data.

28.3.4. Process Capability

Process capability is a way of reporting performance with what are called C_p, C_{pk} measurements. In process improvement efforts, the process capability index or process capability ratio is a statistical measure of the ability of a process to produce output within specification limits, assuming a state of statistical control.

- C_p process capability index is a measure of the capability of a process, that is, what it could produce.
- C_{pk} process capability index adjusts the C_p index for the effect of a noncentered distribution.

Capability statistics are basically a ratio between the width of the specification limits, that is, the tolerance, and the actual process spread. C_p estimates what the process would be capable of producing if the process could be centered assuming the process is approximately normal.

$$C_p = \frac{USL - LSL}{6 \cdot \sigma}$$

The upper specification limit minus the lower specification limit, called the tolerance, divided by six times sigma is the capability of the machine. That is, the machine is capable of operating within the specified tolerance. In a case where the process spread is greater than the tolerance, the system must be considered to be incapable of meeting specifications. A C_p of 1 or greater means the system is capable of operating within tolerance. The C_{pk} takes into account off-centeredness.

$$C_{pk} = \min\left[\frac{USL - \mu}{3 \cdot \sigma}, \frac{\mu - LSL}{3 \cdot \sigma}\right]$$

Process capability charts can have important applications to backtesting as well since they show whether or not a process is capable of remaining in control.

A process with a low C_{pk} should be thought of as a process that will require constant monitoring.

28.4. LOOP 1: Perform SPC Analysis on Single Metrics

All inputs and single factor ouputs should be monitored. The monitoring of these signals allow an operator to determine if a fundamental shift in the predictive nature of the factor has occurred. When an out-of-control situation occurs, the team needs to focus on a quality process method such as Ford 8D to first contain and then fix the root cause.

28.5. LOOP 2: Perform SPC on Attribution Metrics

The output of attribution is normally considered to be stationary and nonstochastic. We believe the output to be stochastic and should be monitored with SPC. The number of standard deviations that an algorithm is over or under weighting a sector is meaningful information. Even more meaningful is whether the over/under weighting is a normal occurance or an out-of-control signal. These results should be fed back into the kaizen system.

28.6. LOOP 3: Perform SPC on VaR Metrics

The output of the VaR calculations, day to day, are stochastic. We recommend the use of SPC to analyze and control VaR outputs. An example of this is the 95% loss threshold. If, for example, seven days in a row, the VaR number has crept up, SPC would say the underlying process mean is shifting, so risk managers should look at the machine to find root causes. In traditional VaR, risk managers would otherwise wait until the VaR number hits some prespecified limit.

If you take the kaizen approach, then VaR allows a risk manager attributes or variables, the largest influencers of the overall process variation, which need either model enhancements, better hedging strategies, or a kaizen team to figure out the root cause.

28.7. Summary

The concept of SPC for process monitoring is very old. The idea of monitoring a machine, person, or algorithm is common in everyday life. Using SPC charts to monitor and control a trading/investment process has not, however, been openly discussed in finance.

We recommend all three types of risk outputs be monitored using SPC. We also recommend risk managers use SPC to monitor and adjust trading limits in a scientific manner; and we recommend the use of SPC to identify problem areas, as a start to the kaizen process. Finally, we recommend that the trading/investment industry follow the manufacturing world by aggressively rooting out abnormal sources of variation in the performance of trading/investment systems. We expect the removal of variation to produce even higher reward to risk ratios similar to continuous improvements for better quality cars, appliances, and electronics over the last 40 years.

28.7.1. Best Practices

- Use Xbar and R charts to monitor metrics.
- Use d and p charts to monitor things such as number of losing trades.
- Use C_p and C_{pk} charts to measure the capability of the system to operate within tolerance.
- Examine control charts for out-of-control signals other than just crossings of control limits.
- Include SPC charts as part of backtesting processes in Stage 2 to understand what normal performance is.

CHAPTER ◆ 29

Determine Causes of Variation

Determining causes of special variation, or nonconformance, in a trading/investment system requires root cause analysis, a set of problem solving techniques that are part of a continuous improvement process. A trading system has two continuing goals: increase returns and decrease risk (i.e., variation) versus the benchmark. Reducing variation increases a system's Sharpe ratio and unmasks new sources of alpha. Correcting or fixing a root cause will eliminate the nonconformance and reduce variation. The point is to solve problems by taking corrective action to fix root causes, rather than just treating or masking the obvious symptoms.

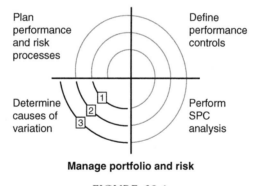

FIGURE 29-1

Often there is more than one root cause for a given nonconformance. However, complete prevention of recurrence, called a "fix," by a single inquiry is often not possible. Like all methods in K|V, root cause analysis should be an iterative, systematic process, where conclusions are based on facts. Root cause analysis consists of many different tools and processes, such as the fishbone diagram (a fishbone diagram shows cause and effect). Nevertheless, for all continuous improvement techniques, a basic outline can be followed for performing root cause analysis:

- Define the special variation, or nonconformance, using evidence from K|V 4.3.
- Identify issues that potentially contributed to the nonconformance.

- Identify root causes.
- Test and confirm using simulations of the effect of the root cause.
- Develop recommendations for fixes as part of kaizen.
- Revert to previous stages to reresearch, retest, and reimplement the fixed trading solution.
- Begin again Stage 4 to manage the fixed trading/investment system.

29.1.   Failure Mode and Effects Analysis

Failure mode and effects analysis organizes brainstorming, the first activity toward finding root causes, by systematically identifying potential points of failure in a trading/investment system. Failure modes are the ways in which a trading/investment system has or might fail in the future. Effects analysis refers to studying the consequences of those failures. Failures are prioritized according to the severity of their consequences, how frequently they occur (or may occur), and how risk managers may detect them. Furthermore, effects analysis should document current knowledge of and actions taken to mitigate risks. Which is to say, the product can use effects analysis to guide strategy design in Stage 1. In this stage it is used for process control, before and during ongoing operation of the trading/investment system. Optimally, though, it should begin during the earliest stages of research, the fuzzy front end, and continue throughout the trading/investment system life cycle.

29.2.   The Five Whys

While simple in its brainstorming approach, Sakichi Toyoda's Five Whys technique (later used at Toyota) asks questions to uncover root cause and effect relationships between inputs and nonconforming outputs. By asking "Why?" five times or more, risk managers dig past symptoms of nonconformance to root causes. Answers to "Why?" questions lead to other problems and further questions. Sometimes, however, risk managers may only be able to answer questions with existing knowledge, when new knowledge may hold the true solution. Asking the right questions is not always obvious; different people may arrive at different root causes for the same problem. Each cause or contribution of the causes needs to be tested until the problem is explained 100%. Nevertheless, as a first pass toward determining root causes, the Five Whys method can be a powerful technique to guide more statistical analysis.

29.3.   Fishbone Diagram

Kaoru Ishikawa's cause and effect diagram, usually now called a fishbone diagram, helps identify special causes of variation. A fishbone diagram provides a framework for adding and subtracting different inputs and analyzing the effect of inputs on your model's outputs. The results in this case are returns, standard deviation, Sharpe ratio, Sortino ratio, as well as other performance metrics. Fishbone diagrams work by testing the input variables on the branches and the outputs in the result area, then using a blending algorithm to modify the inputs and record the outputs.

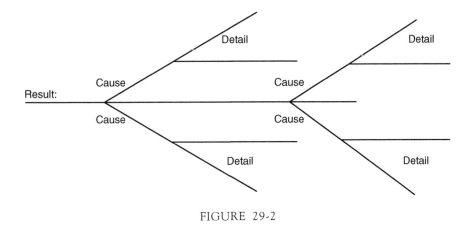

FIGURE 29-2

Ishikawa identifies five steps to making a fishbone diagram:

- Decide the quality characteristic, for example, dispersion of returns or ranges.
- Write the quality characteristic, or result, at the head of the fish.
- Write the main factors that may be causing the dispersion.
- On each cause/branch, write in the details of the causes. On each successive branch, or twig, write more detail.
- Finally, check that all possible causes are represented on the diagram.

In the end, a fishbone diagram will expose what environmental factors affect the returns, standard deviations and ranges of returns, and Sharpe and Sortino ratios for a trading/ investment strategy.

29.4. Pareto Analysis

A Pareto bar chart, named after Vilfredo Pareto, plots values in descending order. The Pareto principle, usually called the 80/20 rule, postulates that 80% of the nonconformances on a system come from 20% of the causes. On a Pareto chart the left-hand vertical axis represents frequency of occurrence, the right-hand vertical axis the cumulative percentage. This arrangement should highlight the most important among a typically large set of sources of nonconformance, the highest occurring type of nonconformance.

Pareto analysis is a statistical technique that should identify a limited number of causes that produce significant nonconformance. The intent is to focus attention on important courses of corrective action. In essence, the risk manager can estimate the potential benefit each course of corrective action may yield. Three steps enable Pareto analysis:

- Create a table listing the causes and their frequency as a percentage.
- Create a Pareto chart with causes ranked by importance.
- Draw a line at 80%. This point will separate the important causes from the unimportant ones.

A secondary result of using Pareto analysis is that the largest sources of variation are attacked first. Through the continuous reduction in variation we can focus on forecasting to produce higher alpha indicators.

29.5.   Design of Experiments

Six Sigma's five step DMAIC—Define, Measure, Analyze, Improve, Control—is a data-driven quality methodology for improving a process. To analyze and subsequently improve a process, Six Sigma uses design of experiments (DoE) combined with analysis of variance (ANOVA).

Design of experiments is a structured, organized approach to measuring the relationship and interactions between factors, that is, controllable independent variables, that affect a process and the output of that process. DoE has been successfully applied to many different types of process including the standard mixture model products. In financial markets it is difficult, if not impossible, to reproduce financial market data and trading/investment system performance exactly. Comparisons between data sets is much more reproducible. This is why the product team should perform experiments between the backtest results and the index benchmark as a baseline.

By comparing results, analysis of variance breaks down total variation into components. In financial markets, we sometimes call these components noise and signals. There is a signal component for each controlled variation and a noise component representing variations not attributable to any of the controlled variations. By looking at the signal-to-noise ratio for a particular variation, analysis of variance will provide clues and answers about root causes.

In trading/investment system management, risk managers are confronted by significant degrees of uncontrollable variation in data and environmental conditions. Such problems can be overcome by running properly constructed experiments. Fortunately, the ease of capturing market data and trading system performance make meaningful experiments possible, if systems for performance analysis have been built in over the stages of development and testing. Modern statistical software packages will perform the appropriate analysis of variance at the click of a mouse.

Design of experiments depends upon the selection of appropriate factors and responses, inputs and outputs, factor ranges, and as always documentation of experiments and discoveries. We believe that interaction between trading/investment signals should be perceived within the framework of design of experiments. There are then three bets a system may make (and this applies especially to filter and multifactor systems):

- Getting the sector right, which may, for example, be best implemented by buying ETFs.
- Getting the individual stocks right, which forces an equal weight or an underweighting of the sector versus the index.
- Getting the interaction right, where ideally the system picks both the sector right and the stocks right.

Our view of interaction and its importance is common in industrial statistics, where the use of design of experiments to tune industrial processes is common. Perhaps the most interesting fact is that many of the primary contributors to the development of DoE— Box, Cox, Jenkins, Hunter, and Montgomery—did so toward the end of their long, prestigious careers in industrial statistics, which included invention of many standard techniques for time series analysis currently used in finance.

29.6. Analysis of Variance

ANOVA is a collection of statistical models where observed variation is partitioned into components explained by different inputs plus an error term. What is called one-way ANOVA compares several independent groups of observations, with potentially differing means and variances. A test can prove whether all the means are equal. What is called two-way ANOVA studies the effects of two factors separately, including their individual main effects and their interaction effect. Total variation, SST, can be partitioned into a component, SSR, that represents variability which is explained by the slope of the regression equation, and another component, SSE, that represents the random or unexplained deviation of points from the regression line. That is:

$$SST = SSR + SSE = \sum_{i=1}^{n} (y_i - \overline{y})^2$$

where

$$SSR = \sum_{i=1}^{n} (\hat{y}_i - \overline{y})^2$$

and

$$SSE = \sum_{i=1}^{n} (y_i - \hat{y}_i)^2$$

Design of experiments techniques provide an efficient means for product teams to optimize a mixture process. The organization must keep records of nonconforming trading systems, including the types and nature of nonconformities, and actions taken to fix the nonconformities, or to preclude the system's continued use. Before it can be put to use, the organization must reverify the implementation of the containment of fix by stepping through the appropriate stages of K|V.

29.7. Sources of Assignable Causes

The root causes of special, or assignable, variation in trading/investment systems often come from one of the following (in no particular order):

- Legal changes, such as Sarbanes-Oxley.
- Regulatory or GAAP changes.
- New, competing systems come online.
- Changes in exchange matching algorithms.
- Technology changes, such as new server technology or FIX or FAST version changes. (A trading/investment machine, unlike a real, physical machine, does not wear down; parts do not become corroded. Technology can, however, become obsolete.)
- Economic shifts.

- Political changes.
- Index composition changes.
- New, tradable contracts are offered.
- Better designed signals that reduce forecasting error.

29.8.   LOOP 1: Determine Causes of Variation in Single Performance

Loop 1 should determine if the working system conforms to the backtest, and what are currently normal results. Again, the purpose of a *t*-test or ANOVA is to find out whether outputs from the backtest and the current system are the same. That is, to determine whether the groups are actually different in a measured characteristic such as profit, win/loss ratio, etc. In trading/investment systems, *t*-tests will determine if a system conforms to its backtest, that is, are the performance metrics of the system from a common distribution as those of the backtest.

The question as to whether the system is working as designed or has the investment environment changed in a manner that affects the model needs to be continually asked. We also need to continuously seek out new ways to increase the forecastability of the trading/investment strategy by removing explainable variation from the process. In many systems the transformation of the system's outputs can greatly decrease the variation.

29.9.   LOOP 2: Determine Causes of Variation in Attribution

A factorial design is used to evaluate two or more factors simultaneously. The advantages of factorial designs over one-factor-at-a-time experiments are that they are more efficient and they allow interactions to be detected. After the attribution analysis is completed and we understand all of the bets we are placing to beat the benchmark, we need to build one final set of tools. These tools are based on statistical process control—namely, design of experiments and ANOVA.

The goal of these tools is to determine the causes of variance in a portfolio's returns and increase the excess returns. If you accept that the best you can do is beat your benchmark by several 100 basis points by placing better bets then you should also accept the fact that the majority of the variance in your portfolio is driven by macro market conditions. Therefore, by applying SPC to monitor your portfolio selection algorithm and the benchmark you can hopefully determine when the algorithms are not working properly. During the times when the algorithms do not work properly you should either scale down your bets or revert back to benchmark.

John Brush showed that the difference between other published studies and his studies was that he deliberately removed data from Decembers and Januarys from his result set. He claims that is why most articles showed that systems did not perform well and his results showed that they could. This can be described as a clean application of ANOVA between months and a group of t-tests to identify the months that have different means, or processes. Brush showed an algorithm that worked versus classical finance academics who did not perform ANOVA and stated that the algorithm did not work.

Just as in manufacturing the only way to find these anomalies is to apply SPC theory to results of the process. Once the process becomes out of control then a cause of the out-of-control condition can be found. If we can find the cause of the process being out of control then we can fix the process and have theoretically less variance than the benchmark. Sometimes in finance all we can do is identify the out-of-control state since we cannot determine what has caused the algorithm not to perform properly. This is also useful since we then can adjust our bets accordingly.

A close friend of ours, Peter Krause, discussed with us a unique anomaly. A high frequency trading system's win-to-loss ratio dropped in half for a single stock in one week. The next week the ratio dropped for ten stocks. Then it dropped for 100 stocks. Finally, the ratio dropped for all the stocks in the SPX and QQQ, which a friend was trading. Half of the profit disappeared from the trading system within two months. A competitor had turned on a duplicate system. The interesting point our friend made, however, was that his friend's firm did not foresee what was going on; they only knew they were making less money. Only after investigating the data did they see the pattern, but by then it was too late. It would have been nice to know ahead of time so the firm could have defended its algorithm by actively driving the other firm's test results through active trading.

This is why we recommend the use of SPC to control the algorithms. Had the firm produced SPC charts for win/loss ratio by stock and by sector, they would have seen the shift in the underlying process. The firm should have already developed a strategy that would drive the profit in these first stocks to zero or negative. The firm should have implemented this strategy quickly in the hopes the other firm would be confused by the results and go back to the drawing board. If this failed, the firm should have had a new system built and waiting to be implemented when a competing algorithm was placed into production. However, without monitoring the process and using kaizen to improve the process, the firm was stuck with half the profit until the next system was turned on, then one-third the profit, then one-quarter the profit until the business becomes a low cost business. If a firm is not the low cost trader, it will be driven out of the marketplace, not due to the trading/investment strategy, but due to the fact that its profit margin has been cut.

While new in financial markets, this view is consistent with the new Lanchester strategy (discussed in Chapter 4), which was originally developed in 1916—constantly looking for changes in the environment, including new machines coming online. Do not rule out new hardware to fight the war until the war is on. This is widely known by the U.S. military. Use the weaponry needed to win the war. Always keep another layer of new technology ready to go. SPC will tell you when the competition has rolled out a new machine.

29.10. LOOP 3: Determine Causes of Variation in VaR

We also recommend the use of DoE and ANOVA and what-if scenarios to investigate and determine causes of variation in Value at Risk. Monte Carlo simulation for Value at Risk will provide the most flexibility for what-if scenarios.

A major benefit of building out a VaR system is the ability to perform what-if analysis. Ideally, VaR identifies the securities, sectors, credit ratings, etc. that result in the greatest shocks to the portfolio. The goal is to use the information from VaR to construct hedges. The goal of hedging is to make returns more stable and the reduce downside deviation. If properly built and implemented, a firm should be able to significantly reduce drawdowns and increase returns, and therefore limit redemptions during market shocks. In a perfect world, a firm can profit during market meltdowns and beat the benchmark during normal markets by using well-constructed hedges and superior trading/investment systems.

29.11.   Summary

A firm's goal should be to continuously improve their profit-to-risk ratio. This should be done by both launching new products and improving the performance of existing ones. Both in trading and manufacturing, once a product matures, the focus needs to switch to continuous improvement to boost profit margin and extend its life. The goal should be to be the firm with the highest profit margin, so when the group consolidates due to pricing pressure, the firm wins.

29.11.1.   Best Practices

- To find sources of special variation, start with brainstorming techniques.
- Use DoE and ANOVA processes to uncover root causes.
- For identified root causes, follow through with kaizen which will require a reversion to a previous stage in our methodology.
- Use a cross-functional kaizen team with both a team leader and a quality facilitator to research and find root causes of variation.
- Errors must be reproducible to be considered fully understood.

CHAPTER • 30

Kaizen: Continuous Improvement

In Japanese, kaizen means continuous improvement. As a business strategy, kaizen aims to eliminate waste in business processes. For our purposes, kaizen is the process of continually searching for and implementing new quantitative methods, new data cleaning techniques, new optimization routines, new technologies, and new risk management methods that will lengthen the maturity stage of a trading/investment system. (Kaizen can also mean continuous improvement of new trading system design and development processes, but we will stick to the former definition for this chapter.) Kaizen, then, really started in Stage 4, where SPC of performance and risk metrics discovered nonconformances and analysis found root causes.

As with all quality processes, top management must lead the way to create a culture of continuous improvement. Kaizen succeeds through systemic thinking versus the current programming "scrum-only" view of producing small, incremental software changes. It is not the programming technique that is wrong, but the lack of a process improvement methodology.

> *Variation is like the water level in a stream. A high water level hides big rocks under the surface. Lowering the water level will expose the big rocks. At that point, the big rocks can be cleared before they wreck the boat. Removing big rocks lowers the water level, revealing more rocks, which can also be cleared; and you keep on going until there are just pebbles left.*
>
> *The rocks are the undetected root causes of variation in a trading/investment system; they cause performance to drift out of control or crash during periods of market stress. The hidden rocks are creating variation and hindering performance; removing root causes lowers variation, which will in turn reveal other root causes, and you keep going until there are no root causes left. Toyota invented this methodology and it is used at every major Lean/Six Sigma organization. It inevitably leads to innovation (i.e., discontinuous improvement) through jumps.*

A culture of continual improvement will eventually also yield large innovations in the form of compounded improvement. Kaizen includes making changes to trading/investment systems, retesting, implementing, and again monitoring results.

30.1. Continuous Improvement Processes

Continuous improvement is an ongoing effort to improve benchmarked methods and technologies that are no longer able to implement their competitive advantage. Several methodologies exist for continuous improvement. The most widely known is the four-step quality model—plan-do-check-act (PDCA) cycle:

- **Plan.** Identify an opportunity and plan for change.
- **Do.** Implement the change on a small scale.
- **Check.** Use data to analyze the results of the change and determine whether it made a difference.
- **Act.** If the change was successful, implement it on a wider scale and continuously assess your results. If the change did not work, begin the cycle again.

Other widely used methods, such as Six Sigma, Lean, and Total Quality Management, extend the PDCA model to emphasize management involvement and teamwork, measuring processes, and reducing waste and lowering cycle times. Six Sigma models for process improvement include DMAIC and DMADV.

- **DMAIC** stands for Define-Measure-Analyze-Improve-Control, and is applicable to an existing system.
- **DMADV** stands for Define-Measure-Analyze-Design-Verify, and is applicable to new systems.

30.2. ISO 9000

According to ISO 9001:2000, the organization shall take action to eliminate the cause of nonconformities in order to prevent recurrence. Corrective actions shall be appropriate to the effects of the nonconformities encountered:

- The organization must take action to eliminate the cause of nonconformities in order to prevent their recurrence.
- Corrective action taken must be appropriate to the seriousness of the effects of the nonconformities encountered, including shutting the system down and returning invested funds.

The organization must document corrective action procedures that define requirements for:

- Reviewing nonconformities.
- Determining the cause of nonconformities.
- Evaluating the need for action to ensure that nonconformities do not recur.
- Determining and implementing the action needed. (Return to previous stage.)
- Recording results of actions taken.
- Reviewing corrective action taken.

Prevention:

- The organization must determine action needed to eliminate causes of potential nonconformities in order to prevent their occurrence.

- The organization must document preventive action to define requirements for:
  - Determining potential nonconformities and their causes.
  - Evaluating the need for action to prevent occurrence of nonconformities.
  - Determining and implementing the needed preventive action.

30.3. Ford 8D Problem Solving Process

The 8D process (8 Disciplines) is a team-oriented, problem solving method that can be applied for trading/investment system and development process improvement. We have already seen the 8D process in K|V 4.4, but here we add the problem solving or kaizen team to the structure.

1. Establish a problem solving team.
2. Describe the problem.
3. Contain the problem. Which is to say, protect investors from the effects of the problem.
4. Investigate the root cause, in K|V 4.4.
5. Choose corrective action. A corrective action to a working trading/investment system will require a reversion to Stage 1 and rebacktesting in Stage 2.
6. Implement corrective action and verify its effectiveness. These are K|V Stages 3 and 4.
7. Prevent recurrence, with SPC in Stage 4. We recommend sharing corrective actions with other product teams. This should be part of firmwide, best practice deployment.
8. Recognize the 8D team.

30.4. Continuous Improvement and Innovation

Robert E. Cole, in his paper "From Continuous Improvement to Continuous Innovation," identifies the primary benefits of continuous improvement:

- Continuous improvement mobilizes large numbers of employees.
- Small wins, occurring in parallel and serially, in large numbers magnify results.
- A series of small wins often precedes and follows large changes.
- Many revolutionary changes are based on a series of small ones.
- Small wins encourage learning that is rooted in daily work routines.
- Small wins by different groups are uncorrelated.
- Small wins are not easily recognized and imitated by the competition.

The common assumption is that improvement is continuous and small scale while innovation is discontinuous and large scale. In reality, continuous improvement and innovation are complementary concepts. The trading and money management industry, though, often gives incentives to traders and portfolio managers for one or the other—improvement or innovation—which then draws ability and attention to one or the other. This is a problem.

> *Toyota, GE, 3M, Apple, SAS, and Honda all confirm that it is the reduction of variation that allows a firm to find breakthrough innovations and new processes.*

Innovation is discontinuous improvement. Innovations appear when process variation is low. In K|V, product teams focus on innovation. After Gate 3, a product team should be freed to focus their efforts again on discontinuous innovation, on finding new strategies for new trading/investment systems. Risk managers and kaizen teams should be responsible for continuous improvement of existing systems, for uncovering root causes of variation, and new technologies that will extend the maturity stage of a trading/investment system.

In the hypercompetitive financial markets, where the importance of technological superiority is increasing, the speed at which firms develop and roll out new trading/investment systems is becoming an increasingly critical competitive issue. Shorter product cycles mean that firms have less time to recoup their investments and be first to market with the right trading/investment system and quality confers major competitive advantage.

The question is the following: can continuous improvement and systematic innovation, which appear to require elaborate steps, exist in a speed-driven world? Competitive advantage is built through innovation. Nevertheless, continuous, incremental improvements are necessary to defend existing strategies against competitor's new systems and digest changes to the economic environment. In our view, the product team should focus on innovation, not monitoring or looking from incremental improvements to existing systems. Speed of product development is most often found where management emphasizes concurrent engineering of many trading/investment systems involving staged development. The focus of these efforts is on streamlining and simplification.

When applied to a trading environment, a continuous improvement strategy involves management, kaizen teams, and reformulated product teams, working together to make small improvements continuously. It is top management's responsibility to cultivate a professional environment that engenders kaizen. A culture of sustained continuous improvement will focus efforts on optimizing trading/investment systems and, furthermore, processes of a trading or money management organization. Intelligent leadership should guide and encourage firms to continuously improve profitability, to increase efficiency and reduce costs.

Through small improvements and innovations from research and entrepreneurial activity, financial firms can discover breakthrough ideas. This includes, among other things, the creation of new trade selection algorithms, application of existing systems to new markets, and the implementation of new technologies for more efficient trade execution.

During a trading/investment system's maturity stage, the available funds are fully invested and performance should conform to test results and/or the benchmark. Maintaining maturity requires continuous improvement to prevent decline. During the decline stage, trading/investment system performance fails to conform to test results and/or the benchmark. Continuous improvement measures may not be effective and the trading/investment system may be shut down.

30.5.   In Conclusion

The trade selection, the order management, and the risk management processes as well as the technology can be enhanced or improved over time, until the useful life of the trading system is over. As you define all control metrics in Stage 1, and build them to monitor, review, and understand the system that you built, we gently pointed you in the direction of how your system needs to evolve due to changing economic conditions and realities. Hence, we start again at Stage 1 with a new system or to slowly modify an existing one.

Results from SPC can be fed back into a redesign and redevelopment process for continuous improvement. In a K|V world for trading/investment systems, risk is process control. Risk management is really a quality control problem and investors benefit from better, higher quality, longer lasting, and more capable systems as lower cost.

Continuous improvement is fundamental to success in the global financial markets. Companies that are just maintaining the status quo in such key areas as quality, new trading system development, the adoption of new technologies, and process performance are like a runner standing still in a race. Competing in the global financial marketplace is like competing in the Olympics. Last year's performance records are sure to be broken down this year. If a firm is not continually improving its trading/investment systems, it will not stay in the top quartile very long. Investor demands are not static. They change continually. A special strategy today that is innovative will be run of the mill tomorrow. The only way a money management firm can hope to compete in the modern capital markets is to improve constantly.

In Chapter 1, we presented a list of seven deadly diseases for trading/investment system design and development. Using the topics discussed in the ensuing chapters, we presented methods to prevent the occurrence of these diseases. Additionally, the goal of our methodology is Quality Money Management.

- **Build trading/investment systems that deliver better performance to investors.**

By following a rigorous process of discovery, evaluation, and development, financial firms can deliver better quality trading/investment systems.

- **Shorten the trading/investment system design and development cycle, the time it takes to turn a trading idea into a finished, working system.**

By following a rigorous process, financial firms can more quickly develop new systems.

- **Formalize the process and increase the speed with which new trading ideas are evaluated and either discarded or promoted, called "strategy cycling."**

By following system documentation and portfolio evaluation processes, firms can use standardized processes for considering many systems under development.

- **Formalize the process and increase the speed of recognizing and shutting down trading/investment systems that no longer have a competitive advantage.**

Using statistical process control, firms can recognize more quickly when a running system is no longer performing to specification.

- **Reduce the total cost of trading/investment system design and development.**

A repeatable development process will reduce the amount of seed capital necessary to move new trading systems from idea to implementation.

- **Provide seed capital investors with a real options model for capital burn rates and stepped commitment of capital.**

Gate meetings allow top management to monitor progress of product teams and to assess the value of each trading system and whether or not it is worthy of additional resources for further development.

- **Formalize a process of developing, building, and packaging working trading/ investment systems for sale to larger institutions.**

Well-documented trading strategies built with well-documented technology are far more easily salable than those without.

- **Enable seed capital providers to better allocate scarce resources and prioritize individual trading/investment systems within a portfolio of competing systems.**

Given a portfolio of systems, top management can optimize resources to the most promising projects.

- **Lengthen the maturity stage of the life cycle of working trading systems through continuous improvement.**

Through continuous improvement, a firm can defend their strategies against competitors launching their own systems.

- **Satisfy the demand by investors and regulators for greater transparency through greater and standardized documentation.**

By standardizing the process of research and documentation, a firm will be better able to meet the demands of regulators as well as investors for increased transparency.

- **Create a taxonomy of risk for trading/investment system development and management and employ best practices to reduce risks.**

At each step along the development process there is both risk of failure and opportunity for competitive advantage. By understanding risks, firms can benchmark processes and define best practices to mitigate risks. Through a Capability Maturity Model, as described in Chapter 2, external observers can evaluate disparate firms on their abilities to deliver competitive advantage.

- **Provide a mechanism for effective self-evaluation, the preferred form of oversight in the financial industry.**

Lastly, development of industry standard best practices is far better than external oversight and regulation by the government. In this text, we have provided many best practices that will, at a minimum, begin to define areas of concern that should be addressed by firms that engage in the development and operation of trading/investment systems.

We will end as we began. In the financial markets, the competition gets tougher every day. The largest problem facing trading and money management firms in the twenty-first century is not the lack of mathematical or technological understanding but rather an inability to manage the entrepreneurial processes of systematic innovation, development, and continuous improvement. By evaluating our methodology and applying those principles that are relevant to your particular business model, you can strengthen your firm's practices.

This book offers a framework and guidelines, not rigid formulas. We recommend you tailor our standard process to suit your projects and your organization's culture.

Firms that learn quality will thrive at the expense of firms that do not. Organizational survival should be the incentive for systematic innovation, quality, and continual improvement. Implementing quality is not easy, nor is it done through simply reading this book. It takes a lot of work, but now is the time to start. We expect that many of you will succeed in changing your approach to building trading/investment systems. Others of you, however, will continue to put projects on the fast track and blame the financial engineers and the traders and the programmers for failure. Only in retrospect, then, will you learn the true value of quality.

Endnotes

Chapter 1

1. Drucker, Peter F. 2002. "The Discipline of Innovation." *Harvard Business Review*. August.
2. Hamilton, Dane. 2006. "S&P may form hedge fund operational risk service." Reuters. December 20.
3. Goetsch and Davis. 2000. *Quality Management: Introduction to Total Quality Management for Production, Processing and Services*. 3rd edition (Upper Saddle River, NJ: Prentice-Hall).
4. Deming, W. Edwards. 1982. *Out of the Crisis*. Cambridge, MA: MIT/CAES.
5. Deming, W. Edwards. 2000. *The New Economics*. 2nd edition. Cambridge, MA: MIT/CAES.
6. Smith, Larry R. 2001. "Six Sigma and the evolution of quality in product development." *Six Sigma Forum Magazine*. November. web.archive.org/web/20020612074338/http://www.asq.org/pub/sixsigma/evolution.html
7. Wilmott, Paul. 2006. "The use, misuse and abuse of mathematics in finance." Submission for: *Science into the Next Millennium: Young Scientists Give their Visions of the Future*.
8. Thomke, Stefan. 2002. "Innovation at 3M Corporation (A)." *Harvard Business Review*. July 23, p. 2.
9. www.SAS.com, http://www.sas.com/corporate/worklife/index.html
10. Brogan, John A. 1973. *Clear Technical Writing*. McGraw-Hill. p. xi.
11. Cascio, Joseph. 1996. *The ISO 14000 Handbook*. Fairfax, VA: CEEM Information Services, p. 200.
12. Martin, Robert C. 2003. *Agile Software Development: Principles, Patterns and Practices*. Prentice-Hall.
13. Webb, Andy. 2004. "High frequency automated trading." *AIMA Journal*. December.
14. Hoffman, Douglas. 2002. *Managing Operational Risk*. Wiley Finance. New York.
15. Shafer, Don. 2004. "Software risk: why must we keep learning from experience?" *Dynamic Positioning Conference*. September 28–30.
16. Hulett, David. 2007. Hulett and Associates, LLC. www.projectrisk.com/Welcome/Project_Risk_Analysis_Approach/project_risk_analysis_approach.html
17. Goetsch, David L., and Stanley B. Davis. 2000. *Quality Management*. 3rd edition. Prentice-Hall.
18. McGrath Goodman, Leah. 2006. "Algorithmic trading inflates costs."*Wall Street Journal*. Monday, September 25.
19. Hamilton, Dane, quoting Paul Roth, partner in Schulte Roth & Zabel. 2006. "S&P may form hedge fund operational risk service." Reuters. Dec. 20.
20. Bogle, John C. 2005. *The Battle for the Soul of Capitalism*. Yale University Press. p. xxii.
21. Pyzdek, Thomas. 2006. Six Sigma and Beyond. "The value of Six Sigma." http://www.isixsigma.com/offsite.asp?A=Fr&Url=http://www.qualitydigest.com/dec99/html/sixsigma.html

22. Bogle, John C. 2005. *The Battle for the Soul of Capitalism.* Yale University Press. p. xxii.
23. Womack, James P., and Daniel T. Jones. 2003. *Lean Thinking.* Free Press. p. 19.
24. http://www.iso.org/iso/en/iso9000-14000/understand/qmp.html
25. Bogle, John C. 2005. *The Battle for the Soul of Capitalism.* Yale University Press. p. xxii.
26. Johnson, Perry L. 1991. *Total Quality Management.* Southfield, MI: Perry Johnson, Inc. p. 1-1.

Chapter 2

1. Sofianos, George. 2006. "Choosing benchmarks vs. choosing strategies: Part 1—Execution benchmarks: VWAP or pretrade prices." *Algorithmic Trading II.* Insitutional Investor Journals.
2. http://www.asq.org/learn-about-quality/benchmarking/overview/overview.html
3. Camp, Robert C. 1989. *Benchmarking: The Search for Industry Best Practices that Lead to Superior Performance.* Milwaukee: ASQC Quality Press, p. 14.
4. DeVito, Denise, and Sara Morrison. 2000. "Benchmarking: a tool for sharing and cooperation.*" The Journal for Quality and Participation.* Fall. Association for Quality and Participation.
5. Hill, Cathy. 2000. "Benchmarking and Best Practices." *ASQ's 54th Annual Quality Congress Proceedings.* American Society for Quality.
6. Best Practice. Wikipedia.com. http://en.wikipedia.org/wiki/Best_practice. (Accessed: December 6, 2006.)
7. FX Alliance, LLC. 2006. *Best Practice in Foreign Exchange Markets.*
8. Wilmott, Paul. 2006. "The use, misuse and abuse of mathematics in finance." Submission for: *Science into the Next Millennium: Young Scientists Give their Visions of the Future.*
9. Boehm, Barry. 1981. *Software Engineering Economics.* Prentice-Hall.
10. Document. Dictionary.com. 2004. *The American Heritage® Dictionary of the English Language, Fourth Edition.* Houghton Mifflin Company. http://dictionary.reference.com/search?q=document (Accessed: August 28, 2006.)
11. www.iafe.org. 2006.
12. Cooper, Robert G. 2001. *Winning at New Products.* Cambridge, MA: Basic Books. Stage-Gate is a registered trademark of R.G. Cooper & Associates Consultants, Inc., a member company of the Product Development Institute. See www.prod-dev.com
13. Process. Dictionary.com. 2004. *The American Heritage® Dictionary of the English Language, Fourth Edition.* Houghton Mifflin Company. http://dictionary.reference.com/search?q=process (Accessed: August 28, 2006.)
14. Deming, W. Edwards. 2000. *The New Economics.* The MIT Press. pp. 95–96.
15. *Capability Maturity Model for Software, Version 1.1*, Document No. CMU/SEI-93-TR-24, ESC-TR-93-177 (Carnegie Mellon University Software Engineering Institute, Pittsburgh, Pennsylvania, 1993).
16. Paulk, Mark C., Charles V. Weber, Bill Curtis, and Mary Beth Chrisses. 1994. *The Capability Maturity Model: Guidelines for Improving the Software Process.* 1st edition. Reading, MA: Addision-Wesley, pp. 15–17.
17. Womack, James P., and Daniel T. Jones. 2003. *Lean Thinking.* Free Press. p. 19.

Chapter 3

1. Royce, Winston W. 1970. "Managing the development of large software systems." *Proceedings of IEEE WESCON* (August), 1–9.
2. Boehm, Barry W. 1988. "A spiral model of software development and enhancement." *Computer*, Volume 21, Number 5 (May), 61–72.
3. Cooper, Robert G. 2001. *Winning at New Products.* Cambridge, MA: Basic Books. Stage-Gate is a registered trademark of R.G. Cooper & Associates Consultants, Inc., a member company of the Product Development Institute. See www.prod-dev.com

Chapter 4

1. Bogle, John C. 2005. *The Battle for the Soul of Capitalism.* Yale University Press. p. xxii.
2. Goetsch, David L., and Stanley B. Davis. 2000. *Quality Management.* 3rd edition. Prentice-Hall. pp. 48 and 274ff.
3. Gundling, Ernest. 2000. *The 3M Way to Innovation: Balancing People and Profit.* Kodansha International, p. 23.
4. Cooper, Robert G., Scott J. Edgett, and Elko J. Kleinschmidt. 2001. *Portfolio Management for New Products.* 2nd edition. Basic Books.
5. Cooper, Robert G., Scott J. Edgett, and Elko J. Kleinschmidt. 2001. *Portfolio Management for New Products.* 2nd edition. Basic Books.
6. Cooper, Robert G., Scott J. Edgett, and Elko J. Kleinschmidt. 2001. *Portfolio Management for New Products.* 2nd edition. Basic Books.
7. Managed Funds Association. 2005. *MFA's 2005 Sound Practices for Hedge Fund Managers.* www.mfainfo.org/hedgefunds.htm
8. Scholtes, Peter R. 1991. *Total Quality Management.* Peter Scholtes, Inc. Southfield, MI.
9. http://safari.peachpit.com/0131857258/part01
10. http://www.isixsigma.com/offsite.asp?A=Fr&Url=http://www.prosci.com/team_selection.htm
11. Marietta, Martin. 2007. http://www.martinmarietta.com/Investors/pdf_Ethics.pdf. May, 2004.
12. Goetsch, David L., and Stanley B. Davis. 2000. *Quality Management.* 3rd edition. Prentice-Hall. pp. 48 and 274ff.
13. Thomke, Stefan. 2002. "Innovation at 3M Corporation (A)." *Harvard Business Review.* July 23, p. 3.
14. Poppendieck, Mary, and Tom Poppendieck. 2003. *Lean Software Development: An Agile Toolkit.* Addison-Wesley.
15. http://www.isixsigma.com/offsite.asp?A=Fr&Url=http://www.prosci.com/team_selection.htm
16. Goetsch, David L., and Stanley B. Davis. 2000. *Quality Management.* 3rd edition. Prentice-Hall. pp. 48 and 274ff.
17. Goetsch, David L., and Stanley B. Davis. 2000. *Quality Management.* 3rd edition. Prentice-Hall. pp. 48 and 274ff.
18. Massa, Massimo, Jonathan Reuter, and Eric Zitzewitz. 2006. "The rise of teams in fund management." *European Finance Association 33rd Annual Meeting.* Zurich, August.
19. Womack, James P., and Daniel T. Jones. 2003. *Lean Thinking.* Free Press.
20. Massa, Massimo, Jonathan Reuter, and Eric Zitzewitz. 2006. "The rise of teams in fund management." *European Finance Association 33rd Annual Meeting.* Zurich, August.
21. Kim, J., and D. Wilemon. 2002. "Sources and assessment of complexity in NPD projects." *R&D Management*, pp. 16–30.
22. Koen, Peter, *et al.* 2001. "Providing clarity and a common language to the 'fuzzy front end'." *Research Technology Management*, pp. 46–55.
23. Cooper, Robert G., Scott J. Edgett, and Elko J. Kleinschmidt. 2001. *Portfolio Management for New Products.* 2nd edition. Basic Books.
24. Herstatt, Cornelius, and Birgit Verworn. 2003. "A causal model of the impact of the 'fuzzy front end' on the success of new product development." EIASM, *Proceedings of the 10th International Product Development Management Conference.* Brussels.
25. Drucker, Peter F. 2002. "The discipline of innovation." *Harvard Business Review.* August.
26. Thomke, Stefan. 2002. "Innovation at 3M Corporation (A)." *Harvard Business Review.* July 23, p. 3.

Chapter 7

1. McConnell, Steve. 1996. *Rapid Development.* Redmond, WA: Microsoft Press, p. 61. Citing research by: The Standish Group 1994. "Charting the seas of information technology." Dennis, MA: The Standish Group.
2. McConnell, Steve. 1996. *Rapid Development.* Microsoft Press.

3. Hall, Sarah. 2006. "What counts? Exploring the production of quantitative financial narratives in London's corporate finance industry." *Journal of Economic Geography*.
4. Wiegers, Karl E. 2003. *Software Requirements*. 2nd edition. Redmond, WA: Microsoft Press.

Chapter 8

1. Brogan, John A. 1973. *Clear Technical Writing*. McGraw-Hill, p. xi.
2. McCrehan Parker, Carol. 2006. "Writing as tool for critical thinking." academic.udayton.edu/aep/TA/TA03.htm
3. Frankfurter, George M. 2004. "The Theory of Fair Markets (TFM): toward a new finance paradigm." *International Review of Financial Analysis*. Elsevier. February, pp. 130–144.
4. Brogan, John A. 1973. *Clear Technical Writing*. McGraw-Hill, p. xi.
5. Iyasere, Marla Mudar. 1984. "Beyond the mechanical: technical writing revisited." *Journal of Advanced Composition*.
6. Booth, Wayne C., Gregory G. Colomb, and Joseph M. Williams. 2003. *The Craft of Research*. 2nd edition. The University of Chicago Press.
7. Ernst, Michael. 2005. http://pag.csail.mit.edu/~mernst/advice/write-technical-paper.html
8. Read, Nick, and Jonathan Batson. 1999. "Spreadsheet modelling best practices." *Business Dynamics*. Published by the Institute of Chartered Accountants for England and Wales.
9. Prescott, J.E., and P.T. Gibbons. 1993. "Global competitive intelligence: an overview." In J.E. Prescott and P.T. Gibbons (eds.), *Global Perspectives on Competitive Intelligence*. Alexandria, VA: Society of Competitive Intelligence Professionals.

Chapter 9

1. Booth, Wayne C., Gregory G. Colomb, and Joseph M. Williams. 2003. *The Craft of Research*. 2nd edition. The University of Chicago Press.
2. Camp, Robert C. 1989. *Benchmarking: The Search for Industry Best Practices that Lead to Superior Performance*. Milwaukee: ASQC Quality Press, p. 4, pp. 142–145.
3. Camp, Robert C. 1989. *Benchmarking: The Search for Industry Best Practices that Lead to Superior Performance*. Milwaukee: ASQC Quality Press, p. 4, pp. 142–145.
4. Frank, Mary Margaret, James M. Poterba, Douglas A. Shackelford, and John B. Shoven. 2004. "Copycat funds: information disclosure, regulation and the returns to active management in the mutual fund industry." *Journal of Law and Economics*. vol. XLVII. October.
5. Frank, Mary Margaret, James M. Poterba, Douglas A. Shackelford, and John B. Shoven. 2004. "Copycat funds: information disclosure, regulation and the returns to active management in the mutual fund industry." *Journal of Law and Economics*. vol. XLVII. October. Citing: Gasparino, Charles. "Vanguard's cutback of fund data may mean it fears a market drop." *Wall Street Journal*. October 14, 1997.
6. Aware. 2006. "Competitor analysis—a brief guide. The basic principles of competitive intelligence." http://www.marketing-intelligence.co.uk/resources/competitor-analysis.htm. Middlesex, UK.

Chapter 10

1. Sloane, Paul. 2003. "The Leader's Guide to Lateral thinking skills." Kogan Page
2. Read, Nick, and Jonathan Batson. 1999. "Spreadsheet modelling best practices." *Business Dynamics*. Published by the Institute of Chartered Accountants for England and Wales.

3. Taina, Juha. 2005. "A brief introduction to function points." www.cs.helsinki.fi/u/tiana/ohtu.fp.html. October.

4. Atwood, Jeff. 2005. "Are all programming languages the same?" www.codinghorror.com/blog/archives/000365.html

5. Prechelt, Lutz. 2000. "An empirical comparison of C, C++, Java, Python, Rexx, and Tcl." Submission to *IEEE Computer*.

6. Read, Nick, and Jonathan Batson. 1999. "Spreadsheet modelling best practices." *Business Dynamics*. Published by the Institute of Chartered Accountants for England and Wales.

7. McConnell, Steve. 1996. *Rapid Development*. Redmond, WA: Microsoft Press.

8. McConnell, Steve. 1996. *Rapid Development*. Redmond, WA: Microsoft Press.

9. www.eusprig.org. 2007.

10. Cullen, Drew. 2003. "Excel snafu costs firm $24m." TheRegister.com. June 3. http://www.theregister.co.uk/2003/06/19/excel_snafu_costs_firm_24m/

11. Boehm, Barry, and Victor R. Basili. January 2001. "Software defect reduction top 10 list." *Computer*.

12. Hesse, Rick. 1996. *Managerial Spreadsheet Modeling and Analysis*. Richard D. Irwin, p. 19ff.

13. Grossman, Thomas A., and Ozgur Ozluk. 2004. "A paradigm for spreadsheet engineering methodologies." European Spreadsheet Risks Interest Group, 5th Annual Symposium, Klagenfurt, Austria.

14. Hesse, Rick. 1996. *Managerial Spreadsheet Modeling and Analysis*. Richard D. Irwin, p. 19ff.

15. Grossman, Thomas A., and Ozgur Ozluk. 2004. "A paradigm for spreadsheet engineering methodologies." European Spreadsheet Risks Interest Group, 5th Annual Symposium, Klagenfurt, Austria.

16. Gordon, V. Scott, and James M. Bieman. 1994. "Rapid prototyping: lessons learned." *IEEE Software*.

Chapter 11

1. McConnell, Steve. 1996. *Rapid Development*. Redmond, WA: Microsoft Press, p. 69ff.

2. McConnell, Steve. 1996. *Rapid Development*. Redmond, WA: Microsoft Press, p. 69ff.

3. McConnell, Steve. 1996. *Rapid Development*. Redmond, WA: Microsoft Press, p. 69ff.

4. McConnell, Steve. 1996. *Rapid Development*. Redmond, WA: Microsoft Press, p. 69ff.

5. Panko, Raymond R. 2006. "Recommended practices for spreadsheet testing." *EuSpRIG 2006 Conference Proceedings*, p. 73ff.

6. Fagan, M.E. 1976. "Design and code inspections to reduce errors in program development." *IBM Systems Journal*, pp. 182–211.

7. Fagan, M.E. 1986. "Advances in software inspections." *IEEE Transactions on Software Engineering*. July, pp. 744–751.

8. Panko, Raymond R. 2006. "Recommended practices for spreadsheet testing." *EuSpRIG 2006 Conference Proceedings*, p. 73ff.

9. Grossman, Thomas A. 2007. "Source code protection for applications written in Microsoft Excel and Google Spreadsheet." *EuSpRIG 2007 Conference Proceedings*, p. 84.

Chapter 12

1. Dunham, David J. 2007. "Gate meetings: speed bump versus acceleration ramp." www.pdma.org/visions/print.php?doc=jul99/dunham.html

2. Cooper, Robert G., Scott J. Edgett, and Elko J. Kleinschmidt. 2001. *Portfolio Management for New Products*. 2nd edition. Basic Books, p. 22.

3. Cooper, Robert G. 2001. *Winning at New Products*. 3rd edition. Basic Books. p. 246ff.

4. Cooper, Robert G. 2001. *Winning at New Products*. 3rd edition. Basic Books. p. 246ff.

5. Cooper, Robert G. 2001. *Winning at New Products*. 3rd edition. Basic Books. p. 246ff.

6. Cooper, Robert G. 2001. *Winning at New Products*. 3rd edition. Basic Books. p. 246ff.

7. Cooper, Robert G. 2001. *Winning at New Products*. 3rd edition. Basic Books. p. 246ff.

Chapter 13

1. Pyzdek, Thomas. 1999. "SPC guide: process capability in English." *Quality Digest*. http://www. qualitydigest.com/jan99/html/spcguide.html
2. Bohlen, Reiner. 2007. "Automating the investment process: the joy of backtesting" *Barra Newsletter* #167. http://www.barra.com/Newsletter/nl167/aip.asp
3. OPEN Process Framework. 2007. http://www.opfro.org/index.html?Components/WorkProducts/ DesignSet/DatabaseDesignDocument/DatabaseDesignDocument.html~Contents

Chapter 14

1. Wong, Raymond K. and Patty N. Ng. 1994. "A hybrid approach for automated trading systems." *IEEE*.

Chapter 16

1. Ishikawa, Kaoru. 1976. *Guide to Quality Control*. Tokyo: Asian Productivity Organization.

Chapter 20

1. IEEE. 1998. "IEEE recommended practice for software requirements specifications." Software Engineering Standards Committee, IEEE Computer Society.
2. IEEE. 1998. "IEEE recommended practice for software requirements specifications." Software Engineering Standards Committee, IEEE Computer Society.
3. Hussain, Amanat. 2000. *Managing Operational Risk in Financial Markets*. Butterworth-Heinemann Finance, p. 186ff.
4. Agile Project Planning. 2006. "3 ways to meet your software project deadline." http://www.extreme-planner.com/blog/2006/02/3-ways-to-meet-your-software-project.html

Chapter 21

1. Clements, Paul, Rick Kazman, and Mark Klien. 2002. *Evaluating Software Architectures*. Addison-Wesley.
2. Fowler, Martin. 1999. *Refactoring: Improving the Design of Existing Code*. Addison-Wesley.

Chapter 22

1. McConnell, Steve. 1996. *Rapid Development*. Redmond, WA: Microsoft Press, pp. 64, 65.
2. McConnell, Steve. 1996. *Rapid Development*. Redmond, WA: Microsoft Press, pp. 64, 65.
3. McConnell, Steve. 1996. *Rapid Development*. Redmond, WA: Microsoft Press, pp. 64, 65.

Chapter 24

1. Camp, Robert C. 1995. *Business Process Benchmarking*. Milwaukee, WI: ASQC Quality Press, p. 21.

Chapter 25

1. Rice, Chris. "Best practices in algorithmic trading." *Active Equity Essays & Presentations*. www.ssga.com/library/esps/chrisricealgorithmictrading20050809/page.html

Chapter 26

1. Bacon, Carl. 2004. *Practical Portfolio Performance Measurement and Attribution*. John Wiley and Sons, Ltd. p. 29

Chapter 27

1. Bacon, Carl. 2004. *Practical Portfolio Performance Measurement and Attribution*. Wiley.
2. Laker, Damien. 2002. "Fundamentals of performance attribution: the Brinson model." MSCI Barra. http://www.mscibarra.com/resources/pdfs/PerfBrinson.pdf
3. Laker, Damien. 2002. "Fundamentals of performance attribution: the Brinson model." MSCI Barra. http://www.mscibarra.com/resources/pdfs/PerfBrinson.pdf
4. Laker, Damien. 2002. "Fundamentals of performance attribution: the Brinson model." MSCI Barra. http://www.mscibarra.com/resources/pdfs/PerfBrinson.pdf

Chapter 28

1. Goetsch and Davis. 2000. *Quality Management: Introduction to Total Quality Management for Production, Processing and Services*. 3rd edition. Upper Saddle River, NJ: Prentice Hall. p. 556.
2. Amsden, Robert T., Howard E. Butler, and Davida M. Amsden. 1998. *SPC Simplified: Practical Step to Quality*. 2nd edition. Productivity, Inc.

Index

287

Printed and bound by CPI Group (UK) Ltd, Croydon, CR0 4YY

08/05/2025

01865016-0002